THE LOST GETTYSBURG ADDRESS

THE LOST *Gettysburg* ADDRESS

Charles Anderson's Civil War Odyssey

DAVID T. DIXON

B-List History
SANTA BARBARA, CALIFORNIA

Cover design by Peter O'Connor
Book design and production by BookMatters
Maps by Hal Jespersen
Printed in the United States of America
ISBN 978-0-9861551-0-9 (hardcover)
ISBN 978-0-9861561-1-6 (electronic book)
ISBN 978-0-9861551-2-3 (paperback)

David T. Dixon
P.O. Box 30923
Santa Barbara, CA 93130
davidtdixon.com

To my parents,
William B. and Peggy A. Dixon

Contents

Illustrations follow page 134

THE LOST GETTYSBURG ADDRESS

The Accidental Historian

Anthropologist rob tolley gasped when he realized what he held in his hands.

One bright summer day in 2002, several tattered cardboard boxes had arrived at Bartley Skinner's remote Wyoming ranch. Skinner's eyesight was failing, so he asked his friend Tolley to help him sort through the collection. The presumed author of this morass of nineteenth-century material was Skinner's great-grandfather, an obscure Ohio governor named Charles Anderson. As Anderson's saga emerged from a mountain of loose ephemera, the anthropologist became an accidental historian.

Tolley toiled for several years to preserve the Anderson legacy. He painstakingly identified, cataloged, and donated pieces of the collection to various archives and historical societies. After sifting through nearly four hundred crumbling, forgotten documents, Tolley was still puzzled by one particular artifact. A thirty-nine-page manuscript written in dark brown ink on a gray-lined legal pad appeared to be a speech written at some point during the Civil War, yet no title or date hinted at its secret. Even after the untitled speech was gifted to the Ohio Historical Society, Tolley continued to try to unravel its mysterious origins.

The breakthrough came when Tolley found an old journal article featuring Anderson's participation in the Gettysburg Memorial ceremonies on November 19, 1863. Edward Everett of Massachusetts, one of the era's most celebrated orators, was the keynote speaker at the consecration. His two-hour address was too long to remember. Lincoln's two-minute masterpiece was impossible to forget. Following the dedication, Lincoln and the other dignitaries attended a rally at Gettysburg Presbyterian Church, where Charles Anderson, then a well-known orator in his own right, thrilled the audience with a fiery speech.

Everett's oration was published soon after the event. Lincoln's brief address was destined to become sacred scripture to generations of American schoolchildren. The president congratulated Anderson on his fine speech, and the Ohio delegation requested that it be printed. That never happened. Curiously, biographical summaries of Anderson ignore the speech. His great-grandson, Bartley Skinner, never spoke of it. Anderson himself apparently did not consider it significant. Only after Tolley read excerpts of the oration published in contemporary newspapers did he realize that the mystery speech included in that box of ephemera was indeed the long-lost original manuscript of Anderson's address at Gettysburg.

Tolley was stunned. Had he really stumbled upon an important piece of Gettysburg history in the middle of the Wyoming wilderness? As an anthropologist and archaeologist on the faculty of Indiana University East, Tolley subscribed to the notion that such significant discoveries are the result of careful research, detailed planning, and diligent fieldwork. The more he thought about the history of archaeology, however, the more he realized that many explorers happened upon their discoveries by accident or coincidence.

How Tolley came to know the Skinners, and to eventually become the custodian of Charles Anderson's papers, was pure serendipity. Years before his chance discovery of Anderson's speech, Tolley and his climbing party had just finished an expedition in the Wind River mountain range in western Wyoming. After weeks spent traversing peaks and glaciers in this rugged wilderness, the weary explorers could think of little else but ending their monotonous routine of freeze-dried meals with a celebratory feast. Locals claimed that the Fort William Guest Ranch near Pinedale had the best steaks around. They warned, however, that it was a little off the "beaten path."

Tolley and his intrepid band had almost given up hope as they traversed a series of gravel roads, passing through numerous cattle guards and gates. They finally wandered into the place at the end of a long dirt track five miles from town in the posted ranchlands. Bartley and Rose Skinner, a spry and elderly couple, greeted them. Grilling steaks over an open aspen wood fire, Skinner sipped gin and spun tales of his great-grandfather, Governor Anderson. The hearty fare and warm fellowship was a pleasant end to an arduous journey, and the ranch became a regular stop during Tolley's frequent outings in Wyoming. As the years passed, Tolley and his family grew close to the Skinners.

Fort William was a virtual museum shrine to Bartley Skinner's ancestors. Paintings, military artifacts, and family relics were his prized possessions. Guests perused Anderson's personal library, complete with the governor's penciled notes written in the margins of nearly every volume. The hidden treasures at the ranch, however, were documents that helped tell the story of Charles Anderson's eventful life. Anderson was a leader among a class of Southern men whom Lincoln viewed as critical to the preservation of the Union. A Kentuckian by birth like the president, Anderson also shared Lincoln's great obsession. Anderson may have been the most zealous of all Southern Unionists. By chance or design, he kept turning up at critical events, both in the run-up to war and during the conflict itself. His oration at Gettysburg was just one of a series of dramatic encounters that kept the Anderson name in the press and in the minds of Americans in both the North and the South, particularly after Anderson's brother Robert surrendered Fort Sumter.

Lincoln's subsequent martyrdom meant that his masterful address was destined to be carved in stone and memorialized as secular scripture, while the featured orations of Edward Everett and Charles Anderson were largely forgotten. Anderson was just one of many important Civil War figures whose stories were overshadowed by a public consumed with the legacies of Abraham Lincoln, Robert E. Lee, Ulysses S. Grant, and Thomas "Stonewall" Jackson. Some of these stories have yet to be told. They may be lying dormant in a collection of unread manuscripts in an archive, or in an even less likely location such as Pinedale, Wyoming, waiting for an enterprising researcher to uncover their significance.

In 2014, Rob Tolley gave me the opportunity to share in the excitement of his archival adventure. He asked me to look at a random assemblage of Anderson's notes and papers that he had been unable to identify. Among this heap of material were eight manuscript pages in Anderson's own hand. These documents had entire sections crossed out. Some of the phrases used on these pages sounded familiar. Upon closer examination, I confirmed that these notes were actually part of an early draft of Anderson's Gettysburg oration. Despite the voluminous studies of this iconic event, to my great delight, fresh surprises and insights still turn up.

The story of Lincoln's Gettysburg Address remains incomplete even after 150 years. When Anderson's speech disappeared from view, part of the context of Lincoln's words was also lost. By considering the major orations that came before and after the president's brief remarks, one may better understand the purpose of Lincoln's speech and the political strategy behind all three addresses in promoting the administration's wartime agenda. For a brief instant, Anderson became famous as a former slave owner who had sacrificed nearly everything to help save the Union. His remarkable yet almost forgotten life story helps explain why he shared the spotlight with Lincoln on such an important day in the middle of the Civil War.

CHAPTER ONE

→→ ←←

Patriot Legacy

THE STORY OF CHARLES ANDERSON begins with the memorable experiences of his father, Richard Clough Anderson, who became the dominant influence and example in Charles's life. The Anderson family had emigrated from Scotland to the Virginia Colony sometime in the seventeenth century. Born in 1750 at the family plantation on Gold Mine Creek in Hanover County, Richard was the third son of Robert Anderson and Elizabeth Clough. Robert was an accomplished hunter and spent much of his time in woods outside of Richmond with his friend John Findley, who owned a pack of hunting dogs.

Young Richard made due with a tutor and the common schools of Richmond, while his older brother was in England earning the education required to manage their father's Virginia farm. He preferred to be out chasing game with his father, or simply exploring the countryside near the James River. Richard surprised his parents when, at just sixteen years old, he accepted a position in the counting house of wealthy Richmond merchant Patrick Coots. Robert Anderson was appalled. Although Coots was a friend of the family, they considered the merchant trade to be beneath the son of a gentleman. Richard ignored his parents' advice and, within a few years, became a valued and trusted employee. When Coots needed a reliable man to supervise his cargo and represent him in overseas transactions, he chose nineteen-year-old Richard for the important office. It was a dream job that satisfied the young man's keen taste for adventure.[1] The merchant assistant traveled throughout the West Indies, London, and various European ports, learning the French language that was vital to conducting international business at the time. On December 16, 1773, Richard Anderson happened to be in Boston Harbor when a band of protestors, some disguised as Indians, started dumping tea from the British East India Company into the water. He took little notice of the incident. He did not understand then how his presence foreshadowed a series of important moments when happenstance would place him on the scene of critical events in America's war of revolution. Richard returned to Richmond just as the war that would shape his future was about to begin. Virginians were forced to take sides in the contest, and the Andersons of Gold Mine were steadfast to the patriot cause. Their fellow parishioners in St. Paul's Church may have had some influence on their allegiance. The minister's son, Patrick Henry, was their friend and neighbor. Henry, like Robert Anderson, was in the middle ranks of the colony's landed gentry. His skill and passion as an orator, combined with his radical views, made him the logical choice as Virginia's first postcolonial governor in 1776.

Patrick Coots had no intention of risking his immense fortune in a rebellion against what was then the strongest nation on earth. When his young protégé resigned and expressed a desire to join the Continental Army, Coots tried to talk Richard Anderson out of it. Professional British soldiers would crush the rebellion in a matter of months, the merchant reasoned. Leaders like Patrick Henry would be hanged. The Anderson farm, along with the property of other disloyal English citizens, would be confiscated. Revolution promised ruin. When it became clear that Coots could not change Richard Anderson's mind, he recommended the young man to Patrick Henry, who urged Richard to accept the office of paymaster general. Anderson refused, instead insisting he serve in the line and fight alongside his brothers. His commission as captain of the Fifth Battalion, Regiment of the Virginia Line, arrived in March 1776. By this time, Anderson had enrolled most of his men from Hanover County.

The twenty-six-year-old captain was well prepared for the rigors of war. He was of medium height but endowed with broad shoulders and a muscular frame. His blue eyes sparkled with intelligence, and his countenance was generally cheerful though serious. Richard was known for being cool under pressure and braver than most men. Years spent hunting in the woods of his childhood had made him strong and resourceful. Life aboard ship had steeled his constitution to disease and hardship. As he marched his troops north to meet General Washington, Anderson expected that his men would soon be tested.

Washington was reeling from the British success following the Battle of Long Island. Forced repeatedly to retreat, the Continental Army found itself facing yet another defeat at the Battle of White Plains, New York, on October 28, 1776. Anderson's troops saw limited action. Morale was low, the army poorly trained, and the entire state of New York about to be lost. Ninety percent of the troops who had fought at Long Island were gone. Many had deserted. Washington himself confided to his cousin, John A. Washington, "I think the game is pretty near up." Perhaps Coots was right. This revolution appeared to be over.[2]

Continental troops retreated into New Jersey and Pennsylvania while General Washington prepared for one final attempt at reversing his fortunes. The opportunity came near Trenton in December 1776. Washington's bold plan involved crossing the Delaware River in terrible weather conditions to mount an attack on an inferior force of Hessians. The main crossing was planned for the night of December 25. General Adam Stephen had ordered Anderson to cross the previous evening, scout in various directions for enemy pickets, avoid any engagement with a superior force, and return via Trenton. It was a dangerous and risky mission. The company had completed its reconnaissance and was returning to camp when they passed a Hessian outpost in the midst of a violent hail storm. Anderson's troops killed the sentry, wounded five others, and raised the alarm, which carried back to the city. A few Hessians made a weak pursuit, but the Continentals escaped back across the river. Those were the first shots fired in the Battle of Trenton.

On the march back to camp, Richard Anderson met Washington's main force, then in motion toward its fateful crossing. The commanding general rode up and was visibly angry when he was told of Anderson's recent advance. He sent for General Stephen and demanded an explanation, reportedly saying, "You sir, may have ruined all my plans." After Stephen admitted that he was responsible for the action, Washington dismissed the general, exonerated Anderson, and ordered his weary troops to the rear of the column. The young captain never forgot Washington's fair treatment during this episode. Ironically, General Stephen's poor judgment and Anderson's unauthorized scouting expedition actually worked in Washington's favor. Hessian colonel Johann Rall, thinking he had repulsed the planned attack, relaxed his guard thus enabling the surprise attack that ultimately would defeat him.[3]

Washington took nearly nine hundred enemy prisoners that day and moved back across the Delaware River to prepare for a British counterattack. To thwart the movements of General Charles Cornwallis and his five thousand soldiers, Washington again moved his six-thousand-man army across the river and established camp south of the Assunpink Creek near Trenton. The Second Battle of Trenton, as this contest came to be called, occurred on January 2, 1777. It was another smashing success for the Americans. Washington's troops won this victory, a subsequent battle at Princeton, and then retired to winter quarters near Morristown, New Jersey. When the news of these unexpected triumphs reached the other colonies, enlistments swelled and the rebellion was saved.

Captain Anderson did not accompany his troops to their winter camp. He had taken a ball from a large-bore German Yager musket in the hip and was transported to a hospital in Philadelphia on a gun carriage. While he recuperated in Philadelphia, he contracted a severe case of smallpox. Not a handsome man to begin with, his absurdly long nose and pock-marked face later earned Anderson the dubious distinction as one of the ugliest men in the American army. He finally left the hospital in May and rejoined his regiment at Morristown. Thanks to General Washington's heroics at Trenton, the war for American independence continued, and Anderson was right in the middle of it.

Richard Anderson served with General Nathanael Greene at the ill-fated Battle of Brandywine Creek in the fall of 1777. There, Washington made a strategic error, leaving his right flank exposed and nearly losing his entire army. Greene's division held off British general William Howe's advance long enough for the Americans to escape and fight another day. That day came three weeks later at Germantown, Pennsylvania, when Washington tried in vain to dislodge the British from their occupation of Philadelphia. Anderson retired with his troops for a long, hard winter at Valley Forge, content in the knowledge that the French, Poles, and other Europeans were supporting their cause. The troops drilled and trained under the Marquis de Lafayette and Friedrich William von Steuben, and emerged from their winter quarters a much more effective fighting force.

Anderson was promoted to major of the First Virginia on February 10, 1778. He and his new regiment saw action at the Battle of Monmouth, New Jersey, in late June. It was a standoff that proved that the American army was disciplined enough to hold its own in a protracted, large-scale engagement. As the war continued, Anderson's services were always in high demand. In the fall of 1779, an alliance between more than five hundred white, free black, and slave soldiers from Saint-Domingue under the command of French Admiral Comte d'Estaing and American troops commanded by General Benjamin Lincoln devised a plan to recapture the port of Savannah from the British. Lincoln wanted Anderson and the First Virginia to join the expedition. On the morning of October 9, the attack began.

The First Virginia was ordered to assault the British siege defenses at the Spring Hill redoubt. The earthworks were soft and between sixteen and eighteen feet high. Anderson admonished his troops to refrain from firing until they reached the top of the embrasure. After the bugle sounded, Anderson led his men in a scramble up the mountain of soil. Very few made it. Major Anderson scaled the parapet and was rewarded with a sword through the shoulder. The force of the blow caused him to slide feet-first down the mound, striking the ground so hard that he ruptured his abdomen. The attack was abandoned. It was small consolation when Anderson's body servant, Spruce, shot and killed one of the defending grenadiers before dragging his master from the ditch.

On his retreat, Major Anderson encountered Polish-born brigadier general Casimir Pulaski, later called the "father of American cavalry." Pulaski was credited with saving the life of General Washington as the result of his brave stand at Brandywine. The Polish hero had been mortally wounded by grape shot as he tried to defend retreating forces at Savannah. Anderson and Pulaski were taken to the privateer *Wasp*, where Anderson stayed with him day and night. Before he died, Pulaski gave his sword to Anderson in gratitude for his friendship and service. The Savannah campaign was a dismal failure. French and American forces blamed each other, and the French admiral sailed away, leaving General Lincoln to his own devices. The Americans retreated to Charleston to spend the winter, while Anderson made another journey to the hospital. The major was still recuperating when British generals Henry Clinton and Charles Cornwallis and a force of fourteen thousand men and ninety ships laid siege to Charleston on April 1, 1780.

Lincoln finally surrendered the city and his five thousand troops on May 12. It was the greatest defeat suffered by the Americans in the war. The invalid Anderson was thrown into Fort Moultrie and given only three spoons and a tin plate. British officers gave him a permit to fish for his own food, but a British guard tore it up, saying that the fish were "too damned good for any rebel against the king." Anderson was finally exchanged after nine months of captivity. He joined General Daniel Morgan's command and eventually reached Richmond, where he received yet another promotion, this time to lieutenant colonel of Virginia's Third Regiment.[4]

As the focus of the war shifted to Virginia, Richard Anderson's knowledge of the countryside became highly valued. Washington appointed him aide-de-camp to General Lafayette. The French marquis was under pressure from Cornwallis, so he abandoned Richmond in order to protect his stores of supplies at Albemarle Court House. With more than seven thousand British troops pressing him, Lafayette called on General Anthony Wayne for assistance. "The boy cannot escape me," crowed Cornwallis. When Wayne was delayed, Lafayette sent Anderson to urge him to move faster. Three days passed with no movement, so the marquis ordered Wayne to move by forced march and instructed Anderson to send him hourly reports of troop movements.[5]

Anderson entered Wayne's tent and immediately requested a pen, ink, and paper. He told Wayne that he had been asked to repeat the order to advance and asked what the contents of his first hourly report should contain. Wayne was taken aback. "Do you mean to insult me?" he asked Anderson. The aide replied that he was only carrying out the orders of a superior officer. "Superior!" Wayne fumed. "Superior! Do you dare call any damned foreigner, and a boy, too, my superior?" A torrent of obscenities followed, in which Wayne impugned Anderson for associating himself with a "fortune-seeking Frenchman." The general eventually lost all control, pacing up and down in a ferocious rage. Little wonder his nickname was "Mad Anthony." After four such tirades had concluded, Anderson suggested that the only hope for success in their cause was for every officer to obey the orders of a superior. Wayne seemed about to explode. Suddenly his expression changed from anger to excitement. He responded to Anderson's request by shouting, "I'll jine him! Tell him I'll jine him! By God! Tell him I'll jine him tomorrow!"

Wayne and eight hundred muskets arrived at Lafayette's headquarters and the Marquis took the offensive. He forced Cornwallis to retreat to Yorktown as part of Clinton's ill-advised attempt to hold both New York and Virginia. Lafayette wrote to Washington: "It is the most beautiful sight which I may ever behold." Anderson had grown close to Lafayette during six months of service. When Washington ordered the aide to help Governor Thomas Nelson Jr. organize the state militia, Anderson and Lafayette said their reluctant goodbyes. Cornwallis surrendered and the war ended, but Lieutenant Colonel Anderson stayed with the army until it disbanded in 1783.[6]

Richard Anderson had served with great honor and bravery for seven and a half years. He had witnessed many of the most important events of the young nation's fight for independence and was on intimate terms with many of its most important military leaders. As significant as his individual contributions to the Revolution were, Anderson's greatest legacy was the direction he gave to his children. He had suffered many hardships to help win freedom for his fellow Americans. His sons and daughters were expected to honor him by making their own sacrifices in the service of their country.

➤➤ ◄◄

Bear Grass Lessons

RICHARD CLOUGH ANDERSON returned home to Virginia a changed man. His adventures on the high seas and on countless battlefields were over. Only thirty-three years old, he could not see himself leading a quiet life in the Virginia countryside. His fellow founding members of the Society of the Cincinnati decided that Anderson was the logical choice to take charge of land grants due Virginia's Revolutionary War veterans. In December of 1783, Anderson signed a contract to become surveyor-general of two tracts of land in the west. The first was in Kentucky, between the Green and Cumberland Rivers. The other tract lay between the Little Miami and Scioto Rivers in Ohio's Northwest Territory. When spring came, Anderson loaded his belongings on seven pack horses and set out for the Falls of Ohio (now Louisville) accompanied by three slaves. He built a log cabin at the headwaters of Bear Grass Creek on a grant of five hundred acres in what later became Jefferson County.[1]

From the beginning of his residence in this largely unsettled area, Anderson attempted to impose civility and order on what was essentially a raw wilderness. He founded the first masonic lodge west of the Allegheny Mountains in 1784. Indian tribes dominated the Ohio land tracts and frequently followed game into Kentucky, making settlement there a risky proposition. Anderson's surveyors were especially vulnerable. Mountains of paperwork chained Anderson to his office most of the time. When he did get out, he often accompanied George Rogers Clark, the founder of the Commonwealth of Kentucky, on hunting expeditions in the deep forest. In 1787, Anderson married Clark's sister Elizabeth. Three years later he began building his dream house, a Georgian-style stone mansion that he dubbed "Soldier's Retreat."

Anderson waited to occupy his new home until the Indian threat had lessened. In the fall of 1789, Indians raided Chenoweth Station, killing several members of that family. When Anderson arrived on the horrible scene the next morning, he encountered a four-year-old child, apparently unharmed. "We are all dead here, Colonel Anderson," the little girl said. This looked to be true as a servant and three of the child's brothers lay dead on the cabin floor. The girl had been spared when her bed was overturned by the intruders, throwing her against the wall and sheltering her behind the mattress. Further investigation of the grisly scene found little Jamie Chenoweth lying by the wood pile with a tomahawk gash in his forehead. He rose, fully conscious. Mrs. Chenoweth was found in the woods nearby, still alive despite her missing scalp. She had played dead when the Indian tomahawk thrown at her missed its mark; she had endured the heinous operation without crying out. Both survived. In 1793, Anderson's former acquaintance, "Mad Anthony" Wayne, defeated a combined force of Indians at Fallen Timbers. Settlement of the countryside began in earnest.[2]

Elizabeth Clark Anderson gave her husband five offspring before dying shortly after her namesake daughter was born in December 1794. The grieving widower had four surviving children to raise and a large business and farm to oversee. In September 1797 he married Sarah Marshall, the cousin of his old friend and Revolutionary War comrade John Marshall. Marshall was destined for greatness in his role as chief justice of the United States Supreme Court. Sarah Marshall Anderson bore the old colonel's next twelve children. She christened her ninth child and youngest surviving son with the name Charles. The family called him Charley.

One of Charley Anderson's earliest memories was accompanying his slave "nurse boy" Frank on an errand to deliver a dinner basket to his older brothers and sisters at the schoolhouse a few miles away. Frank held Charley's hand as they inched their way across the knee-deep Bear Grass Creek on a long board, just below Uncle Tompkins spring. The young slave boy stopped abruptly and pointed down at the waters below. Charley was amazed at what he saw. There, reflected in the quiet clear pool, was a young boy clothed in a blue and white calico girl's gown with a red morocco skull cap, replete with a cotton knot and tassels. Fine, curly white hair cascaded down from the comical hat and framed the face of the innocent youngster. Dirty bare feet and creamy white skin completed the visage. Charley giggled with glee as he realized that he was gazing at himself for the very first time. What a delightful surprise indeed. Life on the Bear Grass for the youngest son of Richard Clough Anderson and his wife Sarah was languid and luxurious. Charley's mother and sisters doted on the bright little tot, and he loved being spoiled.[3]

A few weeks later, when the boys were on a similar excursion, the bucolic bubble that had sheltered young Charley for most of his brief existence suddenly burst. Before him, under the massive limbs of an ancient elm, stood his skinny teenaged brother Robert and a huge, burly boy named Ben Dorsey. The boxing tree was known throughout the county as the appointed place to settle scores. A crowd of noisy boys, and even a few adult male spectators, had assembled on the north side of the lane by the elm to watch the pitched battle and cheer for their favorite. As Robert and Ben stripped off their shirts, Charley clung fast to Frank, and the two youngsters withdrew out of sight of the battle, but not beyond hearing distance. The fight raged on for what seemed like an interminable time. Finally it ended. Frank and Charley ran home to tell the tale of a contest they had not seen. It would not be the last time that Robert Anderson, who later surrendered Fort Sumter, faced overwhelming odds with courage in defeat. The coddled youngsters realized that life was not always a pastoral fantasy. Such lessons took years to reemerge to the forefront of Charley's consciousness. For most of his childhood, times were sweet indeed.

When guests entered the big house at Soldier's Retreat, they understood how hard Charley's father had worked to replicate some semblance of Virginia's colonial elite society in his new environment.

Neighbors and visitors marveled at the sheer size and elegance of Colonel Anderson's mansion. It seemed out of place with the rude log cabins and modest frame dwellings nearby. From its beginning, the Anderson plantation became a must-see attraction for all who journeyed to the developing region. The sixteen-room house was constructed of local gray limestone, with walls three feet thick. Ascending a five-foot staircase through a pair of folding black walnut doors, visitors encountered a passage eighteen feet wide, which led due south to a corresponding set of doors and steps. To either side of the hall passage were various rooms, each about twenty feet square, including parlor, office, dining room, and Sarah Anderson's bedroom. Steps from the rear of the dining room led outside to kitchen, smokehouse, bathhouse, and other outbuildings. In this arrangement the residence was similar to other large dwellings of wealthy plantation owners of the day.

The stone exterior was certainly an unusual feature in this frontier area, but it was the second floor that revealed a truly lavish surprise. The upper hall had a banister staircase to the attic and various doors to other bedrooms. The unique feature of this private home, however, was a ballroom twenty by forty-two feet, lighted by five windows running along the mansion's south side. Large, high-backed cherry chairs, carved in the latest fashion, graced the vast expanse. This room was constructed for one purpose only: dancing. Colonel Anderson hired a professional master to teach his children and neighbors during weekly dancing classes. Slave fiddlers furnished the music. Regularly scheduled balls drew young men and women from as far away as Louisville, some ten miles distant. Participants danced Virginia reels and "contre" dances and often spent the night on the property. Colonel Anderson, a stern and stoic man, never danced himself, but his wife Sarah danced as often as she could. In the midst of this atmosphere of refined frolic, Soldier's Retreat became the center of elite social life in Jefferson County.

Despite fathering his first child at age thirty-eight with his first wife, Elizabeth Clark Anderson, Richard Clough Anderson had eighteen children in all, thirteen of whom lived to adulthood. His last child, Sarah Jane, was born in 1822, when the colonel was seventy-one years old. Sarah Marshall Anderson, his second wife, was nearly thirty years his junior. When Charley arrived on the scene on June 1, 1814, he shared the household with his parents, six siblings, various paid servants, and twenty slaves. Though their father's important duties kept him busy, the children had a close relationship with both parents. This was especially true of the youngest children, who grew up after their father had retired from his office as surveyor-general. Colonel Anderson wanted the best for his family, and a little clean fun was always part of his parental recipe.

The colonel's sons inherited his love of the hunt. Wild turkeys, ducks, and other birds were their favorite quarry, but during squirrel migration season, killing the incalculable hordes intent on devouring the corn crop was first priority. The object was to shoot the squirrels only in their heads, so as not to ruin the meat. This practice created an entire generation of skilled marksmen in Kentucky who would become famous during the Civil War as "squirrel hunters." In the fall the Anderson boys would sometimes beg off the long trip to school in bad weather only to gladly accompany the slave Stephen in his efforts to net partridges. In wet weather, partridges abandoned the field for the safety and shelter of the forest floor, aligning themselves in circular coveys and mimicking dead leaves. The boys used many forms of trickery to herd the prey into Stephen's net. The conquering heroes usually brought back a delicious dinner. When they arrived home, the colonel always insisted that a few partridges be released to ensure a future supply.

Christmas corresponded with the end of hog-killing season on Bear Grass Creek. Since fresh meat was as rare as hard currency in this part of Kentucky, bacon was "laid up" in great quantities each winter after the first frost. In a typical year, more than a hundred hogs fattened on bluegrass, beech nuts, acorns, and white corn were killed and processed. Besides the feasting that ensued from all of the delectable parts not used for bacon, the most treasured remnant for the children was inedible. Choosing the hogs that would carry the largest bladders became sport and science among both the children of Soldier's Retreat and their slave accomplices. The pig bladder was the key enabler of their favorite Christmas tradition. Sons, daughters, and slave children waited impatiently for the butcher to do his duty. Once they were awarded their treasured organ, they proceeded to blow air into its lower orifice until it became, in the best cases, a balloon larger than their own heads. The hard work accomplished, the proud owner of the inflated pig bladder had their mother, Sarah, inscribe it with the child's name and hang it to dry in her special locked closet. The wait for Christmas morning was excruciating. When the joyous day finally arrived, the little scamps grabbed their pig bladders, positioned themselves outside the doors and windows of the older members of the family, and punctured the balloons. It sounded like a small cannon. Following the cacophony, the children, white and black, would cry out, "My Christmas Gift, Sister!" or "Christmas Giff, my ole Massa!"

Joy was plentiful on the Anderson plantation where innumerable delights awaited the curious and social Charley. Melon season was one of the year's highlights, and Colonel Anderson took especial pride in his annual bounty of cantaloupes and watermelons. Each day at exactly noon, Charley's father assembled family and guests to enjoy the treats that he had hand-picked himself at first light and sent by gardener or slave to the springhouse for cooling. Their small vineyard, like their large apple orchard, produced wonderful fruit but "abominable wines." The rural life was one of young Charley's earliest passions. As an adult, he would yearn to return to these days of simple farm pleasures.

After supper, the patriarch of Soldier's Retreat would take his customary walk down an allée of locust and walnut trees to a massive yellow poplar, eight feet in diameter and more than one hundred feet tall. During these walks, father and children would talk about far-ranging topics. The colonel loved his children and they worshipped him. The family's comfortable lifestyle lent itself to the sharing of many intimate parental moments during which plenty of advice was gleaned. Lessons in duty and morality were tops on Colonel Anderson's list. His codes were strict, and he enforced the rules. One such rule was the colonel's insistence that his children avoid too frequent or intimate associations with the slaves. Given the daily interactions between blacks and whites on the plantation and the colonel's fairness to all his dependents, heeding this admonishment was nearly impossible.

Richard Anderson's slaves had a life that was better than most of their peers in the region and substantially better than most slaves in the Deep South. The colonel ruled his entire household with a sense of justice that led more zealous slaveholders to remark that the old soldier was "just ruining all the slaves in the county." His sons and their slave counterparts played innumerable games, ran races, and occasionally fought with each other as boyhood pals often do. When one of the colonel's young pugilists tiptoed into the house with a bloody nose from one of these illicit affairs and sought comfort from the ladies in the household, the master of Soldier's Retreat was called to adjudicate. He usually began his trial by repeating his oft-broken family law prohibiting close associations with the servants. Since one of his sons, by playing and fighting with a slave, chose to place himself as an equal with the servant, "they must stand to the bitter end by their own chosen colors." Colonel Anderson would not treat the offending slave with injustice; nor would he have his boys "indulged into becoming cowardly tyrants." After a fair hearing, the guilty party, slave or son, was taken to a special peach tree near the family graveyard to endure "whaling" with a tree switch. Fights were frequent but usually kept secret to avoid the master's sentence.

Colonel Anderson fought a losing battle against familiar relations between his brood and his servants. He believed, like most of his contemporaries, that the system of slavery was warranted by innate deficiencies in character and ability among the blacks. He forbade slaves telling ghost stories and traditional tales to his children, as these "lies" worked against his standards of "good morals, good manner, and good English." He tried to avoid what he felt were the "demoralizing and vulgarizing" influences that close fellowship with the slaves engendered. Despite his rules, daily life on the plantation encouraged intimate relations between masters and servants. White children were wet-nursed by their black "mammy" from infancy. Patsy was Charley's nurse. She was one of three black women of child-bearing age on the property. The birth of Patsy's son Richmond in 1817, like the other slave births, were recorded in the family records. Patsy nursed Charley in her slave cabin bed, loving him, as he later wrote, "with more than a maternal love." She was, in Charley's opinion, "a woman whom for mental and moral qualities I rate with any woman of any race or sphere."

When each Anderson child was old enough to walk, they were assigned a "nurse boy," and later a personal servant, to attend to their every need. Charley's servant, Edom, was just a year older than Charley, his master. As was the custom among the slaves, each personal servant invented a nickname for his young master. Edom dubbed Charley "Marse Chunk"—not for his appearance, but rather for his habit of scrounging for a piece of wood to use as a chair in their frequent trips to the woods. The practice of assigning personal servants to the master's children led to ardent friendships between child and slave. It also promoted what Charley called "the servile vices." The Anderson children were spoiled. They rarely engaged in hard labor of any sort. A slave saddled their horses, blackened their shoes, chopped their wood, and fetched their clothing. Charley later blamed some of his poor work habits on the slave system, but there were other factors at play, not the least of which was his unquenchable curiosity. He loved learning much more than work.

Young Charley was fascinated by aspects of the African slave subculture. He often stole away to watch the slaves perform the juba, a dance set to the rhythmic clapping and patting of hands and feet, rather than to music. He called this dance a "marvel of artistic perfection." Their own "uncle" Benjamin was the most accomplished juba performer in the county. Looking back as an adult, Charley claimed that Ben gave the best lessons in the art of oratory that he ever had. The plantation hierarchy was suspended on rare occasions such as during large corn-shucking festivals, where master and servant competed together for top honors. Despite the temperate colonel's best intentions, rewards of corn whiskey led to nights of revelry when customary rules of slave fraternization were somewhat relaxed. To Charley, the African race possessed the "most social, genial, amicable, peaceable, and fun-loving traits of personal character of any peoples inhabiting the earth." As he matured, he began to view slavery as his father's "one, but most grave, parental error." Such feelings were unusual for a southern man from a slaveholding family. Charley grew to become "a strong anti-slavery man" in moral matters but would struggle to reconcile this stark example of American injustice with the political exigencies of his tumultuous times.

Colonel Anderson's patriot connections and honored position meant that Soldier's Retreat became a way station for many important visitors to Kentucky. Social and political circles of the early nineteenth-century elite were small. Intimate friendships were maintained long distance by letter, and when old friends came to call, they sometimes stayed several days or even as long as a week. As the colonel and his Revolutionary War comrades advanced in age, they often made strenuous efforts to see each other one last time. In the fall of 1819, when Charley was just five years old, one of his father's old brothers-in-arms came to see him. On this occasion, James Monroe (now president) visited. The two rehashed past times, reopening the old wounds each had suffered at the Battle of Trenton. Eventually the large retinue dispersed across the lawn and around the property.

One of the party guests was the famous hero of New Orleans, Andrew Jackson. While General Jackson and Colonel Anderson traded recollections of wars in the republic's young history, Charley's eight-year-old brother, John, sauntered up to meet the general. The colonel immediately interceded, suggesting that Jackson might not wish to speak to the lad. "He got drunk—dead drunk—in the harvest field with all the other hands yesterday," Anderson explained. "Did he though?" Jackson inquired. "Come to me, my lark!" he beckoned. Jackson grasped the boy by the shoulders with his strong hands and gazed intently into his eyes. The general then placed his palms over the boy's ears and raised him to eye level, presumably as a show of punishment. Setting the lad back down, he patted him on the head and cried, "By the eternal, you are a little Hickory of a fellow." The slaves took the cue and followed with a nickname. They rechristened young John as "Marse Hickory." John and his brother Marshall became life-long devotees of Jackson and his political allies from that day forward.

Jackson visited Soldier's Retreat again nearly eight years later. It was April 1825, and the election of John Quincy Adams by the House of Representatives had recently denied him the nation's highest office. Colonel Anderson's health was failing at the time, and this visit was an appropriate way to honor the old patriot. A month later, another longtime friend arrived somewhat delayed after his steamboat sank on the Ohio River. The Marquis de Lafayette was in the middle of a two-year triumphal tour of America, nearly forty years after his service during the American Revolution. It was a touching scene as the two old friends kissed each other and renewed their close bonds in the twilight of their lives. After this visit, Anderson traveled with Lafayette to Frankfort, Kentucky, for a ceremony honoring Lafayette. It was his last trip away from home.[4]

Charley's entire world was turned upside down in his twelfth year. The first blow came with the sudden death of his oldest brother, Richard Clough Anderson Jr. The colonel's namesake son was serious and diligent, much like his father. Like all of Colonel Anderson's children, Richard had attended only the best schools. He received his earliest education from a tutor in Louisville. A brilliant boy, he graduated from the College of William and Mary at the age of sixteen. An attorney by vocation, Richard had been elected to the Kentucky House of Representatives in 1815, and he served in the U.S. Congress from 1817 to 1821. He reentered Kentucky's House of Representatives in 1822 and was elected its speaker. President Madison appointed him minster to Colombia in 1823. He contracted yellow fever while returning to his post in Bogotá and died on board a ship on July 24, 1826. His heartbroken father, already failing from a hernia related to his old war wounds, died less than three months later.

When news of the colonel's imminent demise broke, Anderson's eldest son, Larz, was away at Harvard. Robert, a recent graduate at West Point, was at his post with the Second U.S. Artillery. The only son of age in the state at the time was nineteen-year-old William Marshall Anderson, then a student at Transylvania University in Lexington. Marshall raced home in record time, via a relay of three swift horses. His father died in his arms. Marshall served as executor of the colonel's estate, which took three years to sort out. Suddenly he was the man of the household, caring for his mother, four siblings, and twenty slaves for whom it seemed there was less and less work. The isolated farmstead barely produced enough to support itself.

The older Anderson brothers—Larz, Robert, and Marshall—became Charley's role models. Although all three shared their father's core values and sterling character, they were very different from each other. As Charley walked the meandering path toward manhood, his brothers guided him; they remained his three closest confidantes throughout most of his life. The colonel's sons did much more than merely honor his patriot legacy. They developed into leaders themselves. The Andersons were destined to become one of the most accomplished families in the region.[5]

↦ ↤

CHAPTER THREE

Born to Lead

Larz Anderson was thrust into the role of family patriarch at the age of twenty-three. It was a job that perfectly suited his talents and temperament. Brilliant like his late brother Richard, Larz was also warm and compassionate like his younger brother Charley. Larz's shrewd business sense and laser focus made him a financial success. He guided his brother Marshall's Transylvania College education, even sending money to Marshall on his father's behalf while Larz himself was a student at Harvard College in Cambridge, Massachusetts. "Be not the least niggardly in your expenses," he advised Marshall, "but be prudent."

Acting as executor of Richard Jr.'s estate in the summer of 1826, Larz found that his ill father's affairs were a mess. He hired out slaves to other plantations where they could at least generate some income. By the summer of 1827, it was clear that something had to be done about the plantation at Soldier's Retreat, so Marshall left college to help his mother manage the farm. Marshall was dutiful but extremely unhappy in his captivity back home. While Robert may have been a likely candidate to manage the struggling plantation, he would need to resign his commission to do so. This he just would not do. Larz refused to throw away his father's investment in his children's education. He planned to place sixteen-year-old John in a customs house job in the fall; to move his mother, Charley, and his two sisters to Louisville; and to sell the place after the estate was settled. His mother refused to leave the farm, however, so Larz sent Charley off to board at the famous Pickering School in Cincinnati, Ohio.[1]

Larz was a pragmatic man. He was determined to advance in society, and he needed a wife to do that. In a letter to his sister, Maria Latham, in late August, Larz vowed to be wedded by Christmas, though the identity of the lady was "yet a secret even to myself." A week later, he revealed that he had identified the "contenders" for his spouse as Misses Prather, Armant, Bullitt, and Steele. Larz seemingly had it all planned out, but he had forgotten one critical element—love. That emotion hit him unexpectedly when visiting Louisville during Harvard term break in late February 1828. He met a girl whom many contended was the most beautiful and accomplished young woman in the state. Miss Ann Pope, the daughter of a wealthy Jefferson County farmer, was known not only for her great beauty but was said to have a quick wit and acerbic tongue, which made her charming in social situations. Larz had to have her. After graduating in June 1828, he rushed home to Kentucky and married his sweetheart. Back at home, Larz found that Marshall was "disgusted" with farm life and had "pretty much abandoned it." Marshall spent more than half his time in Chillicothe, Ohio, working with his brother-in-law, Alan Latham, who had assumed Colonel Anderson's land office responsibilities. Larz insisted that his mother get an overseer or take herself and Charley off the plantation.[2]

Nineteenth-century families faced many challenges, but serious illness was certainly one of the most threatening. Nearly everyone in the Anderson household contracted a gastrointestinal malady known as "bilious fever" at some point during the 1820s. Larz's and Marshall's cases were so severe that both nearly died. Charley developed asthma in childhood and lived with it all of his life. Childbirth was also dangerous. Larz's wife Ann gave birth to their only son, Richard Clough, in 1829, but she was too weak to nurse him. The infant was nursed by a slave woman while Ann tried to recover from the birth. She never did. Heartbroken, Larz buried his first love in the Bear Grass neighborhood, where both had grown up. He threw his energies into a legal career; he and Marshall passed the Kentucky bar and set up a law practice in Louisville.[3]

With the estate finally settled and the farm and slaves sold, the widow Anderson packed her belongings and moved to Chillicothe, where she remained for the rest of her life. Charley, not yet fifteen, immediately left for college at Miami University in March 1829. He planned to complete his final term of preparatory courses there, before matriculating in the fall. Journeying upriver from Louisville, he stopped at the great metropolis of Cincinnati. The "Queen City" of the West boasted more than twenty-nine thousand inhabitants and dwarfed all other cities in the region. Young Anderson was awed by the wax figures of Aaron Burr shooting Alexander Hamilton and the figure of the great Indian Chief Tecumseh in the Western Museum. Soon after he arrived on campus, Charley had befriended most of the inhabitants of the small town of Oxford, who appreciated his gregarious nature and keen wit. There were so many things to learn and so many new people to meet. For the bright youth from rural Kentucky, college days were among the happiest of his life.

Ohio had set aside land for a university as early as 1803, but it was not until 1824 that the college was actually founded. The board of trustees, on which Anderson would later serve as an adult, envisioned a Harvard of the West, hewn out of the raw wilderness and attended by the most promising young minds in the region. Half of the students in Charley's class were from wealthy Southern families. The South's dearth of first-class higher education was readily acknowledged. Despite its rural setting, Miami University was no backwoods institution. Two literary societies were founded just a year after the university opened. Charley chose the Erodelphian Society as his social club and was elected its secretary in his second year.

He flourished in this new environment. The club raised money to expand their growing library, and Anderson read everything he could get his hands on. The Erodelphians often engaged their rivals in the Union Literary Society in lively debates, ranging from philosophy and history to current events. A classmate recalled a time when Charley debated a young man who lamented the lack of a large standing American army. Anderson overwhelmed his debate opponent with his booming voice, denouncing militarism as "hostile to human liberty." Another debate considered whether the citizens of

Ohio should prevent free blacks from settling in the state. One student thought Anderson's frequent passionate outbursts were a sign of an "impetuous and impulsive nature." This charge followed Charley most of his adult life, as he exercised his political independence on a larger stage.

Young Charley Anderson was a precocious teen with many talents. He was among a select few, in the opinion of one classmate, who ranked "far above their fellows in superior mental endowments, high-toned morality, and upright conduct." Most people agreed that Anderson's finest attribute, however, was his "genial warmth and gladsome society." Charley seemed to be everyone's boon companion. He was the "soul of social life and the center of its circles," as another former student described him. Colonel Anderson's youngest son discovered that he was a natural leader, and that he could use that power for all manner of ends. This sometimes resulted in a practical joke with Charley as the instigator. One such instance occurred at the house of a Mr. Bingham in Oxford, where Anderson first boarded. A skittish young man named Solomon Mitchell was one of his housemates. In May 1832, U.S. Army troops, including some led by Charley's brother Robert, were fighting the Sauk Indian chief Black Hawk in Illinois. Just a short distance away in Indiana, Native American villages predominated, and the threat of Indian attack was a constant concern. A rumor circulated that Black Hawk was fifteen to twenty miles from Oxford and advancing. Anderson was following the war and knew this was extremely unlikely, but Mitchell was beside himself with apprehension. Charley gathered a band of friends, dressed them as Indians, trained them to yell and "hoop" like warriors and made a mock assault on the boardinghouse room where young Mitchell was sleeping. Once he had recovered from the shock, the "victim" was too humiliated to report the incident.

After the Union Society unveiled a portrait of university president Dr. Robert Hamilton Bishop in the fall of 1829, the Erodelphians racked their brains for a way to outdo their rivals. Anderson recalled the lifelike wax figures he had seen recently in Cincinnati and proposed that they procure a statue of Bishop for their hall. "Too costly," the members retorted. "Then perhaps a bust," Anderson replied. When the members asked Charley who would create the work, Anderson suggested that the artist who made the wax figures could accomplish the task. The society voted to allocate seventy-five dollars in subscriptions for a plaster bust and sent Charley, William Woodruff, and James Stagg to find the artist. The boys found a handsome young man in a dirty apron named Hiram Powers and offered him the commission. Powers agreed to make the bust for one hundred dollars, and his clay-covered handshake with Anderson sealed the deal. The bust was a hit with both Bishop and the Erodelphians. Then unknown Powers later gained the patronage of Larz Anderson's father-in-law, self-made millionaire Nicholas Longworth, and became a world-renowned sculptor. Powers's masterpiece "The Greek Slave" was viewed by more than one hundred thousand people on its American tour in 1847. The sculpture became a potent symbol for the abolitionist movement.[4]

When the time came for Charley to graduate, he was near the top of his class. In fact, only his inability to master Hebrew kept him from achieving the top rank. The young man rose to deliver his commencement oration on September 25, 1833. It was customary for select graduating seniors to give a brief address on a topic of their choosing. This particular student stood out among his twenty peers. Over six feet tall, with reddish-blonde hair, a prominent nose, and a booming voice that belied his nineteen years, the popular youth had a magnetic stage presence. He was not bound for the ministry, where half of his classmates would end up. While all the student speeches were serious, Charley's effort was particularly earnest.

As Charley announced the title of his address—"An Oration on the Influence of Monumental Records upon National Morals"—his friends may have cringed. The young graduate began by claiming that "the commemoration of illustrious individuals and events has ever been the delight and glory of past ages." He maintained that every soul "burns for immortality" and that "marble is made to speak lessons of piety, patriotism and philanthropy." Honoring the patriots that built this great nation, Anderson argued, is as noble and virtuous as the biblical admonition to honor one's father and mother. Such monuments promote a "national morality." In the America of

1833, he asserted, the young country's greatest hero had no lasting memorial to glorify his past deeds and instruct future generations. His speech was a plea for the creation of the Washington Monument. The young baccalaureate extolled "the obelisks of fallen Egypt" and suggested that the memorial be "simple, towering, sublime," bearing Washington's name aloft, "bright with the beams of immortal glory." How did this mere lad foresee the precise aspect of an iconic shrine that was yet to be designed and would not stand complete for another fifty years? The answer lies in Charles Anderson's family history.[5]

By the time young Anderson graduated from college, John Marshall had been chief justice of the U.S. Supreme Court for more than three decades. It was Marshall who first organized and chaired the Washington National Monument Society just weeks before the Miami University graduation festivities. Charles must have thought it his patriotic duty to help "Uncle John" spread the word and raise money for the project. At least one member of the audience at the Miami University commencement ceremonies listened to Anderson's oration with rapt attention. Sixteen-year-old Eliza Jane Brown would later say that she fell in love with Charles that very day. He dedicated his speech to her, and they would share the marital bed for sixty years.

There was another woman who, despite Eliza's sacrifices and devotion, would hold the preeminent place in her future husband's heart. Lady Liberty was Charles's first and most ardent love. He was betrothed to her by his father's legacy. He would never abandon her at any cost. Anderson's graduation speech may have been dedicated to Eliza, but it was really a solemn oath to Union and country and set the course for the rest of his eventful life. The young man with so much potential ignored his guardian Larz's advice to prepare for the ministry. Larz had found that religion soothed the heartache of his wife's untimely death and made a declaration of faith. Charles had other plans: he had been devising a business partnership by correspondence with his brother Robert, who by now was seriously considering retirement from the military and getting back to farming. Charles yearned to return to the rural life of his boyhood. The root of his desire ran all the way back to his earliest memories.

When Colonel Anderson's youngest son was only three years old, his sister Maria presented him with three unusual gifts: an almond, a pecan, and a dinner knife. Charles was to plant the nuts and grow his own trees, which might someday bear the fruit of his juvenile efforts. He did as he was instructed and the little seedlings grew for about four years, until a particularly hard winter killed the almond. The pecan tree, on the other hand, would outlive the boy. Charles later recalled this feat with some irony, as his "sole great success in life's works." The toddler arborist often heard his father speak of his lands on the Ohio River opposite the Wabash, which included a huge island full of ancient pecans. Repeated begging led Colonel Anderson to deed the land to his youngest son. Charles dreamed that one day he would build his own bucolic country seat on that very spot. He convinced his brother Robert to join him in the venture. In October 1833, not long after graduation, Charles boarded a steamboat and headed for Wabash Island. There he found a former Shawnee town with huge tree stumps remnant of an urgent contest to clear the land. Fever raged in this remote outpost. There were no schools, no churches, and no polite society of any kind. When Charles reached the tract that he owned, he discovered that a tornado had recently cut a mile-wide swath directly through the property. The pecan trees, along with his childhood dreams, were obliterated.

Undaunted, Charles and Robert purchased a farm on Gravois Creek, near Jefferson Barracks, Missouri, in 1834. That effort also ended in failure. As Charles was preparing to leave, an old man advised him to return to Louisville and become a lawyer. It was clear to the aged stranger that Charles Anderson "was no farmer." Charles took the old man's advice and headed to Louisville, where he studied the law and joined Larz's firm, Pirtle and Anderson.

Robert accepted an appointment as instructor of artillery at the United States Military Academy at West Point, New York. He had made many important connections there while he was a student. In the Black Hawk War, Robert had mustered Abraham Lincoln in and out of service. Winfield Scott had become Robert's loyal champion and closest friend. Mississippi native Jefferson Davis (the future president of the Confederacy) had served as Robert's aide. William T.

Sherman had been Robert's junior first lieutenant when they were both stationed in South Carolina. Robert's friends became Charles's friends. The brothers were that close. Some of these connections proved valuable as Charles's life progressed.[6]

Jefferson Davis and young Charley shared more than mutual admiration for Robert's character and abilities. They also shared a sweetheart. As a boy on the Bear Grass, Charley's playmate from early childhood (and his first crush) was Sarah Knox Taylor. She was the daughter of career military officer, Louisville resident and future U.S. president Zachary Taylor. It was an innocent tryst that existed more in Charley's imagination than in reality. When the dashing young Lieutenant Davis met sixteen-year-old Sarah at Fort Crawford in Wisconsin territory, sparks flew. It took nearly four years for Davis to convince Zachary Taylor to allow Davis to marry his daughter.

In the meantime, Davis took every opportunity to rendezvous with his secret fiancé. One such opportunity came with the marriage of Charley's cousin Anne Bullitt and Major Thomas L. Alexander in 1833. Charley was visiting his cousin Mary, the wife of General Henry Atkinson, at Jefferson Barracks when he attended an "infair," a wedding reception in honor of the newlyweds. He had met Davis on several occasions. Charley's customary room at headquarters was occupied by other Louisville guests, so Lieutenant Davis invited the young man to room with him at his quarters across the parade ground. While Charley sat in the general's headquarters the next day, Lieutenant Colonel Stephen W. Kearney of the First Dragoons entered and asked to speak to the general on urgent business. Kearny pleaded with Atkinson to help persuade Colonel Taylor to allow Davis to marry Sarah Taylor. It was an awkward moment for the nineteen-year-old Charley Anderson, as he was compelled to listen to the man urge a marriage between his "best friend" Sarah and his "then bed-fellow" Davis. When the two lovebirds finally tied the knot in 1835, Charley was in attendance. The new bride died of malaria just three months later. Davis was a changed man. The twenty-five-year-old officer whom Anderson later described as "witty," "sportful," and "captivating" became a "sober, grave, philosopher-thinker."[7]

Yellow fever had nearly claimed the life of Charley's brother

Marshall the year before, during a visit to Robert Anderson's post at Baton Rouge. A friend of the family convinced Marshall that upon his recovery, a trip to the Oregon Country might help to restore his health. It seemed like a rather rash remedy, given that the route Lewis and Clark had taken just thirty years before was rarely traveled by anyone other than fur traders and mountain men. The daring trip, later published in diary form, kindled a spirit of adventure in William Marshall Anderson that would never be extinguished. Marshall returned to Ohio in 1835, married the daughter of former Ohio governor Duncan McArthur, and settled into a legal career. Like his youngest brother, Charley, Marshall loved learning more than working and became a renowned archeologist. His valuable collection of Indian tools and artifacts from the burial mounds of Ohio were later donated to the Smithsonian Institution.[8]

Charles Anderson became someone different from each of his accomplished older brothers. Richard Jr. was the enshrined model and facsimile of their father—the beau ideal of a son. Larz represented industry and achievement and was the most respected brother of the clan. Robert represented faith, constancy, and duty, achieving lasting fame for his lifetime of sacrifice in the service of his country. Marshall was most like his youngest brother in his interests and independent temperament. These traits eventually cleaved huge divisions in the family over faith and politics. In the end, however, brotherly love prevailed over seemingly irreparable differences. With the support of these mentors, Charles prepared to enter the real world and face his own great challenges.

His chosen partner on this lifelong journey was the sister of two of his Oxford roommates. Eliza Jane Brown was still finishing high school when she and Charles pledged their troths to each other. They married in 1835 after a two-year engagement. The young couple settled in Dayton, where her Patterson ancestors had founded a prosperous and growing community. Eliza was an educated woman, a loving companion, and a dutiful, traditional wife. Anderson's ego required a partner and a helpmate, not someone who would oppose or challenge him. Their first son arrived the following year, and they named him Allen Latham in honor of Anderson's brother-in-law. Like his brothers, Charles pursued a career in the law. It was not his first choice, nor his calling in life, but he had a family to support and his first duty was to them.

→→ ←←

Devilish Whispers

L ARZ ANDERSON WAS TROUBLED by what he had observed over the previous five years. Since graduating from college, his youngest brother appeared to be wasting his talents and squandering a promising legal career. Despite the rare advantages of a first-rate classical education, superior intelligence, and the fine examples set by his older brothers, Charles Anderson lacked diligence and commitment. By December 1840, Larz could no longer stifle his opinion. He sent his little brother a long letter with a decidedly parental tone. He suggested that Charles read a short essay by the English Baptist minister John Foster titled "Decision of Character." It was intended to be a wake-up call to the young attorney. Charles had, by his own admission, accomplished nothing since he married and embarked on his chosen profession. Perhaps he had forgotten his father's favorite maxim, Larz suggested, "that whatever is worth doing at all, is worth doing well."[1]

According to his older brother, Charles spent most of his time "discoursing and castle-building," instead of applying himself in earnest. He was living beyond his means and constantly in debt. Neglecting his practice with no plans for alternative employment amounted to a disservice to his family, his community, and his legacy. It was high time for Larz's little brother to stop daydreaming and to get serious about a career. Larz knew that his brother harbored regrets about his short-lived experiment at farming. If Charles really examined his conscience, Larz insisted, he would find that agriculture lacked the excitement and social interaction that he sorely needed. Politics was an enduring interest of men in the legal profession, and Charles often wondered if that was his true calling. Larz dismissed the idea. Charles disliked law because he hated the "low acts" that attorneys often resorted to in order to win cases. How then, Larz asked, could Charles possibly stomach "the paltry means, the vile intrigues, the hypocrisy" of the politician? The elder brother had considerable experience in both realms. One could be successful in law without sinking to such levels, Larz reasoned, but "it is next to impossible for the politician to preserve himself pure, amid the despicable shifts and maneuvers" that elected officials subject themselves to. "Put it down as certain," Larz advised, "that you can never be a politician."

Larz urged his former ward to do something. "I want a purpose, an end, a plan," he pleaded. The plan itself was not nearly as important as the effort and perseverance behind it. Larz could set Charles up in Cincinnati, or across the river in Covington, Kentucky, where the prospects for financial success were good, if Charles could "exorcise the demon of Politics." But Charles was firmly rooted in Dayton, where Eliza's family property offered at least a small measure of security in their uncertain financial situation. As for the devil on Charles's shoulder, he found that it kept whispering sweet entreaties into his ear until he could no longer ignore the temptation.

It was his fellow citizens, rather than Satan himself, who demanded that Charles Anderson become a public figure. From the beginning of his time in Dayton, he had been actively involved in community affairs. This was expected of a man of his education and talents. It was also a virtue that his father had stressed and his siblings honored. Charles served a term as clerk of Dayton Township, an office he took on in order to help implement a new common school law. He commanded the local militia, called the "Dayton Grays," until his paid work made holding that position impossible. A year after receiving Larz's admonishing letter, Charles succumbed to peer pressure and agreed to run for the office of Montgomery County prosecuting attorney. "Tomorrow I begin one of the most disagreeable tasks of my life," he wrote to his sister Maria in September 1841. His opponent in the race was an old mentor and friend, Judge George B. Holt. Charles defeated the judge but, like many former and future adversaries, retained the friendship for the rest of Holt's life.[2]

Despite Charles's foray into elective office, Larz was not overly perturbed. His brother's star was rising in legal circles and the new-found recognition led to a partnership with successful Dayton attorney John Howard. The new partners were a good match. Howard was one of the most successful practitioners at the Dayton bar. He was bright, extremely well-read, and possessed a tireless work ethic. He overcame a slow, awkward manner of speaking by connecting in an intimate and folksy way with the jury. In many ways, Howard and Charles made an ideal team. Clients calling on Anderson often found him absent, as he preferred to sit on the river bank and fish or tend to his small farm, rather than endure the tedium of office work. But Charles was magic in front of a jury. The same star qualities that made him so persuasive in arguing cases before his peers made him attractive to political operatives.[3]

Charles Anderson was a prototype leader. Tall, handsome, and articulate, with an engaging personality and a quick wit, he was as effective in intimate gatherings as he was impressive on the podium. Anderson was a man of learning and ideas and was not shy to offer an opinion or take a stand on an issue. He was a public-spirited citizen whose heart was unquestionably committed to his neighbors and his countrymen. A man like him did not need to seek office. Such actions were considered crass and vulgar to a gentleman's sensibilities. Rather, the opportunities came to him. Much to Larz's dismay, when Charles was called to serve, he rarely resisted.

The seed of Charles Anderson's political interest had been germinating since childhood. Like his brother John, the visit of Andrew Jackson to Soldier's Retreat when the boys were mere tots made him an early disciple of Old Hickory. That all changed one summer day when the fifteen-year-old Charles was in Cincinnati visiting Larz. His brother brought the college-bound boy to hear a political speech by a fellow Kentuckian and fierce opponent of Jackson. Charles was captivated by both the man and his message. After the speech, he had the opportunity to shake the hand of Henry Clay. At that moment, Charles Anderson became a party man and one of the region's most ardent followers of Whig principles. He followed Clay and his party faithfully until his death.[4]

By 1829, Clay was a titan on the American political scene. His work on the Missouri Compromise was critical in keeping the Union together. The North and South had grown increasingly belligerent over such issues as banking, tariffs, and slavery. Clay had run for president twice and did not win his party's nomination on either occasion. When the opportunity came to help Clay win the presidency as the Whig nominee in the summer of 1844, Anderson took down his shingle and became a full-time politician. It turned out to be a short career.[5]

Usually a key battleground state in national elections, Ohio was no exception in the contest of 1844. Determined to help Ohio fulfill what they felt was its political destiny as kingmaker, the state Whig machine trotted out an impressive ticket of candidates for the legislature and statewide office. Their mission, in addition to reversing recent Democratic Party gains, was to ensure that Clay carried Ohio. Voting a straight-line party ticket was encouraged in these days. Local candidates often made the difference in the decision to vote for a presidential hopeful whom very few had seen or heard. When Whigs in Montgomery and Warren Counties nominated Anderson for the state senate, they knew that they were securing a devoted and effective spokesman for Clay. The previous year, Anderson had lost his bid for the Whig nomination to the U.S. House of Representatives to his good friend Robert C. Schenck. This time, however, he did not disappoint.

Charles Anderson was a dynamic force on the stump, traipsing all over the state to assist in the Whig Party crusade. At one point, an exasperated Eliza complained to her mother-in-law that her husband was "out electioneering again." She hated politics and yearned to see Anderson return from the road.[6] His extraordinary efforts paid off, as he was elected by a comfortable majority. Whigs dominated the state senate but were badly outnumbered in the house. Whig gubernatorial candidate Mordecai Bradley outpolled popular Democrat David Tod by a mere thirteen-hundred votes. Clay won Ohio's twenty-three electoral votes by a margin barely exceeding six thousand with more than three hundred thousand ballots cast. The celebration was short-lived. After all the returns were in, the grand prize had eluded the Kentuckian yet again. James K. Polk was reelected president. Clay's destiny was to be one of the greatest American political leaders to never win the nation's highest office.

Newly elected Senator Anderson traveled to Columbus in December 1844 to begin a short and stormy stint in the legislature. The great national issue of Texas annexation loomed large, overshadowing state business. Some Whig hardliners even suggested that such an event, which Polk would surely accomplish, might be grounds for immediate disunion. Although Anderson strongly opposed annexation, he was not in that radical camp. The freshman state senator focused on his new role, immersing himself in typical Whig concerns: railroads, turnpikes, and benevolent institutions. While he achieved some minor success in these efforts, Anderson took a position of conscience that was so controversial and so offensive to most of his constituents, that it would seal his fate as a one-term senator while he was still learning his way around the statehouse. A bomb exploding on the floor of the senate might have caused less noise than that which Anderson created near the start of the Forty-Third Ohio General Assembly.

Many whites feared a sudden influx of what they perceived to be ignorant, immoral escaped slaves and free blacks into the free states of the West. This concern led many border states to pass a series of codes restricting the freedom of their black neighbors. The Ohio "Black Laws" were enacted in 1803, shortly after the territory achieved statehood. A wide range of sanctions required free blacks to register with local authorities and to provide proof of freedom upon demand. The statutes proscribed harsh penalties for harboring undocumented persons of color. Technically free, the black population of Ohio had few of the privileges of white residents. Being exempt from the yoke of slavery did not mean that one was a full-fledged citizen. The status of nominally free black residents was troubling to Anderson. His own views on race were a confused muddle of conflicting emotions, experiences, and principles. He was certainly not a radical abolitionist like firebrand fellow senator Benjamin F. Wade, yet his own moral principles urged him to find ways to ameliorate the poor condition of these "wretched beings." Anderson resolved to take action.

He proposed a measure that would do away with one provision of Ohio's codes for black people. Statutes prohibited blacks from testifying in civil and criminal cases. Eliminating one provision that so clearly stood in the way of fair trials might be a first step toward gradually eroding the entire odious collection of laws. The senate erupted in heated debate. Anderson gave an eloquent speech on the senate floor that sent the opposition press into hysteria. "Niggers! Niggers!! Niggers!!!" screeched the Dayton *Western Empire*, whose editors accused Anderson of turning his back on his Kentucky heritage and engaging in "Niggerology." Helped by an overwhelming Whig majority, the bill passed on February 20, 1845, and was referred to the house. It was a dead letter when it arrived, however, given the thirty-two to four seat dominance of the Democrats there. The annexation of Texas drowned out all other news just two weeks later, and Anderson's effort was all but forgotten.[7]

One man who did not forget was rising political star Salmon P. Chase. Chase was disappointed that Anderson had refused to align himself with the new Liberty Party. He wrote the young state senator, chastising him for not having the same kind of zeal against the extension of slavery as he did in opposing the Black Laws. Liberty Party editors sneered in silence at such Whig actions they felt avoided the more pressing issues of the day. Anderson ignored them. As long as Clay was alive, Anderson would remain his loyal disciple and follow his lead.[8]

Unaccustomed to working every day in the public eye, Anderson simply toiled in the statehouse until he ruined his health. The asthma that plagued him his entire life was back, despite an arsenic solution that his doctor had prescribed. What Charles needed was some time away in a healthier climate. Friends recommended a sea voyage, and Anderson jumped at the idea. He was granted a leave of absence and left Columbus in early March. The trip turned out to be much more than an extended period of convalescence. It was the trip of a lifetime.

Anderson spent nearly six months alone in Europe indulging his insatiable desire to advance his learning in art, history, and nature.

Landing in Barcelona in late April 1845, his sojourn took him through northern Spain, southern France, and down the Rhone River. He cruised in the Mediterranean Sea, visiting Italy, Greece, and Turkey. He met with the sultan twice in Constantinople. From the Black Sea, Anderson ventured up the Danube River through Germany and northern France, ending his long odyssey in London. The trip exceeded his grandest expectations and kindled a lifelong dream of a diplomatic appointment. By October the dreamer had nearly run out of money, and responsibilities beckoned back home. When the Ohio legislature opened session in January, Anderson returned to his seat and resumed his place in the middle of controversy.[9]

A petition from the Society of Friends of Whitewater, Indiana, just across the state border, motivated Anderson to renew his attack on Ohio's unfair Black Laws. These codes restricted free movement of blacks between the two states, obstructing commerce. According to the young senator from Dayton, these statutes were "unconstitutional, grossly wrong and unjust in principle and integrity." The restrictions were "brutal and inhumane in practice," Anderson exclaimed, amounting to "a stain of disgrace blotting our laws." He urged their immediate repeal. Anderson's fellow Whigs saw little opportunity to pass any such legislation, however, as the lower house was still dominated by Democrats. The petition went nowhere, and Anderson's political reputation ebbed.[10]

The problem with Anderson, as his peers saw it, was that he stood so firm on principle while ignoring the cardinal rules of republican politics. Legislative success required artful compromise and prescient timing. Anderson was deficient in both areas. Former colleague George F. Drake recalled that Anderson's "brilliant talents" were diminished by his "dogmatic and to some extent intolerant" stands that too often left him in the minority. When Ohio's Black Laws fell just a few years later, it was not the result of furious assaults from true believers like Anderson or abolitionists like Joshua Giddings, but rather through the crass political deal-making that Anderson so abhorred. When his term ended, no one dared suggest that he run for reelection. By refusing to play the game by the politicians' rules, Anderson had alienated all parties. His nascent political career appeared to be over.

It was time to follow his brother Larz's advice and commit himself fully to his chosen profession. Cincinnati was the logical place to begin anew.[11]

Larz Anderson made sure that his youngest brother would not fail in this latest attempt to restart his career. Now that Larz was no longer a practicing attorney, he spent most of his considerable energy managing the estate of his father-in-law, Nicholas Longworth. Longworth was not just the richest man in Cincinnati. He was the second wealthiest man in the nation. His personal attorney, Rufus King, took Charles Anderson in as partner, and the family moved to the Queen City in 1847. This placed the younger Anderson brother under the watchful eye of his mentor and squarely in the middle of elite society in the burgeoning metropolis. The results were just as Larz expected. Anderson was an immediate success at the bar and in social circles. He and his partner shared a love for the arts and a dedication to public service. King is remembered as the father of the Cincinnati library system and left a considerable endowment to various charitable organizations.[12]

Anderson flourished in his new environment. He used Larz's connections to gain access for himself and his friends to the highest places of power, both in the West and in the nation's capital. With family friend Zachary Taylor now in the White House, the Andersons of Cincinnati, backed by the Longworth fortune, wielded considerable influence. In the summer of 1849, Anderson reported being "quite enamored of Old Zack and his family," while making the high society rounds in Washington City. He spent time with Thomas Ewing, the foster father of his good friend William Tecumseh Sherman, and Ewing's daughter Ellen, who was destined to become Sherman's wife. It was a tight little circle in the capital city, and Anderson relished the opportunity to peek into the salons of power. The allure was irresistible to him.[13]

While Charles and his oldest brother discussed paintings and sipped sherry with polite society, their brother Robert was once again doing his duty, despite fighting for a cause he thought unjust. The annexation of Texas had started a war with Mexico that lasted the better part of two years. Robert and his longtime friend Winfield

Scott played key roles in the conflict. The wounded Robert emerged as a hero, but these accolades were bittersweet. Charles was closer to Robert than any of his brothers, and it pained him to know that his favorite had suffered so much for such an ignoble purpose. What was this national delusion called "manifest destiny," the thing that sparked such boorish imperialism on the part of his beloved country? Anderson the scholar decided to study the issue in his usual painstaking manner. After he had finished his analysis, he parsed out all of the illogical rhetoric of this immensely popular notion. He delivered a masterful demolition of the manifest destiny concept, thus placing himself virtually alone among contemporary white intellectuals on the subject of race theory.[14]

The issue of race had perplexed Charles Anderson from childhood. He found it nearly impossible to reconcile his moral misgivings concerning slavery with the political expediency that enshrined the peculiar institution into the Constitution. It was a repugnant bargain, yet it held the Union together. The innate superiority of the white race was a nearly uncontested scientific fact to practically every white American, from John C. Calhoun to renowned abolitionist William Lloyd Garrison. Pseudoscientists calling themselves "phrenologists" claimed that skull measurements proved that innate differences made the Negro race akin to a separate species. Historians and politicians of the day added fuel to the fire when they suggested that the natural characteristics of an Anglo-Saxon "race" meant that white people were chosen by God to rule lesser humans. This was more than Anderson could stand. He launched a withering attack on the idea of an "Anglo Saxon destiny" at the Philomathesian Society at Kenyon College on August 8, 1849. Few if any in the audience that day had heard anything remotely like it.

The speech itself was a tour de force of logical argument and probably the finest rhetorical effort of Anderson's life. Unlike his peers, Anderson did not oppose manifest destiny merely because of its crude violence or its potential impact on the balance between slave and free states. Rather, he questioned the rationale behind the doctrine, dismantling the argument point by point. This false creed was so universal in its adoption and so insidious in the way it pandered to the pride of elite and poor whites alike that it created huge barriers to anyone bold enough to challenge it. The first error that Anderson exposed was the myth of an Anglo-Saxon race. Ancient historians like Tacitus never mentioned the Saxons. Neither the Saxons nor the Angles ever represented a majority of peoples inhabiting the British Isles. Like the Americans, according to Anderson, the British throughout history were composed of the most "mongrel and heterogeneous stock of people on earth." There could hardly be an Anglo-Saxon destiny when that race itself did not exist.

The mere idea of racial destiny was preposterous, in Charles Anderson's view. First, it was more than presumptuous for any people to claim that they could divine God's will. Throughout history, one empire after another felt convinced that it was destined to rule. Many justified violence and even genocide in the name of racial superiority and destiny. All of these empires eventually fell. The great achievements of ancient cultures and those of the British-American people were due mostly to circumstance. Who was to say, for example, that the achievements of Americans in constructing a free and prosperous republic were any greater than the artistic triumphs of the Italians or the technical advances of the ancient Chinese? Was the successful American experiment the result of a providential racial destiny, or the product of great leaders seizing a moment in time? Americans who continued to believe in what Anderson described as "a fallacy in philosophy, and untruth in history, and an impiety in religion" would someday face a harsh reckoning.

Anderson went on to challenge even the most sacred tenet of this racial philosophy: the idea that blacks, or Mexicans, or any other ethnic group were inherently inferior to white people. Here he used his audience's own religious beliefs to support his case. The Bible taught the unity of the species, Anderson argued. At various times throughout history, different races of men achieved dominance—not by virtue of any inherent superiority but as a matter of favorable circumstance. In other words, conditions in certain areas of the world allowed their residents to develop more quickly than others living in a less-than-ideal environment. This nurture-versus-nature view clashed forcefully with the self-serving arguments of manifest destiny adherents. Even America's lowly nineteenth-century Catholics—despised by many—saw themselves as the Jews of old did: "a royal priesthood, a people set apart." Anderson's logic suggested that free blacks who competed with whites for jobs, or even slaves (considered vile and ignorant by some), could achieve as much as whites given the proper circumstances was just too much for some to bear. Others, like Larz Anderson, simply laughed it off. Larz sent a copy of the speech to Orlando Brown, director of the Bureau of Indian Affairs at the time, thinking it would "amuse" him with its "monomania" against Anglo-Saxons.[15]

Charles Anderson's unusual speech drew the attention of the press and public outside of Ohio. He reprised the address before the New England Society of Cincinnati. After hearing it delivered on December 20, 1849, some political leaders insisted the speech be published and widely circulated. As was the case throughout his long life, Charley's penchant for drawing a crowd and delivering compelling, often entertaining orations, made him one of the most popular and controversial speakers in the West.[16]

A talent for public speaking was a useful tool for an attorney. In June 1850 partners Anderson and King represented Dr. William R. Winton in one of the most sensational criminal cases ever heard in Ohio. The wealthy and respected doctor, an 1837 graduate of the Ohio Medical College, specialized in surgery to correct deformities of the limbs. When he was approached by the parents of eighteen-year-old Harriet Keever, Winton offered to treat her club foot in his own home. The unfortunate girl became pregnant and accused the doctor of seducing her. Imagine Charles Anderson reflecting back on his talks with Larz regarding the "low acts" that both despised in the political realm. Was defending a man accused of raping an innocent invalid any less onerous? Still, Anderson agreed to defend the doctor in Preble County Court.

There he faced a hostile jury and a public enraged by the heinous nature of this apparent crime. Anderson used all of his considerable skills of debate and persuasion to create reasonable doubt as to his client's guilt. The alleged rapes took place while the doctor's wife and the local minister chatted in a room next door. The victim did not cry out or attempt to run away after five supposed molestations. She was driven home by the doctor and arranged to see him for a follow-up appointment months after she left his home. She only made her accusation after the birth of her child, nine and a half months after she left the doctor's residence. Despite the lack of credible evidence and the conflicting testimony of the alleged victim and her family, Winton was convicted of "seduction," a lesser charge than rape. Judge Crane's instructions to the jury were clear: they either had to find the defendant guilty or declare that the young woman was nothing more than a "perjured strumpet." Anderson admitted in his closing argument that such a verdict in the face of so little evidence would shake his faith in the legal system. In reality, he knew better than to expect perfect justice in an imperfect world.

Anderson's losses in the courtroom and on the stump did little to tarnish his image or his growing celebrity. His entire thirty-five-page closing argument was published the following year. His rapid rise to prominence on a larger stage did not go unnoticed by state party leaders. Despite being all but banished from political life just four years earlier, a considerable effort was made to nominate Charles Anderson for the United States Senate in 1851. His well-known independence made him a potential compromise candidate, as Whigs and Democrats grappled with the popular Free Soil Party movement in a fast-changing game of party realignment. [17]

Anderson himself appeared a little bemused at the prospect of being used as political barter. The machinations began in November 1850, when Judge Holt, Anderson's older brother Larz, and other prominent Democrats prepared to support Charles's candidacy, rather than allow the Free Soil Party to triumph. "I prefer the weakest Democrat in Ohio, representing a large and honest party," Anderson wailed, "to one of those traitorous fanatics or knaves, though he be Webster in intellect or Clay in statesmanship." A confused mess of backroom dealings concluded at the Whig caucus in January 1851, where Anderson was beaten, as he had predicted, "by some damned small fry" named Hiram Griswold. The vote was twenty-six to twenty. Griswold and the

Whig Party were crushed in the election at the statehouse. Benjamin Franklin Wade emerged as victor on the Thirty-Seventh ballot. Wade went on to serve three terms and become one of the most radical Republicans in Washington.[18]

Charles Anderson traveled to Baltimore in June 1852 for the quadrennial national Whig convention. The Democrats had nominated New Hampshire native Franklin Pierce for president only weeks earlier. Incumbent chief executive Millard Fillmore coveted the Whig nomination, but Anderson and most others felt he had little chance to beat Pierce. They nominated General Winfield Scott after Anderson gave a rousing speech supporting his old friend. Just days after the convention concluded, Henry Clay died of tuberculosis. He was the first person to lie in state in the United States Capitol. Pierce then trounced Scott in one of the most lopsided presidential elections in history. The Whig Party was essentially dead, rendered irrelevant by their divisions over slavery and unable to survive the passing of their founder.[19]

It was appropriate that Anderson delivered his personal and moving tribute to Clay in Cincinnati on the very day of the election, November 2. This was a eulogy for both the man and his party. It was no coincidence, Anderson suggested, that this great leader was born in the first year of his country's independence in Hanover County, Virginia, where so many noble patriots like Patrick Henry and Anderson's own father resided. Like Richard C. Anderson, Clay had made his way to Kentucky early and dedicated his life to the service of his commonwealth and his country. What set Clay apart, according to Anderson, was "an undaunted independence of mind in himself, and a most ardent and philanthropic sympathy with the rights of Liberty in all Mankind." Clay's first vote and speech, Anderson was quick to point out, was in favor of Negro emancipation. Just as Anderson had experienced when advocating against Ohio's Black Laws, Clay had been "howled, by the accustomed outcries, into the seclusion and consequent oblivion of private life." Neither Clay nor Anderson would remain in political exile long. Clay's moral objections to slavery were gradually overcome by "reason and understanding," in Anderson's words, as the Great Compromiser realized that

his dream of general emancipation was both impractical and dangerous to the fragile Union. Anderson called Clay the "model statesman
of the model republic." He was also the model after which Anderson
patterned his public life and most cherished principles.[20]

Cut adrift from the only political party he had ever supported,
Anderson vowed to maintain the principles and legacy of his hero,
describing his newfound status as a "fossil Whig." As the emerging
Republican and American parties competed with the Democrats to
woo former Whigs to their camp, Anderson retained his independence. He would only support good men from any party whom he
felt might help keep the Union intact. This principled stand brought
him praise from a select few as well as derision and scorn from the
vast majority of politicians. They could not understand how he could
avoid party affiliation and stay relevant. Yet Charles Anderson's name
seemed to be constantly on the lips of Ohio's political operatives. He
was still a man of influence, a wild card that might be played in an
uncertain game of power where the players and the rules were in a
state of perpetual flux.

➤➤ ◄◄

Political Outcast

A S THE WHIGS SANK RAPIDLY into the political abyss, Charles Anderson focused on his practice and achieved more success than he had ever enjoyed in his adult life. To display his new-found wealth, he constructed a lavish residence at the southeast corner of Pike and Fifth Streets in Cincinnati, just a few hundred yards from the mansion of Nicholas Longworth, whom many considered the wealthiest man west of New York. Anderson hired accomplished architect John Hamilton, who had designed several public buildings and cemeteries in his native England, to build his dream house. The plan was ambitious. Anderson drew inspiration from his European tour, choosing to design the house in the popular Italian Villa style. The builder took advantage of its picturesque position, perched on the edge of a steep hill, with a commanding view of the city and countryside below. The house impressed visitors, not with scale and opulence, but rather with its tasteful artistic sensibilities, creative use of a difficult building site, and advanced technology.

Approaching the residence from the street, two iron statues of lions copied from those at St. Peter's Basilica in Rome greeted Anderson's guests at the entrance gate. After ascending ten stone steps and proceeding under a double-arched stone portico, visitors entered a modest hall and continued on to an elegant suite of three rooms with fourteen-foot ceilings. The adjoining parlors and dining room were connected by large pocket doors that when opened created a grand expanse nearly seventy feet wide. The parlor fronting Pike Street had a unique feature. Hamilton inserted a huge window directly over the fireplace, accomplished by bending twin flues around a wall opening and rejoining them above the roof line into one central chimney stack. This innovation brought copious daylight to the space. At night, Anderson closed the window via a shutter mechanism concealed in the wainscot. A large mirror graced the front of the closed shutter, mimicking the one over the dining room fireplace at the opposite end of the suite. The twin mirrors reflected the candlelight from custom-made chandeliers. There was nothing quite like it in the entire city.

The private spaces in the house were no less dramatic. From the hall or central parlor, Anderson and his special guests retired to the spacious library. This room, an octagonal retreat accessed at entrance level, was a full three stories above the ground due to the steep rear elevation. Kitchen and servants' quarters were cleverly constructed below in the rear of the house, creating opportunities for light and views unheard of in a basement service wing. Climbing the main staircase past the bedrooms on the second level, one continued upward in a Romanesque stair tower, finally emerging into a beautiful belvedere of open arches. Yellow sandstone tastefully accented architectural elements across the red brick exterior of the house. The highlight of any tour of the Anderson residence was the flat roof deck off the belvedere, which boasted unparalleled views of the Cincinnati environs that delighted everyone who visited.[1]

By the time his new house was completed in 1854, Anderson appeared to have it all. He was surrounded by like-minded people of education and taste. His promising eighteen-year-old son, Allen Latham, was preparing to enter West Point. Daughters Kitty and Belle were busy being instructed in French, music, and the domestic arts. Anderson's services as a celebrated orator were always in great demand. He rarely resisted an invitation to address friends and neighbors on a wide range of topics. He and his law partner, Rufus King, once spent an entire afternoon discussing which works of art they should purchase. While Anderson's prosperity and leisure time increased, however, the nation drifted closer to disaster.[2]

One of the political deals that had held the nation together, the Missouri Compromise of 1820, was essentially repealed in 1854 with the passage of the Kansas–Nebraska Act. Anderson imagined Clay rolling over in his grave after Stephen A. Douglas of Illinois was successful in selling his doctrine of popular sovereignty in the territories to the U.S. Congress and to President Franklin Pierce. The act precipitated a civil war in Kansas, a territory that had been free of slaves, as slave owners rushed in to tip the political balance in their favor. Free Soil men and other Northerners felt betrayed, leading to the birth of the Republican Party on an antislavery platform. While these alignments were taking shape, a gubernatorial election loomed in Ohio in the fall of 1855. Hard-core Union men like Anderson faced a difficult choice between two candidates they could not abide.

Incumbent governor William Medill, a Democrat, and Free Soil/Republican "Fusion" candidate Salmon P. Chase had only one thing in common, according to Anderson and other prominent ex-Whigs such as Judge William Johnston. Their platforms were sectional and threatened to accelerate the momentum toward disunion. Supporting the Democrat was unthinkable. Chase was regarded by his opponents as a radical abolitionist. What could Anderson and his friends do to avoid either undesirable result? Their answer was to trot out seventy-one-year-old federalist ex-governor Allen Trimble and run him under the banner of the American or Know-Nothing Party. This was a tainted compromise, as Anderson was a bitter opponent of this party and their brand of racist nativism. The campaign turned nasty. Judge Johnston was accused of secretly supporting the Democrats in a guerilla effort to defame and defeat Chase. Chase won the governor's race comfortably. Trimble finished a distant third with only 8 percent of the vote. The press had a field day at the expense of Johnston and Anderson, claiming that their political "firm" had been forced into a "hopelessly insolvent state of liquidation."[3]

Although Anderson's friends and critics had grown accustomed to his stubborn independence in the political arena, many were shocked when he came out in support of James Buchanan for president in 1856. "Old Buck" was not only a Democrat but also the man whom many felt had impugned Henry Clay's character. Buchanan had accused Clay of constructing a corrupt bargain to support John Quincy Adams for president in 1824, in exchange for a promise of the office of secretary of state. The charge had since proven false, but the former animus between Anderson's chosen candidate and his departed hero survived in the hearts of many ex-Whigs. The press continued to harass Anderson for his latest and most unexpected alliance. The Dayton *Gazette* compared Anderson to a boa constrictor, somehow swallowing Buchanan after the candidate himself was compelled to stomach Pierce, Douglas, and the Nebraska Bill. "What politician ever," the *Gazette* teased, so completely demonstrated "straining at a gnat and swallowing a camel?"[4]

In his speeches and private letters, Anderson was clear that, despite his unusual endorsement, he was no Democrat. In fact, he had sworn off all parties for the rest of his life. Electing Buchanan was simply the best chance that the nation had to avoid a disastrous breakup and a possible civil war. Anderson's logic was simple. A victory by the Republican candidate John Fremont would push the country to the brink of disunion. American Party candidate Millard Fillmore had no chance to win in the North, as his party took no position on slavery and had alienated recent immigrant voters. This was "no crisis in which to exercise our suffrage as a sort of party sentimentalism," Anderson wrote his friend and former Whig Orlando Brown. "I *must* vote and vote efficiently," Anderson declared, "directly *against* disunion and everything standing that way."

Soon after Buchanan won, Anderson received a visit from Virginia governor Henry A. Wise. Wise assured Anderson that he expected a "national and more conservative" administration from the new president than Republicans and others feared. "I may be perversely wrong in all these hopes and opinions," Anderson wrote to Brown in late November 1856, "but I am as yet quite happy with any delusion if it be delusion. I really believe the Union is now *safe*." Anderson would soon realize that he had been thinking more with his heart than his head. He would later change his opinion and regard the defeat of Fremont as a calamity for his beloved country.[5]

⇥ ⇤

CHAPTER SIX

Texas Fever

CHARLES ANDERSON WAS RESTLESS. The law provided a comfortable lifestyle, but he had always despised it. His asthma had worsened to the point where he was confined to his bed for weeks at a time. When he was finally forced to abandon his profession, Anderson felt both anxious and relieved. He needed to restore his health, find a new career, and support his young family. Cincinnati had experienced devastating epidemics of cholera, tuberculosis, and other diseases typical of emerging industrial cities. It was no place for a person in his condition. He yearned for a diplomatic post. He had alienated many former allies in his bolt to the Buchanan camp in 1856, and he expected that patronage was due him for this sacrifice. As his brother Larz and other influential friends moved behind the scenes, Charles dreamed of an ambassadorship in Berlin or Naples, where he could indulge his love of the arts and become immersed in European culture.

At first blush, Anderson seemed an ideal candidate for a foreign post. He was well-traveled, highly educated, and particularly attuned to the intricacies of American policy. His superior intellect and magnetic personality made him a worthy candidate to develop intimate relationships with world leaders. He had glaring liabilities, however, that frustrated these ambitions time and again over the course of his life. The plum appointments that Anderson craved were typically bestowed on party loyalists or personal friends. By the 1850s he had sworn off party politics and was now an avowed independent. Among the many aspirants to political patronage jobs were lifelong Democrats who had proven their party allegiance over the course of many campaigns. An independent turn of mind could be viewed as dangerous in key diplomatic posts. As Anderson had demonstrated in the Ohio senate, he refused to toe the party line when those platforms clashed with his own conscience. He never fully understood the art of political compromise. Thus national party leaders often liked and even admired him, but few really trusted him to be an unflinching servant to administration policies.[1]

The traditional approach to securing such appointments was to drop hints to influential friends, then stand by for the call from the president or one of his cabinet members. Campaigning for a post was considered undignified. After just a few months of waiting, Anderson surprised his close friends by traveling to Washington City in May 1857 to plead his case. Rufus King felt sorry for Anderson's "vain and hopeless effort" to secure a foreign mission. Despite the encouragement of Anderson's many friends, King concluded that his law partner had "neither game nor any intimation of Mr. Buchanan's will." After nearly a month in the capital, Anderson learned that Governor Joseph A. Wright, a pro-Union Democrat from Indiana, was the president's choice for Berlin. Subsequent posts to Vienna and Naples landed in the laps of two natives of Buchanan's home state of Pennsylvania. Anderson returned home, discouraged.[2]

Frequent illnesses gave Anderson ample time for his two favorite pastimes: reading and learning. He devoured hundreds of books each year, adding copious notes in the margins for future reference. A man he particularly admired for his artistic sensibilities published a travelogue of sorts in 1857 that changed Anderson's life in unimaginable ways. Before he became America's father of landscape architecture, Frederick Law Olmsted made a name for himself as a journalist. His interest in the U.S. slave economy led him to a commission by the New York *Daily Times* to tour the Southern states for six years, beginning in 1852. Olmsted and Anderson shared a passion for adventure. *A Journey through Texas* was one of a series of works recounting Olmsted's travels in the American South. They were instant bestsellers, and this particular edition held Anderson spellbound.

Olmsted described a frontier land, wild and exotic as any Anderson had visited on his European tour, but with the added promise of economic opportunity. As Anderson later recalled, this was the book that "decided [his] fates."[3] Olmsted paid particular attention to the natural landscape in his works. Anderson was easily seduced by reports of fine, sweet mesquite grasses covering river bottomlands in abundance. Olmsted described the San Antonio River as "of a rich blue and pure as crystal." Its spring was in a wooded glen north of town and "may be classed as of the first water among the gems of the natural world"; the river is of such incredible beauty, he wrote, that "[you] cannot believe your eyes, and almost shrink from sudden metamorphosis by invaded nymphdom."[4]

By 1858, Anderson had contracted yet another strong affliction, which his sister-in-law Catherine Longworth described as "Texas fever." The fever intensified, soon becoming an obsession. Anderson concocted a plan to set up the first blooded stock operation in the fledgling state. Despite his failure as an aspiring farmer twenty years previous, Anderson was determined to once again seek his fortune in agrarian pursuits. It was a bad decision. The Anderson brothers shared a life-long passion for horses. Marshall was the family expert and managed his brother's livestock interests in Ohio while Charles was busy with law and politics. If his youngest brother was to follow through with this latest endeavor, Marshall would make sure he had the best stock available. Charles pressed forward with his latest scheme, despite the contrary advice of friends and family. They knew that once he had fixed his mind on a course, any attempt to dissuade him would prove fruitless. That summer, Charles set off on his own Texas adventure to scout a location for his future ranch. What he found delighted him.[5]

The neighborhood that had been the subject of Olmsted's flowery gushes lay four miles north of town on an eminence. To its immediate north were the verdant Worth Springs, where the San Antonio River literally burst forth from the earth and meandered south, past whitewashed buildings of the burgeoning town and the crumbling remains of old Spanish missions. Anderson returned from this scouting trip excited and energized and immediately made plans for the move. Leaving his financial affairs in the capable hands of Rufus King, Anderson set out again for the Lone Star State on January 8, 1859. Eliza and their daughters followed that fall. If any of them expected to replicate some of the finer aspects of their life in Cincinnati, they were in for a shocking surprise.[6]

San Antonio was just beginning to transform itself from what one visitor in 1845 had described as a "dirty mud hole" into a modern town. From a mere thirty-five hundred inhabitants in 1850, the population had tripled just six years later. It was a place of startling contrasts. On the one hand, investment capital from the industrial North and unprecedented profits from the cotton boom in the South were pouring into the town. German immigrant William Menger, who had made a small fortune operating a stable and brewery in the center of San Antonio, opened his namesake hotel that year. It soon received worldwide acclaim for its lodgings, said to be the best in the West. Neat one-story stone houses built by German immigrants were interspersed with new American dwellings of three stories with fancy brick facades, balconies, and picket fences. On the other hand, the city's bleaker sections looked quite different. Older Mexican dwellings were simple huts made of stakes and mud, topped by river grass, or low adobe structures without windows. Olmsted and other observers remarked that San Antonio, with the exception of New Orleans, was the most complex amalgamation of race and language of any city in the nation.

The military post in San Antonio provided a solid economic base and a level of prosperity that was often missing in frontier towns. Goods from Matagorda Bay 150 miles away found their first trading depot in this unusual place. The town bustled with government mule trains, express wagons, and innumerable ox carts hauling all manner of goods in and out. To the casual observer or unabashed optimist, San Antonio looked like a great place to be. In reality, life in southwestern Texas in the middle of the century was hard, primitive, and dangerous. Street fights were a regular occurrence and hardly a week went by without the report of a murder or shooting.[7] This was not the

Kentucky wilderness that Richard Clough Anderson and his wealthy Virginia gentleman peers had tamed and molded into a bucolic paradise of small farms and middling plantations. It certainly was not the tidy little metropolis of Dayton that Eliza's Patterson ancestors had hacked out of a virgin forest.

Despite these challenges, Anderson was determined to create his idealized version of a country estate and leveraged his military connections to build it. The site he chose was one of the most picturesque in the area. Perched on the highest point of land about four miles north of town and nourished by natural springs at the headwaters of the San Antonio River stood a half-finished armory. It had been abandoned by the army and remained standing like a medieval ruin, an eyesore to the citizens of San Antonio. Anderson purchased the property and began transforming it into a ranchero mansion. The building had potential. Laid out in the shape of a Maltese cross, with thick stone walls and lofty ceilings, the home was cool in the summer and cozy in the winter. Anderson relished the opportunity to turn this rough diamond into a sparkling jewel, though it was a mere shell needing flooring, plaster, and decorative accoutrements. Anderson poured his considerable energies and money into the project. He intended to create a showplace. He imagined that it might become one of the finest new residences in Texas.[8]

Anderson brought horses and cattle with extensive pedigrees to his new ranch. They contrasted sharply with the longhorns and Indian palominos prevalent in the region. He branded the bovines with a moon and star. He gave his stallions biblical names like Jehoshaphat and Nebuchadnezzar. He eschewed the black coat and collar typical of his gentlemen peers, preferring instead the traditional vaquero outfit of chaps and a broad-brimmed sombrero. Like a character in one of his favorite Shakespeare plays, Anderson immersed himself in his own period drama. It soon became a horror story. When slave traders began to land their illegal cargo at Indianola and Galveston in blatant defiance of Texas and U.S. laws, Anderson resolved to take action. He would not stand idle and watch his country disintegrate. Despite having no political capital in Texas, he was still a man of talent and influence. Sam Houston and the Union circle in Texas needed him.[9]

Anderson decided to raise a company of "new Texas Rangers" to "cut the throat of every pirate aboard, scuttle their ships," and free the slaves. He had two secret accomplices but needed a third. He chose a close neighbor whom he suspected shared similar political views. Anderson revealed his plan to Dennis Meade and asked for assistance. Meade replied that if Anderson attempted such a rash plan, he would call on the real Texas Rangers to stop him. His ardor thus cooled, Anderson abandoned the scheme. In retrospect, his move to Texas in 1859 appears rash and unwise. He was so smitten with his beloved Lady Liberty that he may have misread fatal flaws in the Constitution as mere hairline cracks in the folds of her otherwise sparkling marble gown. Anderson was not alone. Throughout the tortuous final years of the 1850s, few leaders could actually conceive that sectional divisions and jealousies could lead to the most catastrophic of outcomes.

Union supporters in Texas were bolstered in these delusions in August 1859. The election of Sam Houston to the governor's chair by a majority of nearly eighty-seven hundred votes came amid the largest turnout in state electoral history. Houston had defeated incumbent governor Hardin R. Runnels, whose Democratic Party's platform included formal reopening of the slave trade. Anderson attended several campaign events and felt that Houston's emotional connection with his audience was as great as any speaker he had ever seen. He later stated that Houston was the most courageous Union man that ever breathed. Both Houston and Anderson ended up paying a high price for their patriotism. Strong Union supporters like Houston existed among the most influential public men in almost every Southern state. Such Democrats were busy preparing a conservative platform that, they hoped, would triumph in the next presidential election and save the country. The events of the next twelve months exposed that dream as pure fantasy, however. The most sensational of these events was certainly the seizure of the federal arsenal at Harpers Ferry in West Virginia by radical abolitionist John Brown and his gang in

October 1859. Brown had intended to kindle a slave uprising, leading many Southerners to recall with horror the murders committed by escaped Virginia slave Nat Turner's mob just thirty years earlier.[10]

Back in Cincinnati, Larz Anderson was sure that his youngest brother's Texas adventure was destined to fail. He knew that the only way to persuade Charles to abandon his folly would be to appeal to his latent ambition. With a foreign post unlikely and the prospect of Civil War looming, Larz succeeded in convincing the Buchanan administration that his youngest brother was the right candidate for assistant secretary of state. Postmaster general Joseph Holt, a former judge from Ohio, tendered the formal offer on February 3, 1860. Anderson received it two weeks later. It was a tempting opportunity. The current secretary, Lewis Cass, was said to be in ill health, and this appointment could be a stepping-stone to the Cabinet. The experience would give Anderson national exposure and prepare him for higher office. It turned out to be one of the most important decisions of his life.

After careful consideration, Anderson declined Holt's offer. His old colleague was persistent and urged him to reconsider, but Charles would not budge. He was tired of politics. He could not stomach working alongside fire-eaters like James G. Breckenridge, who actively advocated disunion. Besides, the Union had been endangered before and cooler heads had always prevailed.[11] Later that same month, Senator Jefferson Davis of Mississippi introduced resolutions to affirm that the federal government was obliged to protect slave-holding interests in the territories. Davis knew full well that this issue would split the Democratic Party in the upcoming convention. The resolutions would also blunt Steven Douglas's efforts to establish popular sovereignty in new states and territories. The Union was in serious jeopardy. Anderson realized that the "sham of state equality," as he called it, was no longer the exclusive doctrine of extremists like William L. Yancy of South Carolina. The lie had become the favored dogma of the Southern Democratic Party in what Anderson described as the "morbid madness of their unbridled lust for power."[12]

Anderson's dreams were disintegrating and he could no longer pretend otherwise. In March 1860 he placed an ad in the *Goliad Messenger*, seeking the return of twenty-three Spanish mares, two saddle horses, a roan, and a sorrel pony that had been "lost." Stock not endangered by extended drought, rattlesnake bites, or other natural hazards were continually at risk of being stolen by Indians, bandits, or even unscrupulous neighbors. Lawlessness and violence in Texas was growing as loyalty to the Union ebbed.[13] Independence Day proved melancholy. Anderson called it "our national Holy Day" and exclaimed, "Great God! Is it to be our last?" He could now see that disunion was a distinct probability and his mood was gloomy. "Poor fool," he lamented, "to love one's country to the point of distress." When he looked to the future, Anderson saw "a hell of woes . . . bleeding, blazing, groaning directly and boundlessly beyond." Tragically, this vision would come to pass.

A few days earlier, workmen constructing his house had found one of the Andersons' two slaves, a young black boy named Dan, dead in the river. Charles was convinced that the boy had been murdered. By the end of July, violence against blacks had escalated into one of the most shameful events in the history of the young state. Rumors of imminent slave uprisings and other conspiracies of blacks and abolitionists were routinely planted in newspapers in Texas and throughout the South, concocted by Southern radicals to frighten and inflame readers. The result was horrific brutality in Texas in 1860.[14]

The summer had been a scorcher. Temperatures rose to 110 degrees in northern Texas on the afternoon of July 8, and several large fires broke out. The blazes burned most of downtown Dallas to the ground, razed half the town square in Denton, and destroyed a store in Pilot Point. At first, spontaneous combustion and the recent introduction of phosphorous matches were deemed the likely cause of these unfortunate events. One man, however, saw political opportunity among the ashes. Four days after the fires, the editor of the *Dallas Herald*, Charles R. Pryor, wrote explosive letters to state leaders and newspaper editors. He suggested that the fires had been started by recently expelled abolitionist preachers and their black friends as part of a widespread conspiracy to destroy the entire state. He called the supposed plot "a regular invasion, and a real war." Pryor's letters were printed in newspapers across the state. Many communities formed vigilance committees to capture the alleged instigators. Despite the absence of any evidence that the fires were set by anyone, local lawmen looked the other way while gangs of citizens lynched an estimated one hundred innocent blacks and whites. The panic abated by September, just in time for the presidential election. Southern extremists used what they euphemistically called "the Texas Troubles" to inflame sectional passions, painting Abraham Lincoln as an abolitionist whose Republican Party was behind the events.[15]

Emotions ran so high in San Antonio in the months before the presidential contest that local Unionists like Anderson could not safely promote their candidates in public. In August a courageous twenty-three-year-old Unionist named James P. Newcomb stepped up to the task. He started a Union paper called the *Alamo Express*. In its pages Anderson and other Union men could express their political views through the voice of the young editor. Anderson's motto in the 1860 presidential election was simple: "Anything to defeat Lincoln. *Almost* anything to defeat Breckenridge." He believed that the triumph of either sectional party spelled almost certain disunion. Thus he followed his brother Larz in supporting John Bell of Tennessee and Edward Everett of Massachusetts in the newly imagined Constitutional Union Party. Even Stephen A. Douglas, whom Anderson had despised as the agent behind the repeal of the Missouri Compromise, was preferable to the sectional candidates. The diminishing Union circle in San Antonio waited with apprehension as the election of Lincoln became a foregone conclusion.[16]

➤➤ ◄◄

Debate at Alamo Square

THE DAY AFTER THE NEWS of Abraham Lincoln's election reached San Antonio, handbills appeared on walls and fences around town. The posters called for all Breckenridge men to assemble in Alamo Square and consider next steps in the wake of this momentous event. Within a few days a second notice appeared extending the invitation to all citizens of Bexar County. Unaware that a meeting was scheduled, Charles Anderson rode into town the morning of the rally to purchase supplies at George W. Caldwell's store. Excitement ran high. Several Union men gathered at the store and urged him to stay and speak at the meeting that evening. Anderson's conscience would not allow him to refuse. Forgoing his usual meticulous preparation, this speech would have to come straight from the heart.[1]

Local secessionists fixed the agenda, but the Unionists had their own plan for the meeting. Celebrated Methodist preacher Dr. Jesse Boring began the assembly with a secessionist speech that was as measured and dispassionate as it was firm and confident. He argued that the Union was in effect already dissolved. In the middle of Boring's address, Union men raised the national banner on a flagpole behind the stage, and the crowd erupted in cheers. As soon as Boring concluded his remarks, prearranged calls for Anderson came from the crowd. Anderson felt inspired with "the most inflamed, indignant, outraged specimen of old Clay temper and Patriotism." He calmly ascended the ladder to the stage as if he had been the featured speaker.

Almost no one in the audience had heard Anderson speak in public. Before he launched into a refutation of Boring's central theme, Anderson reminded the audience that he was born and reared in a slaveholding family. He said that his time in the North had given him a broad perspective and a more objective view of the sectional issues. With no political allegiances or entanglements to sway him, Anderson argued that he could divine the truth in this critical matter. He implored his audience to take a deep breath and consider the gravity of the decision they faced. "Have sectional partisans finally *dared* to make, or devise, an assault upon this beloved and most glorious Union, which our fathers of the South and the North shed their united blood to cement and establish?" This was not a popular revolt that was brewing in Texas and other Southern states, according to Anderson. It was a power grab by unscrupulous politicians who wanted to establish their own separate government based on slavery.

If the Union really is dissolved, Anderson asked, what happens next? Do they return to the Lone Star Republic? Should Texans form an alliance with a confederation of Southern states that did not yet exist? "In nature," he explained, "there are no lone stars. They cluster and constellate." The former Republic of Texas "darted upwards with the speed of a comet" to join with the other United States in its constitutional system. Would they just as rapidly abandon this course without just cause? The idea of a Southern constellation of states was equally abhorrent and unwarranted, according to Anderson. Despite the hype and fear mongering from the fire-eaters, neither Lincoln nor the Republican Party had espoused, in words or platform, any desire to interfere with the institution of slavery where it was already established. To say otherwise, as secessionists claimed, was to create a pretext for disunion based on "the figments of a heated and diseased imagination."

A voice in the crowd demanded that they hear "no more of these Black Republican arguments," but Anderson was just warming up. "Nor am I coward enough to fear such taunts, and to prevent me from boldly denouncing such statements," the speaker exclaimed, "when used for such unholy purposes. I have, I say, met and resented assault in other crowds, where to defend your rights, required, at least, real manhood." This may have been true, but Anderson had never made such bold statements under such dangerous circumstances. He tried to appear nonpartisan by enumerating the many hostile actions that abolitionist radicals in the North had taken against Southern states. He chastised Massachusetts for repeatedly nullifying fugitive slave laws. This was cause for righteous indignation, Anderson admitted, but not for national suicide.

Anderson was not above using fear tactics himself when his beloved Union was at risk. If Southerners opt for disunion, he maintained, they must be prepared for disastrous consequences. "Could we then hold three millions of our slaves in their proper bondage and subjection with our left hands, whilst we should smite their pale faced allies with our right?" This was a shrewd attempt to turn existing fears of slave insurrection against the very fire-eaters who had created them. He begged his listeners not to deplore Northern fanaticism while ignoring the same dangerous folly at home. Northern extremists could not trample the Constitution and its explicit protection of the South's peculiar institution. Southern extremists must not use lies and distortion to foment revolution where no proximate cause existed. "Must the true, permanent, invaluable interests of the Southern people," he asked, "be forever made a sacrifice to mere politics?"

Boring's tired assertion that the Constitution gave each state the right to secede for any reason was easy fodder for Anderson's sharp wit. The mere thought of such a no-fault divorce in a bond of national matrimony was unthinkable in nineteenth-century America. "Secession," Anderson explained, "was what General Jackson proclaimed it: only revolution." He finished his speech with the same passionate and eloquent appeal for the Union that his former Ohio neighbors had so often heard. "Let us look again on that banner of beauty and glory," Anderson pleaded. "Oh! May this flag of our Father's Union—our Union—no sister star bedimmed or gone rayless and lost in outer darkness, our whole constellation complete. Oh!

May it thus stand and remain the most loved and treasured legacy to our latest posterity, co-existent with the earth, the air, the very sun himself." The Germans and Irish in the crowd, who had cowered in fear of being branded abolitionists, burst into cheers as Anderson walked from the stage. The Union banner fluttered in the moonlight. The celebration soon died down as the next scheduled speaker took the stand.

Colonel John A. Wilcox, a former Methodist preacher turned Know-Nothing politician, resumed the tirade against the supposed plans of Lincoln's abolitionist allies. Unlike Boring, Wilcox was a bombastic fire-eater of the first stripe. His role in the proceedings was to excite the secessionists. He attacked Anderson and all appeals to a conservative path forward with ferocious fury. Wilcox made point after point, ending with references to "the gentleman" from Ohio. Phrases like "abolition politicians," "stealing niggers," and "nigger equality in railroad cars" dominated his harangue. Wilcox's supporters gathered around the stage and shouted in chorus with each charge: "This no cause for secession? The gentleman from Ohio says not." When the colonel finally accused Anderson of being in friendly alliance with Ohio's most infamous abolitionists, Charles lost his composure. Fuming with indignation, he rushed the stage and pushed his way to the foot of the ladder, intending to physically assault Wilcox for this egregious insult. Fortunately, Daniel Story, a friend and fellow rancher, grabbed Anderson and prevented him from starting a melee.

With bloodshed narrowly averted, Union supporters broke up the meeting by taking the stand and preventing the next scheduled speaker, Christopher C. Upson, from addressing the crowd. They called instead for Samuel A. Maverick, long considered to be a Union man, to take the stage. Maverick finally acceded to the wishes of the crowd but disappointed many by siding with Boring and Wilcox. The time had come for secession, Maverick admitted. Some Union men called for Judge Isaiah A. Paschall, but it was past midnight and the meeting was over. Unionists signaled a band to strike up "The Star-Spangled Banner" and marched through the town singing till the wee hours of the morning. The Union celebration in San Antonio, however, did not last long.

Anderson's speech to the citizens of Bexar County made national headlines. Lincoln and his advisers praised the oration as eloquent, courageous, and truthful but were concerned that it was not vindictive enough toward the South. "It distributes too equally and too justly both blame and censure," said publisher George W. Pendleton, paraphrasing the president-elect's camp. Despite his reservations, Pendleton ordered six thousand copies of Anderson's speech to be printed and distributed to Congress and the public. Before his speech at the Alamo, Anderson had always acted on the principle of unswerving loyalty to his country. After the speech, he became not just a national figure but also a potential tool of the Lincoln administration.[2]

→→ ←←

CHAPTER EIGHT

Treachery and Treason

CHARLES ANDERSON'S TEXAS EXPERIMENT WAS an abject
failure. "I am dead broke," he complained to Rufus King on
December 7. Since his bank account was overdrawn, Anderson
resolved to sell his cattle, lay off two of his vaqueros, and halt construction on his house. The political crisis made loans almost impossible to procure. Without a circle of wealthy friends to support him,
Anderson had few options. He begged King to get him two thousand dollars on a twelve-month term, even if it meant mortgaging his
Dayton, Ohio, property. He owed fifteen hundred dollars on the former arsenal property and his creditors were not inclined to wait. On
the political front, the excitement of the past month had died down.
What emerged was an interesting political alignment. The non-slave-
holders were pushing for secession, according to Anderson, while 70
percent of slaveholders supported the Union. Anderson hoped that
the Union could be saved. He could not imagine the depth of the
conspiracy in motion against it.[1]

The Knights of the Golden Circle (KGC) were already known to
Anderson when he gave his speech in Alamo Square. Founder George
Bickley lived in Cincinnati until he was chased out in the late 1850s.
As Anderson gazed down from the stage on the night of the Alamo
meeting, he saw blue cockade badges adorning numerous hats and
lapels. The Knights had organized in the mid-1850s as a secret society promoting slave states in Mexico, Central America, and the

Caribbean. Members wanted U.S. slaveholding states to secede, join these new territories, and form a new nation. The KGC proved to be the match that lit the fire of Texas secession. San Antonio became the headquarters for Knights of the Golden Circle activities in Texas by 1859, and every substantial town had a branch called a "castle." U.S. military experts claimed that the Knights could call up more than eight thousand men on a few days' notice. Their discipline was said to be stricter than that of the legitimate army. Most of the key players guiding the Texas secession drama were members or had close connections with the covert militia.[2]

The town was also the headquarters of the U.S. Army's Department of Texas. In command was Lieutenant Colonel Robert E. Lee of the First Cavalry. One of the most respected and accomplished officers in the entire army, Lee was fresh off his capture of John Brown's gang at Harpers Ferry when he was assigned to this new command in February 1860. Lee and Charles Anderson were intimate friends. Robert Anderson and Colonel Lee were the great favorites of General Winfield Scott, for whom they served with distinction in the Mexican War. Lee made frequent trips to the Anderson residence north of San Antonio to attend dances and hunting parties. Officers in the San Antonio garrison lived in private residences and had ample time for leisure pursuits. Most socialized with the large circle of Union men and their families, and there were balls and parties almost every evening. Anderson's handsome daughter Kitty danced with Lee and other officers, but her heart was stolen by twenty-four-year-old Lieutenant William Graham Jones. After a brief courtship, the two were engaged.[3]

Two opposing forces, one a formal army and the other a nascent rebel militia, watched and plotted as developments on the national scene evolved. The KGC plot was already in motion. Unbeknownst to Lee or Anderson, Major General David E. Twiggs had already played his first card the day after Lincoln's election. Georgia native Twiggs was on leave from his former command of the Department of Texas and convalescing in New Orleans when he heard the electoral news. Despite his poor health, Twiggs wrote immediately for orders and was directed to resume command in San Antonio. He arrived back in

Texas on November 27, just three days after the Alamo meeting. The man behind this move was Secretary of War John B. Floyd.

Floyd and Charles Anderson had been friends since childhood, although they had become distant in recent years as Floyd moved in lockstep with the Breckenridge set. For months the secretary had been moving federal arms and munitions into the hands of various Southern governors, so that local militias could train and prepare for secession and possible war. Until his resignation from Buchanan's cabinet in December 1860, Floyd's actions had made him one of the most infamous traitors of the times. But he made at least one strategic mistake. Knowing that Charles's brother Robert was a Southerner, and assuming him in sympathy with secession, Floyd had General Scott assign Robert Anderson to Fort Moultrie at the mouth of Charleston harbor. That decision would later come back to haunt Floyd.

Lieutenant Colonel Lee was startled and perplexed by these sudden developments. Twiggs was clearly infirm. Why would Floyd relieve Lee of an important command at this critical juncture? What did his dear friend and mentor General Scott know about this? He did not wait long for answers, for Scott had been plotting as well. Near the end of October, Scott produced a paper intended for private circulation. His monograph outlined potential military strategies for the United States to consider should the Southern states secede. In retrospect, the idea was brilliant and simple. The Union would make the western theater the primary focus of early war efforts. Scott planned to immediately occupy the Ohio, Missouri, and Mississippi Rivers, thus severing Texas, Arkansas, Missouri, and western Louisiana from the rest of the Confederacy. Once that was accomplished, the Tennessee and Cumberland Rivers would be secured in a similar way.

On December 1, Scott sent these views to Anderson in San Antonio, asking that he share them with both Twiggs and Lee. Anderson gave the papers to Twiggs first, who returned them after a week. Twiggs told Anderson that it was "damned strange that General Scott should have sent the papers to you." He then added, "I know General Scott fully believes that God had to spit on his hands to make Bob Lee and Bob Anderson, and you are Major Anderson's brother." Charles Anderson then took the package from Twiggs and delivered it immediately to Lee. A few days after Lee received General Scott's papers, he summoned Anderson to his room at the boardinghouse. Charles brought along friend and confidante Dr. Willis G. Edwards. Lee felt that the publication of the papers might imply that the federal government intended to take preemptive military action, and he made Anderson promise not to publish them. The men talked at length about the secession crisis.

Anderson was violent in his denunciation of the Southern fire-eaters, whom he felt deserved most of the blame for the perilous state of affairs. Lee replied that "somebody is surely at fault, probably both factions." When Anderson restated his opinion and suggested that a broad-based conspiracy was brewing, Lee remained silent. At this point, Edwards pointedly asked whether in such cases a man's loyalty was due to his home state or to his nation. Lee's decision would change the course of history. Lee did not equivocate. Surely this vexing issue had tortured him for some weeks or even months. He chose this moment to declare his intentions to two of his close friends. Lee believed that his first allegiance was due to Virginia. The conversation ended. Lee made preparations to leave for Fort Mason, about 112 miles from San Antonio, and await a fate now held firmly by the very politicians he so loathed. He had scarcely left town when South Carolina voted to secede.

Some politicians were working feverishly behind the scenes to prevent the secession crisis from spreading. In Congress, Senator John J. Crittenden of Kentucky introduced a compromise bill he had conceived with the help of Larz Anderson and others, but it failed at the eleventh hour. The day after Christmas, Robert Anderson, seeing that his position was too exposed to safeguard his men, transported them from Fort Moultrie to Fort Sumter in the middle of Charleston harbor. This move was viewed by some Southerners as an act of aggression. On January 9, the steamer *Star of the West* was attacked by South Carolinians determined to prevent reinforcements from entering the fort. The whole world waited to see what would happen next.

As the nation was coming apart, Union men from all over Texas scrambled to slow the secession momentum. In mid-January, Charles Anderson received a letter from Judge I. A. Paschall requesting an immediate meeting with Governor Sam Houston in Austin. Upon his arrival, Anderson learned that the governor had big plans for him. Houston desired that Anderson take control of all the forts, arsenals, arms and munitions, and other property of the United States within the state of Texas. By preempting the Knights of the Golden Circle, Houston hoped he could scotch the rebellion before it began.[4]

Houston's request to General Twiggs to cede arms to the state was met with evasion. On January 22, Twiggs replied that because he was without instructions from Washington, D.C., he could not fulfill the governor's request. After secession, Twiggs continued, if the governor repeated his demands, he would then receive an answer. Houston did not know that Twiggs had already requested to be relieved of his command nine days earlier. As Houston and Twiggs tried to outfox each another, the flames of disunion grew into a full-fledged conflagration. Four states had seceded by the time a despondent Anderson returned to Worth Springs. He immediately wrote William M. Corry asking for advice. "Our form of government is a failure," Anderson lamented. "The dream is mere mirage. Our system . . . like all other perfect theories, fails in the experience through the amazing irrationality and malevolence of Mankind." Though he still accused the secessionists of igniting the revolution, the abolitionists certainly bore blame as well. "If the people of the North had possessed the requisite capacity for self-government," Anderson argued, "they never would have allowed their *personal* sympathies, envy and other private passions to thrust themselves into a ballot box designed for different motives."[5]

While Anderson brooded, Larz managed to visit their brother Robert at Fort Sumter. He returned to Washington carrying secret messages. Larz had many influential friends in the capital and worked tirelessly to achieve some sort of last-ditch compromise. Meanwhile, Robert E. Lee remained at Fort Mason, awaiting the action of the other Southern states. Texas did not keep him waiting long.[6] Sam Houston, despite doing all he could to forestall a secession convention, was losing the battle. Ultimately he was forced to yield to a petition of sixty-one prominent citizens from all over the state. Nearly all were KGC members. The secession convention was held on January

28. Houston again ordered Anderson to Austin, and the Texas Union leaders awaited the results of the convention. The vote was 166 to 7 in favor of secession, to be ratified by popular vote on February 23. "The deed is done," Anderson wrote to his former law partner Rufus King on February 9. "Texas goes out of the Union to which she never ought to have belonged."[7]

The KGC did not wait for ratification. On January 29, they established a Committee of Safety to begin taking "control of the arms and munitions of war within her limits." They feared "coercion" from the twenty-eight hundred U.S. troops within the state's borders. The committee boldly stated that it expected that General Twiggs, "a Southern man by birth and friendly to the cause of the South," would surrender U.S. Army property. In case he refused, the committee commissioned former U.S. marshal Henry Eustace McCulloch to persuade him otherwise.

It was all a ruse, as Twiggs was in on the plot all along. McCulloch and his band of nearly a thousand armed citizens confronted 160 federal troops. Twiggs was permitted to feign surrender to an overwhelming force of arms on February 16. As it so happened, Lee was returning to San Antonio that very day. When his ambulance arrived at his boardinghouse in the middle of the afternoon, it was surrounded by men wearing a curious red badge that Lee had never seen before. "Who are these men?" Lee asked Mrs. Caroline Darrow. "They are McCulloch's," she replied. "General Twiggs surrendered everything to the state this morning and we are all prisoners of war."

Lee was visibly upset; some later claimed they saw tears in his eyes as he spoke. "Has it come as soon as this?" he asked. Unsure of his status, Lee walked to a nearby hotel, registered, and changed into civilian garb. He then proceeded to army headquarters, now occupied by McCulloch's men. The commissioners told Lee that unless he resigned immediately and joined the rebellion, he would not be allowed to transport his personal effects out of the state. Remorse turned quickly to anger as Lee steadfastly refused to recognize this apparent coup and asserted that he had no obligations to an illegal gang of revolutionaries. He then sought out Charles Anderson and asked him to look after his belongings until they could be sent east. Together they walked to the commission merchant.

While on their way to the warehouse, Lee asked Anderson if he remembered their conversation of a few weeks previous. Anderson said that he did indeed. Lee reiterated his decision. "I still think," Lee insisted, "as I told you and Doctor Edwards that my loyalty to Virginia ought to take precedence over that which is due the federal government. I shall so report myself at Washington. If she stands by the old Union, so will I. But if she secedes, though I do not believe in secession as a constitutional right, nor that there is sufficient cause for revolution, then I will still follow my native state with my sword, and if need be with my life." Anderson felt compelled to respond. "The selection of the place in which we were born," he explained, "was not an act of our own volition; but when we took the oath of allegiance to our government, it was an act of manhood, and that oath we cannot break."

"I know you think and feel very differently," Lee replied, "but I can't help it. These are my principles, and I must follow them." Lee left the following day. On his arrival in Washington City, Winfield Scott made Lee an enticing offer. Scott proposed that he be promoted immediately to the rank of colonel. The president had further authorized Scott to offer Lee command of the entire army, second to only the aged Scott himself. Lee repeated what he had told Anderson and left for his plantation at Arlington, Virginia.[8]

Anderson wondered what the future held for him and his family. A week later, he received a disturbing telegram. His son Latham, an 1859 graduate of West Point and first lieutenant in the U.S. Fifth Infantry, had lost his first battle to a large force of Texas Rangers in New Mexico. He had escaped unharmed. Would Anderson and his family be so lucky? Nerves were fraying inside the Anderson household. Anderson wrote that his terrified wife "now fancies K.G.C.s, Vigilance Committees, or Committees of Safety in every road or street." With Texas voters formally endorsing a secession that had already taken place, Anderson saw all but the most hard-core Unionists jump on the bandwagon or at least cooperate to save their fortunes and their skins. He himself would have none of it.

"In two years more," Anderson wrote King, "my income from horses would probably have begun at between $5 and 7,000 per annum." But rather than be "an alien and an enemy to [his] native land," he vowed to "choose instant poverty." Anderson decided to leave as soon as the Committee of Safety would allow it. He sold Kentucky lands in Madison and Franklin Counties to help finance the move. "I might be off before a month—though it may not be in 6," he predicted. He suspected that leaving would not be so easy. While many hoped for peaceable secession, Anderson did not "expect to see that miracle of miracles," he wrote King on March 24. Two separate republics with a twenty-five-hundred-mile border, separated with such bitterness and animosity and goaded by fanatics on both sides could hardly coexist peacefully. "I am compelled to droop my head and close my eyes against the rising pandemonium of the near future," Anderson admitted.[9]

Two weeks later, Robert Anderson surrendered Fort Sumter and war became inevitable. Late April was the scheduled time for federal troops leaving Texas to leave from the coast on their homeward journeys. The outbreak of hostilities changed those plans. On April 23, Confederate Colonel Earl Van Dorn arrested his counterpart, Colonel Carlos A. Waite, confining him and his staff officers as formal prisoners of war. Other U.S. forces were already on their way to the coast. Van Dorn went after them. It took Confederate soldiers more than two weeks to detain or capture most of the exiting U.S. troops. The last confrontation came about fifteen miles west of San Antonio on the old military road at a place called San Lucas Springs. U.S. commander Lieutenant Colonel Isaac Van Duzer Reeve and 270 men confronted nearly 1,400 Confederate partisans. Neither side wanted bloodshed, so Reeve surrendered his command and marched his troops into San Antonio on May 10. Any hope of Union resistance in Texas was over without a shot being fired.

The U.S. troops held in San Antonio and elsewhere had few options in their confinement. Their captors encouraged them to renounce their allegiance to the Union and join the Confederate ranks. Few did so. An alternative was to sign a "parole of honor" by which they agreed not to take up arms against nor leave the Confederate States until such time as they were either exchanged or released. Before battles raged in the east, the prospects for exchange seemed bright, so most chose this path. The same code of honor that protected U.S. soldiers did not apply to the general public. Union men became particularly vulnerable.[10]

Few Union men were as bold or brave as James P. Newcomb. His *Alamo Express* had been published on and off for about a year. When Newcomb learned of the San Lucas Springs capture, he ran a scathing condemnation of the act in his triweekly paper. A mob consisting of KGC men and Texas Rangers responded by destroying Newcomb's press and burning his building. The next day, a well-armed Newcomb rode down Commerce Street and out of town, headed for Mexico.[11] In Houston, violence against Union men reached a fever pitch. On May 15, two New Hampshire natives were tarred, feathered, ridden out of town on a rail, and hanged. Anderson happened to be in Houston and heard that Dr. K. B. Ayer, also from New Hampshire, had been branded an abolitionist. This was ludicrous, since Ayer owned a plantation in Arkansas employing twenty-four slaves. Charles intervened just in time to convince a lynch mob to spare his friend's life in return for his removal from the state.[12]

Union men and their families began leaving Texas in droves and the rebels were happy to see them go. Whether they chose to make their way to the Texas coast, to New Orleans, or to brave the more arduous journey southwest to Mexico, dangers along the way necessitated that refugees travel in wagon trains. After the first major land battle at Manassas, the Confederate government decided to put a deadline on these emigrations. The Alien Enemy Act of August 8 gave the refugees forty days to leave the state. That deadline was later extended to the end of October in Texas, based on the time it took for the proclamation to reach remote areas. Those who tarried longer were at the mercy of local authorities.

➤➤ ◄◄

CHAPTER NINE

Capture

CHARLES ANDERSON'S FIRST IMPULSE was to flee. Over the course of the nightmare year 1861, however, the opportunity to assist other Union men had caused him to hesitate. Now that the Confederate government was closing that window, Anderson had to get his family out. This was hardly an easy task. War created chaos in financial markets, especially in the South. Compelled to sell his livestock, land, and house quickly in a hostile climate, Anderson braced for the worst. He had spent about thirty thousand dollars creating his beautiful ranch and home. He salvaged only a fraction of that investment.

Anderson first advertised his land for sale in the newspapers, but a scarcity of money and nervous potential buyers made that effort fruitless. He finally came up with an idea. His friend John James had an approved claim against the U.S. government for rent of lands near Camp Hudson, Texas. It was due to be paid in 1861, but the war broke out and the U.S. Senate froze appropriations to Texas. If Anderson could get back to Washington, he could present James's claim and recover at least a thousand dollars. So he swapped some of his property for James's claim on September 14. Anderson exchanged his most valuable land for notes on a house in Louisville, Kentucky. He bartered his prized stallions for land and whiskey in Lexington, Kentucky.[1]

The remaining livestock and personal effects went to auction. The

Andersons ended up selling everything but their most practical possessions. Even Eliza's family Bible went on the block. Fortunately Mrs. Banning Norton, a family friend, bought it and shipped it on to New York. On Friday, September 27, Charles Anderson rode into town, where he met with Confederate general Henry H. Sibley, who urged him to leave by stage for New Orleans the following Tuesday. Sibley gave Anderson till ten o'clock the following morning to decide. When Charles returned home, he found Kitty so sick that she was unable to sit up. She had malaria.[2]

Kitty suffered through chills and night sweats. Since she was unable to travel by stage, the family opted to leave in wagons for Matamoros, Mexico. There they could catch a steamship and eventually make it to the North. Despite Eliza's objections, the family was persuaded to depart on Sunday. Their escorts, two members of Judge Thomas J. Devine's jury, were leaving that day for Brownsville, Texas. That port town was 278 miles away, just across the river from Matamoros. Anderson purchased the fine ambulance of former U.S. Army major James Longstreet so that his wife and daughters could ride during the day and sleep comfortably at night. They went off to an uncertain future.

The family was detained in town as close friends said their good-byes. Most of the paroled Union officers turned out. Kitty's fiancé, Will Jones, packed the wagon with extra comforts for the road. Melinda, the family's twenty-year-old black servant, was in tears as she begged Eliza to take her with them. She had been freed by Anderson just days before. Once the family fled the state, Melinda was abducted and sold back into slavery. They finally departed San Antonio around eleven o'clock. As the Andersons followed the course of the lovely river, passing several missions along the way, they gazed backwards. Their hearts sank as the town slowly vanished.

The little band made twenty-five miles that day. Edward Gallagher and Robert McCarty followed them at first but soon passed, as their mules were stronger and their loads lighter. After an hour, they crossed the Salado River and bade farewell to several of their Mexican friends. The roads were heavy with sand. The Andersons could not catch up with their fellow travelers by nightfall, so they made camp by the roadside. They passed their first evening as refugees uneasily. Kitty and Eliza awoke in the middle of the night to the sound of horses. They were afraid that bandits had come to rob them, as some miscreants in town had threatened to take their auction money. Thankfully, the riders passed and the Andersons rose to breakfast Monday morning relieved if not completely refreshed. The party left early in the morning for the second day of their planned journey.

The Anderson family had been back on the road only four or five miles when they observed soldiers riding toward them. As they drew close to the wagon, the column split in two and filed off on either side of the emigrants. Once surrounded, Anderson asked Lieutenant Arthur K. Leigh if he had seen their escorts. "They are about three and a half miles beyond," replied the officer. "Would you be able to return to San Antonio?" he asked. "I object particularly and prefer to go on and catch up with our company," replied Anderson. Leigh informed him that they had orders to bring him back. Anderson maintained his poise throughout the exchange, stating that he could not imagine why he should be molested in this way. "Well, Felix," he finally said to his driver, "Turn around. We shall go back." Turning to Leigh, Anderson added: "I assure you, if it were possible against such odds, I would resist such a rascally procedure." As the soldiers and their captives returned to town, Anderson looked for opportunities to escape. This might have been easily accomplished as they passed through the thick chaparral, but he feared for the fate of his family should he attempt it.

When the party stopped for dinner, Anderson pretended to make coffee while he burned letters and other papers that might implicate his Union friends. He tried to remove a thorn from a hobbling mule and was rewarded with a kick, followed by a bite from his dog for the same mercies. "Well this *is* Anderson luck!" he exclaimed. Despite his misfortunes, Anderson retained his sense of humor. As they neared San Antonio, however, his mood changed. Leigh had ridden forward to inform McCulloch of his successful mission. Upon his return, the Confederate lieutenant informed Anderson that if he agreed not to leave the city, he would be given a parole and liberty of movement throughout the town. "I refuse to take parole for an inch of space or a moment of time!" Anderson exclaimed. The women were allowed to go wherever they pleased, but they preferred to stay with the prisoner.[3]

Arriving in San Antonio Monday evening, soldiers took the Andersons to the Menger House and placed them in the hotel's finest rooms. Guards monitored the doors and did not allow the prisoner contact with any of his friends. The soldiers confiscated the family's baggage, allowing access to it only by the women under the watchful eyes of Lieutenant George W. Balzer. The family spent the next three days locked in the Menger House hotel. Eliza and her daughters refused to take meals at the public table downstairs, as they were concerned that any contact with their friends might put them in danger too. Confederate colonel Dr. Phillip N. Luckett and Presley J. Edwards came to visit the Andersons on the first day of their captivity and were turned away by the guards. Will Jones, Kitty's fiancé, would not be deterred. He succeeded in visiting the women each day of their confinement. It was cold comfort.

The Andersons woke early on Tuesday morning and awaited their fate. At about half past nine, three officers called for Charles and escorted him down to the vacant room where the family's baggage was stored. Captain D. C. Stith, Major William T. Mechling, and Lieutenant Leigh each questioned the prisoner in turn. Anderson opened all the trunks and unpacked every article. They confiscated all of his money save one hundred dollars and all of his personal papers. Anderson was alarmed. "Some of the money was mine," Eliza protested. "And some mine," Kitty added. Such remonstrations were pointless. Anderson asked his wife if she really thought that McCulloch would recognize her auction proceeds of three hundred dollars for the piano and three hundred dollars for her carriage. "Yes," replied Eliza, "they have no right to take it from me nor will not." Eliza and Kitty also worried that the soldiers would try to take the money they had sewn into their clothing. What was clearly illegal in peacetime had little bearing on the actions of local authorities in a time of civil war.

After dinner, Anderson spent the afternoon being further interrogated downstairs. In the evening, he was allowed to see close friend Presley Edwards for a few minutes. Eliza still refused to see a steady stream of friends who called at Menger House. Kitty received a handful of friends Tuesday night, including her loyal beau Will. Perhaps tomorrow would be better, she prayed. By the next morning, however, her hopes were dashed. Kitty resolved to be quiet and cheerful, but early Wednesday morning her mother came back to their room with tears in her eyes. Anderson had decided that the rest of the family should leave him in Texas and go north. Eliza did not agree and tried to convince him otherwise, but his mind was made up. McCulloch finally informed Anderson that he was considered "an alien enemy and a prisoner of war." No formal charges had been brought, but it was clear to all that the prisoner was not going anywhere.

Luckett was finally allowed to see Anderson, and he began carrying letters back and forth from McCulloch. Anderson sent word to the colonel that he wished his family to embark on their journey, so McCulloch arranged for Lieutenant Leigh to escort them the following day. He suggested that his friend, Cuban lawyer Jose Augustin Quintero, should also accompany them to Brownsville. Quintero called on the family later in the day. Kitty found him polite and charming. She did not suspect that he was a Confederate spy.

Anderson's missives to McCulloch became increasingly combative. These proceedings were illegal by any civilized standard, he declared. He had been denied the privilege of facing his accuser. He could not be both a citizen of Texas and an alien. Martial law had not been declared. Anderson insisted he be remanded to Brownsville, where the Confederate States Court was in session. When again offered parole, the prisoner replied, "I wouldn't give my parole for one minute to save your soul from Hell!" Anderson received his last letter from his captor on Thursday. McCulloch wrote that it was his duty to arrest Anderson. "As your former mild and courteous letters, and the appeals of your friends, have not been able to arouse my personal sympathies," McCulloch wrote, "you certainly will not expect me to be so unmanly as to permit your harsh, bitter, and unwarranted allusions to myself to excite the baser passion of the heart . . . I will exercise all the kindness and courtesy towards you that I can do safely, or that you—in your evident desire to make yourself a martyr—will permit."[4]

McCulloch ordered Anderson to be removed to Captain William T. Mechling's line of camp sentinels and forbade him correspondence or outside visitors. Although the terms of parole allowed Will Jones travel within the Confederate States, McCulloch denied him the right to accompany his fiancé's family to the port. Eliza went into her husband's room alone for what seemed to Kitty like hours. When she emerged, Kitty and her eleven-year-old sister wrapped their arms around their father's neck and said their good-byes. Belle was sobbing quietly, while Kitty stood somber and stone-faced.

→→ ←←

CHAPTER TEN

Exodus

ELIZA ANDERSON WAS CRYING as family friends loaded them into their ambulance for yet another wrenching farewell. As the mules started moving, Kitty's beau, Will Jones shouted, "I will overtake you before you reach there!" to which Eliza responded, "And bring Mr. Anderson with you!" They were traveling the same road that took them back to San Antonio less than four days previous, but the rear view this time looked gloomy and ugly. They never saw their Texas home again. At the edge of town, the little company paused, as Lieutenant Arthur Leigh had gone back to Presley Edwards's house to retrieve some family photographs. They had almost made it to the Salado River when night fell and they were forced to make camp near an ancient little house on the side of the road. Leigh and lawyer Jose Augustin Quintero made every effort to tend to the family's needs, but sadness and exhaustion had enveloped the Anderson girls. They fell asleep immediately.

The party woke early the next morning to repack and reload. Once under way, they made good progress and arrived at the Calaveras River by lunch time. Before the meal, Kitty whispered a private prayer. "Oh father, my dear father, when will I ever see you again? So blessed of God in every way. Kind heaven grant a nobler destiny than this we fear!" Passing the very spot where Charles Anderson had been arrested, the party again made camp. After a brief walk they fell into another dreary, deep sleep. The days passed with little variation.

They woke early and traveled until sundown, making twenty to twenty-five miles on a good day. The refugees and their escorts began to feel more comfortable with each other. Lively conversation provided occasional relief from premonitions of doom. Quintero engaged Kitty in a discussion of politics and was surprised at how much she knew. When he asked her why her father would turn down a parole, Kitty replied, "Do you think my father would take parole now?" All talk of such matters ended abruptly.

At Goliad, Eliza urged Kitty to keep up her singing per her father's wishes. Anderson loved music and the sound of his favorite daughter's voice most particularly. "Every note," Kitty replied, "seems to choke me." So she buried herself in one of her father's beloved Shakespeare dramas. The little book was replete with his characteristic pencil notations. As she gazed at the margins of each page, Kitty could almost hear her father's voice. During the journey she learned that Quintero had an interesting past. Leigh told her that the Cuban and fellow exiles like Narciso Lopez had attempted to overthrow the Cuban government with arms and financial backing from U.S. interests. Quintero continued to work Kitty for information, reading poetry to her and promising her a parrot he kept with Colonel John S. Ford at Brownsville. Ford later pretended to go out of his way to aid the refugees. However, he was actually their sworn enemy.

The landscape past Palo Blanco became more attractive, with bright streams, grassy plains, and post oaks. It was a park-like setting. Leigh sang "How Can I Leave Thee" in his native German as they rode along, his fine voice cheering the emigrant band. If her father was only with them, Kitty speculated, they might actually start enjoying this trip. After a week on the road, the weather changed. Rains came, alternating in drizzles and torrents. The mules were tired from their extra exertion in the wet, sandy roads and hungry due to a scarcity of corn, their favorite fodder. The midday meal for the humans was "beyond barbaric," according to Kitty, and they did not eat it. The day they left San Patricio, where arms were being stored for the Confederate government, the party made only six miles. An unfinished, abandoned house on the prairie served as their lodgings for the night, as the ground was too damp for camping.

On October 12, the company made an arduous seventeen-mile slog, pushed along by a fierce storm, and arrived at the King ranch. Captain Richard King had one of the largest and most prosperous ranches in the state. His sixteen thousand acres included the spring-fed Santa Gertrudis Creek in the middle of the Wild Horse Desert. King and his refined wife, Henrietta, were kind to travelers. The Anderson family enjoyed a brief respite in the comfortable society they were accustomed to. The next day, packed with a supply of fresh meat from their generous hosts, the refreshed travelers again braved the hostile desert. A swift but boring twenty-five-mile ride to Santa Rosa on Saturday was followed by an equally wearisome trek to Taylor's Well on the Sabbath. The only break in the monotony was the addition of Captain James Walworth to the party, he having joined them from King's ranch. Walworth was a clever man and a confirmed bachelor. He was also an outspoken secessionist, so the Andersons kept their distance.

The rain resumed on Monday and continued during the twenty-two-mile crawl to Las Animas (the Ghosts). This stretch of the journey was well named, as they found abandoned vehicles and homesteads nearly as plentiful as the wild turkeys, ducks, partridges, geese, and deer that inhabited the area. After two more days of sandy and sparse wilderness, they stopped at the ranch of Francis W. Latham, who treated them with the utmost kindness. He was a Connecticut native and about to be married to a cousin of Governor William Sprague of Rhode Island. Like so many former Union men, he eventually supported secession. Finally they arrived at the edge of Arroyo Colorado, fourteen miles from Brownsville. Recent rains had flooded the arroyos and made the crossing a difficult proposition. They were forced to wait until the water level subsided.

The next day the party encountered several travelers. Judge Devine met them on his way to court. He expressed mock dismay at Charles Anderson's predicament, telling Eliza that he was "astonished" to hear that her husband had been detained. He was hardly an "alien enemy" and had the judge been in San Antonio at the time, he maintained, the capture would not have occurred. Even if he was considered an enemy of the Confederacy, the judge claimed, it would be his duty to send Anderson out of Texas as soon as practical. But the judge was not shooting straight with the Andersons. He, Quintero, and Henry McCulloch were on the same page. Once his artful evasion with Eliza had concluded, the judge had a private conversation with Quintero. The Cuban insisted that the family should stay in Brownsville and await the certainty of Anderson's release; he urged the Andersons not to worry. His friends would keep an eye on them.

On Thursday, October 17, the anxious family woke shortly after midnight. They were too excited to sleep, knowing that this part of their long trial was nearly at an end. The water in the arroyo was only about a foot deep, so the party crossed and made their way to Victor's, a popular inn, where they were given comfortable rooms for the night. They were greeted by a steady stream of visitors, including Edward Gallagher and Robert McCarty, the family's escorts in their first attempted emigration. Also calling was San Antonio dentist and fellow refugee William G. Kingsbury, a man who proved to be one of the Andersons' most loyal friends. The next morning, they moved to their new lodgings in one of Mr. Latham's boardinghouses. No sooner had they arrived than Quintero and Ford called to check up on them. Kingsbury arrived later that day. He had been across the river in Matamoros, Mexico, meeting with friends sympathetic to the Union cause. There was an English brig set to sail in eight to ten days for New York with a possible stop in Havana. They might be able to secure passage. The competition for berths on any vessel leaving Texas at that time was fierce.

On Saturday, after breakfast Eliza, Kitty, and Belle went out to buy letter paper. Upon their return, Kingsbury called, quite agitated. Colonel Ford was downstairs under orders to inspect their baggage. Ford came up to their rooms in a flurry of apologies and examined the few papers the Andersons had in their possession. His young wife called minutes later and expressed her displeasure with this imposition on their privacy.[1]

Kingsbury returned in the afternoon with two other gentlemen to take the ladies on a tour of Matamoros. The town was unlike anything Kitty had ever seen. She was used to the Mexican culture and people of San Antonio, but Matamoros was so different, so foreign in aspect. She welcomed this small bit of leisure during an otherwise tumultuous time. Ferrymen rowed the Andersons and their tour guides from the wharf across the river in two skiffs. The party climbed aboard carriages for their city excursion. They soon came upon an enclosed square with grass and trees. Kingsbury said that a band played there on Sundays and Thursday evenings. Fine two-story brick mansions with iron railings and balconies fronted the square. Wealthy ladies could be seen "airing themselves" through the tall, grated windows on the second floor. They visited the small but luxuriant gardens of Doña Anna Domingo, landscaped with Spanish bayonet palms, citron, and other fruit trees. Like most cities in Europe or America, Matamoros was a city of contrasts.

Most of the dwellings were one-story structures. Traditional "jacals" composed of mud, sticks, and thatch roofs were interspersed among modern residences, giving the town a picturesque, exotic look. The Central Market House was the largest building in town, surrounded by paved courts and other buildings of various designs and functions. Most of the houses they saw had iron spikes on their windows, suggesting to Kitty "a town of prisons." The town was alive with short Mexican soldiers with red caps. The visitors soon learned that the soldiers were going off to quell an insurrection in some interior village. It appeared that most of the inhabitants of Matamoros were expecting an attack any day from forces loyal to Cipriano Guererro, who had recently lost a hotly contested race for governor of Tamaulipas. The Andersons passed about forty armed cavalry troops, followed by a tiny piece of artillery guarded by a few smallish soldiers in gray uniforms and red caps. This force did not compare favorably to the militia that Kitty and her mother were used to seeing back in Texas and Ohio. The tour complete, Eliza and her daughters returned to Brownsville and called it a night.

The next day was Sunday, and Kingsbury took the Andersons to the Presbyterian Church to hear Reverend Hiram Chamberlain preach. The celebrant was "sensible and plain," according to Kitty, but the music "horrible." No matter. This was their first opportunity for formal worship in more than two weeks. Eliza and her girls prayed ardently for Anderson's deliverance. The very next day their prayers would be answered.[2]

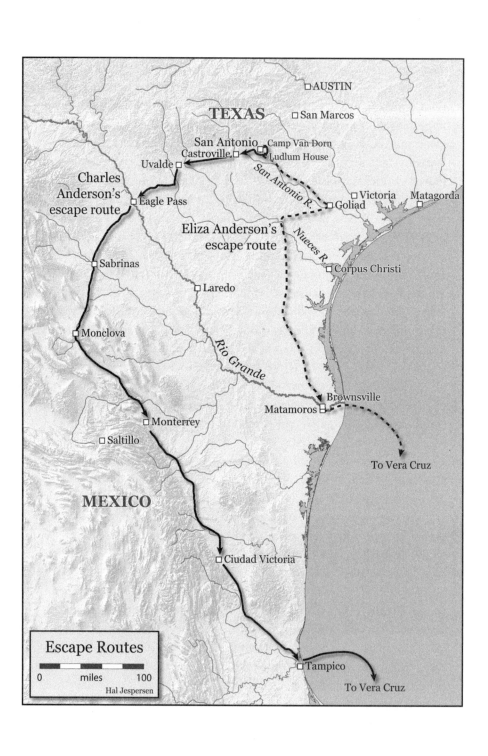

✦

CHAPTER ELEVEN

Escape

THE DAY THAT HIS FAMILY left San Antonio, Charles Anderson was remanded to the custody of Captain William T. Mechling, whose artillery brigade was camped six miles east of town at a place that came to be known as Camp Van Dorn. He was supplied with two wall tents facing each other with a sun shade in between. He slept in one of the tents and had his study in the other. Anderson was under guard twenty-four hours a day. His movements were strictly circumscribed during his first few weeks of captivity, and he ate all his meals with Captain Mechling's family. At first he was allowed no visitors, but as he and Mechling became better acquainted, these rules were somewhat relaxed. Eventually most of the prisoner's officer friends were permitted to visit him and he seemed to be in pretty decent spirits. Of course, Anderson was eager to hear of his family's arrival in Brownsville. One day he remarked to his good friend and fellow captive Lieutenant Zenas R. Bliss that "no bride ever waited more anxiously for the coming of the groom than I do for the return of Lt. Leigh." After a few weeks, Leigh returned with the news that his family was safe, allowing Anderson to plan his next move.[1]

Men frequently escaped from military prisons in the nineteenth century. Suitable facilities for the detainment of large numbers of prisoners often did not exist and certainly could not spring up overnight. Under the European tradition of a parole of honor, prisoners were given some freedom of movement while awaiting exchange.

Once incarcerated, however, soldiers were no longer bound by the conditions of their parole. The first escape from a Civil War prison occurred in Texas just weeks before Anderson was arrested. Three sergeants from Reeve's command who had been captured at San Lucas Spring in May 1861 arrived in Washington City on October 20. T. D. Parker, Franklin Cook, and R. E. Ellenwood of the Eighth Infantry Regiment said that the Confederates had violated their parole agreement by placing them under guard and severely reducing their clothing, blankets, and rations. They made their escape through West Texas and Mexico, eventually boarding a steamer to Havana and thence to New York. They made use of detailed military maps to guide them to safety, the same kind of maps that most of Anderson's officer friends possessed.[2]

Anderson's friends in San Antonio knew that he would rather die than be away from his family for the course of the war, however long that might be, so they began conducting secret meetings to affect his liberation. It was a dangerous business. The escape plan they settled on involved three unlikely accomplices: Ann S. Ludlum, Jean-Charles Houzeau de Lehaie, and William Bayard.

Ludlum was a forty-nine-year-old widow of humble means. Born Ann Manson in Baltimore, she married her first husband, a man named Barry, sometime before 1836. After his death, she wed Cincinnati house painter Wesley Ludlum and lived for many years in the Buckeye State. She moved to New Orleans with her husband and family around 1850, where he died a few years later. By 1860, Ann Ludlum had divorced her third husband, Joseph Coker, and was running a small boardinghouse on the Goliad Road just north of downtown San Antonio. Ludlum barely knew the Andersons. In fact, she had made her first visit to their home just weeks before the family's hasty departure. She was unhappy that her eldest son, Thomas H. Barry, had ignored her wishes and had run off to Houston to enlist in the Confederate Army. Ludlum knew that she ran a terrible risk in even talking about springing Charles Anderson from the military camp, but she was a dedicated Union woman and had to do something. She devised the plan.[3]

One of the renters at the Ludlum boardinghouse was an eccentric, brilliant Belgian astronomer named Jean-Charles Houzeau de Lehaie. The forty-one-year-old Houzeau, as he preferred to be called, was born in the small city of Havre, near Mons. His distinguished career as the director of the Brussels observatory was cut short after he aired his strong political views once too often and was dismissed from his job. His interest in geology led him to Texas, where he settled in Uvalde and organized scientific expeditions to the borders of Indian country. Indian attacks forced Houzeau to abandon his fossils and cherished books and flee to Austin, just as Texas was seceding. Local leaders needed intelligent recruits and offered Houzeau a commission in the Confederate Army. He refused, saying that he "would sooner cut off [his] right hand than serve that cause." Houzeau was a radical abolitionist and decided that San Antonio, with its large contingent of Union supporters, might afford him a safer haven. Naturally, this Renaissance man had become a fast friend of Anderson, whose interests in all things scientific knew no bounds.[4]

The third conspirator in the planning of Anderson's escape was a little-known visitor with important family connections. Twenty-year-old William Bayard was born in New York to a wealthy family with a rich military pedigree. He had been living with his uncle, Dr. J. Yellot Dashiell, since the summer of 1860. Dashiell was not only a wealthy stock raiser but an important town leader who had been mayor of San Antonio. He became adjutant general of Texas during the rebellion. Dashiell's daughter was married to Confederate Captain William T. Mechling, the Confederate officer holding Anderson at Camp Van Dorn. When the war broke out, Bayard declared his Union sympathies and was placed under a sort of house arrest by his cousins. Later he was transferred to the same camp that held Anderson. The two became friends. One day over backgammon, Anderson proposed that Bayard join him in an escape. He readily agreed. With Anderson's young friend on board, the three schemers then resolved to put an escape plan into action.[5]

The first step was communicating the plan details to Anderson. Ludlum decided to trust her neighbor, twenty-six-year-old German saloon keeper Charles Kreische, with this mission. Kreische and many of his German friends were in sympathy with the Union cause. Although not privy to the specifics of the plan, he agreed to pass a coded letter to the prisoner in camp. Kreische and Anderson discussed the philosophy of Kant for a time before the two settled into a game of backgammon. While the guard was busy polishing his saber, Kreische passed the note to Anderson and left at the conclusion of the game. Anderson read the letter, memorized the details, and destroyed it. The plot was simple but dangerous.[6] Anderson was instructed to leave on the first cloudy night of that week and make his way to Ludlum's house, where horses and supplies would be waiting for him. He intended to stay secreted at the boardinghouse for two or three weeks. When the excitement surrounding his escape died down, Anderson would depart to meet Bayard down the road in their mutual escape to Mexico.

If Anderson assented to this plan, he was to exit the tent and bow three times. He waited several minutes after Kreische left his tent, then walked out into the yard. He looked at the sky as if examining the weather, stroked his beard and lowered his head. He paced and bowed inconspicuously, repeating this slow and seemingly innocent behavior two more times. Then he walked back inside the tent, taking care not to look away at any time. Bayard observed the signal and the game was on.

One clear night followed another. The conspirators grew anxious. Kitty Anderson's fiancé, Will Jones, passed the tent one morning and, when the guard was not looking, tossed a satchel into Anderson's study. The purse contained several hundred dollars. The money was collected by Jones from his fellow officer prisoners. Anderson stashed the money and a pair of shoes in a hole under his bed and awaited a change in the weather. His asthma had returned, though not in as serious a form as he had led his captors to believe. The illness gave Anderson the excuse to opt out of the nightly games he had been playing with some of his guards and focus on planning his escape. He sent money to Dr. Ferdinand Herff one day to secure some stramonium, more popularly known as "Jamestown weed." He often smoked the plant to relieve his symptoms and help him sleep. A strong narcotic, stramonium is lethal in large doses.

On the first cloudy afternoon of that week, Anderson approached Captain Mechling with a request. He told the captain that he was supposed to take only small puffs of the intense weed, but that he had smoked an entire pipe full in his desire to get a good night's rest. He asked Mechling to let him sleep undisturbed if he was not up by breakfast. The captain honored the request. Anderson placed his boots outside to be blackened as he had done every night during his confinement, and he retired for the evening.

Anderson waited until everyone in camp was asleep except the guards. He slipped unseen into his study tent with his shoes, money, and little else. When the sentry passed to the side of Anderson's bedroom, Charles crept out under the tent wall of the study. Clouds and rain blotted out the stars and most of the light from the half moon. Anderson was thankful for the darkness but afraid of losing his bearings. As he sneaked away from the Confederate soldiers, he paused each time the lightning flashed, hoping to catch a brief view of his surroundings. Soon he was completely lost. After wandering for a few hours, Anderson saw some lights and decided to approach them so as to determine his position. As he walked toward the illumination, a sentinel challenged him. Anderson remembered that the only other brigade encamped nearby was that of General Henry B. Sibley. Sibley's troops were stationed on the Salado River, preparing for a campaign into New Mexico territory. Some of these troops would ultimately clash with forces commanded by Anderson's son Latham at the Battle of Val Verde.

Maintaining his composure, Anderson answered the sentry, stating that he had important business with Sibley and asking for directions to his tent. The ruse worked, and Anderson walked calmly in that direction. As soon as he was out of the guard's sight, Anderson quickened his pace and headed for the river. After struggling for countless minutes while wading away from Sibley's camp in water up to his neck, Anderson heard the drums beat a general alarm. Since he had failed to show up at Sibley's tent, he was now being hunted. On and on Anderson walked through the driving rain, his cheap, borrowed shoes disintegrating in the process. His feet and hands were bleeding from encounters with the briars and brambles of his trackless flight. The featureless landscape and poor visibility led him to crawl on his hands and knees at various points, trying to feel for a road or a way marker of some kind.

Anderson had been stumbling along until well after midnight when he found himself at the old powder house on the outskirts of town. This was good news. He was in widow Ludlum's neighborhood. Unfortunately he had never been to the house, so he was unsure precisely which of the nearby dwellings was hers. Finding a small abode that seemed to match the description, he took a chance and crept into the courtyard. He saw two horses that appeared out of place in such a small enclosure. He suspected that he was at the right address. Houzeau and Ludlum had been ready for several nights to receive their secret guest. The scientist placed a large book on his bedroom windowsill each evening. Anderson pushed the window open as instructed, and the book fell to the floor. Houzeau sprung from his bed and was dressed in sixty seconds. He went into the courtyard and felt for Anderson's hand in the gloaming predawn darkness.

"He is here, he is here," Houzeau whispered to awaken Ludlum, "and he wants to leave." The escapee was in no condition to travel, however. Ludlum disposed of Anderson's wet clothes and put him to bed. When he woke in a few hours, the widow explained that there had been a change of plans. Some of the bread and meat that Ludlum had hidden away for Anderson's journey was missing. She suspected that her servant, a Frenchman named Esau, had taken it. She went to the servant's room while Anderson was sleeping and found the goods in his possession. Ludlum was convinced that Esau would surely betray them if a substantial reward were offered. Rather than stay a few weeks as planned, Anderson had to leave at once. The widow gave him some of her son's clothes and a revolver. She trimmed the fugitive's red beard close, cut his hair, and dyed both with lamp black. Houzeau assembled the necessary supplies: a pencil and paper, compass, candle, matches, powder, bullets, map, a gourd of fresh water, and a six-day supply of biscuits. He fitted Anderson with a belt containing twelve-hundred dollars, including the money from Jones. Anderson gave Houzeau a few business papers he had somehow hidden from his captors and the October 4 letter from McCulloch. The pair mounted their horses before dawn and vanished.

On the morning of October 23, Anderson failed to show up for breakfast. Captain Mechling thought little of it. Around ten o'clock, the captain stopped by the prisoner's tent and spoke to him. Anderson did not reply, so the officer let him sleep. Finally, fearing that his prisoner had overdosed on stramonium and might be dead, Mechling attempted to jostle a life-sized dummy of Anderson awake. Infuriated by what he discovered, Mechling and a couple of other soldiers on horseback galloped into town.

Mechling spied Zenas Bliss and shouted at him. "Where is Charley Anderson?" he bellowed. "I am sure I do not know," replied Bliss, who figured that Anderson must be back in Mechling's camp as the captain had charge of him. Bliss was not privy to details of the escape plan. Mechling continued in a heated voice, "Well he isn't in my camp, but has violated his parole and escaped. My whole company is out after him, damn him. If they catch him," he added, "they will hang him to the first tree." Bliss calmly replied that the whole town knew that Anderson had never been on parole, having steadfastly refused it when it was offered to him. This appeared to stymie Mechling's aggressive approach, so he tried another angle. He may not have escaped, the captain claimed, but was probably intoxicated by the stramonium he has smoked the previous night. He probably had drowned, Mechling speculated. He ordered his troops to drag the river. They did and found nothing.

While Mechling and his rebel followers scurried around searching for Anderson, the escaped prisoner and his friend Houzeau had made considerable progress. The pair traveled a pre-planned, circuitous route north before turning due west. They made no fires, slept in concealed areas during the day, and rode close to the river bottoms most nights. Houzeau had no saddle. He rode clothed in a ranchero-style disguise with a rope tied around his horse's nostrils. A gentle rain fell most of the time and the first few evenings were favorably dark. The now black-haired Anderson sported buckskin trousers, the jacket of Ludlum's absent son, and a broad-brimmed vaquero's hat. They were emerging from a riverbed very early the morning after he had taken flight, when they were greeted by a young Mexican boy. Frank Chavez recognized Anderson despite the disguise. The boy knew nothing of the escape. If he knew of it later, he never told anyone about his encounter with the fugitive.

San Antonio was alive with rumors concerning Anderson's departure. A reward of one thousand dollars was posted for the return of the prisoner, dead or alive. Captain Mechling was placed in irons, accused of being bribed by the conspirators. Known Union families in town were nervous. Many received menacing visits from Mechling's soldiers, who arrived with guns drawn, hurling threatening epithets. KGC members who had not enlisted in the Confederate Army formed a posse and visited Lorenzo Castro, a prominent resident and suspected Union sympathizer. Castro visibly trembled at the prospect of dying by the rope, but as he knew nothing, he could not betray the runaway and his accomplices.

One man did know something, however, and he finally cracked. The Frenchman Esau, made nervous by Ludlum's discovery of his treachery, could keep his secret no longer. He was disappointed in having lost the opportunity to claim a reward for Anderson's recapture, as he had planned. He told his wife the story. She told one of her friends, and soon Ludlum's role in the conspiracy became public knowledge. Esau was frightened. He went to Anderson's friend W. A. Bennett to ask for advice. Bennett said he was sorry that he could help neither Esau nor Ludlum, as he was concerned about his own neck. Esau then simply disappeared. Ludlum fled to the mountains but remained there only a short time. She still did not feel safe, so she eventually made her way to the Rio Grande.

Meanwhile, the time had come for Anderson and Houzeau to part ways, as the authorities would surely come looking for a known abolitionist. When they discovered that he was a lodger at Ludlum's house, things would really heat up for him. Anderson found it difficult to express his gratitude for the risks that the Belgian had taken in freeing him. Houzeau merely folded his hands and said, "God bless you." He listened to the sounds of the hoof beats in the mud dissipate as Anderson's horse trotted away.

The following morning, the filthy escapee decided to wash himself in the stream near his encampment. As he splashed the water on his face, Anderson noticed that the water had turned black. Feeling foolish for having washed off the most effective part of his disguise, he shrugged his shoulders and mounted his horse. He had just started riding when three Texas rancheros came into his view, driving a herd of cattle. Anderson attempted to detour around them, but was soon face to face with one of the men. A man named Travis recognized him at once, and greeted him with a shout. "How are you, Mr. Anderson?" the cowboy inquired warmly. Anderson replied by drawing his pistol and exclaiming, "Gentlemen, I will not be taken alive." The men responded saying that they had no intention of interfering with Anderson's journey. They warned him, however, that Confederate pickets were closely guarding the crossing at Laredo, so he may want to try another route. That information may have saved Anderson's life. He changed his plans and headed for Eagle Pass.

Union men had established safe houses along various routes of escape from San Antonio, much like the Underground Railroad stations that slaves used to avoid capture. Anderson used a password to gain admittance to several of these houses before he left the bounds of civilization. They fitted him with fresh horses every ten miles or so. After dining with Charles Hood at Atascosa, fourteen miles west of San Antonio, Anderson spent a night with William Reuter near Castroville.

Just after noon one day, a traveler came to San Antonio from the west and was immediately brought to the Menger House for questioning. Had he come across any detachments in pursuit of a fugitive? The man replied that he had not. Confederate authorities pressed him. Had he met any strangers on the road? "Oh yes," the man replied, "toward the end of the day a stranger near the fork of the Medina told me to warn the locals that their chickens had been sold." When he passed this message on to the local farmers, they seemed utterly confused. When asked to describe the man who had made this puzzling statement, the traveler described Anderson. The coded message was designed to reassure his friends that he was safe.

Four days after his escape, Anderson was riding a fine black horse when he met another east-bound traveler. Clay Willis encountered Anderson on the road west of Castroville. They were strangers to each other. Anderson told the young man that his name was "Wilson" and that he was riding to Brownsville to negotiate a large contract with the Confederate government. Anderson asked Willis not to disclose the details of their meeting until a few days after the youth's arrival in San Antonio, as he did not want competition for the contract. When Willis arrived home and finally recounted the story, Anderson had been gone more than ten days.[7]

A week later, a farmer brought a horse into town. Anderson had exchanged the horse on the far side of the Nueces River. Now it stood in the center of Alamo Plaza with a sign around its neck. Local authorities were offering a one-hundred-dollar reward to anyone who could identify its owner. No one claimed the bounty. Since this particular horse was branded, it did not take long to find the man who had sold it to Anderson's friends. A Polish man admitted he sold the horse in question for cash to some unknown gentleman several weeks past and had thought nothing more of it. By refusing to identify Houzeau as the purchaser, this man probably saved the astronomer's life. San Antonio authorities were not satisfied, however. They took the horse and walked him around the square, then up and down the entire length of Main Street. During the parade, the town herald proclaimed that it was the duty of every good citizen to come forward and identify the animal. No one did. Anderson's trail had grown cold by this time, but Confederate officials still had reason to hope. William Bayard had ridden out of town on November 1 with soldiers and spies hot on his trail. Perhaps he would lead them to Anderson.[8]

The most difficult part of Anderson's journey was just beginning. Leaving the planned safe houses of friends in neighboring ranches and towns, he now faced an environment that was mostly empty, hostile desert. Contemporary maps detailed the military route to Eagle Pass. It lay 117 miles from Castroville. If he traveled too close to the road, Anderson risked discovery and recapture. Losing sight of the way promised almost certain death from Indian or animal attack or dehydration. Standing on a small rise and looking west, Anderson could see nothing but a featureless plain that extended beyond the horizon. He rode his horse through the west Texas chaparral, stopping every eight to ten miles to water the animal at a river or stream. He first passed Quihi, a town with a small lake that was a frequent target of Comanche raiders. After crossing Hondo Creek, the route turned to the southwest. Anderson forded the Seco and Frio Rivers and came to a fork in the road just past the Lenora River. Here he exercised special care, since to his west was a busy thoroughfare that led to Fort Clark, forty miles away. Anderson took the left fork and continued riding to the southwest.

Near a stream crossing, Anderson's horse began to wear out. The last thing he wanted to do was to shoot the animal and continue on foot. An exchange of horses at this part of the trip would be dangerous, both for him and for his friends back in Castroville. Having few options, he decided to call at a small, isolated house for rest and supper. A wild-eyed young woman met the refugee with a familiar greeting. "Oh yase, I know ye," said Anderson's host. He was surprised and nervous until he realized that the poor woman had mistaken him for a local preacher. While his host was cooking the dinner, Anderson relaxed on the floor and soon fell sound asleep.

When he woke, Anderson heard a young man's voice discussing him. The man seemed suspicious, even after Anderson had introduced himself as "John Wilson," a man on important Confederate government business. Officials were well aware of the recent Indian depredations in this region, Anderson explained. His mission was to gather troops to defend this road against future raids. If he could exchange his pony for a fresh mount, the government would be most obliged. The young man directed him to a ranch down the road where Anderson repeated his fib. They did not believe him at first, but after "Wilson" repeatedly emphasized the urgency of the situation, they finally agreed and sent him on his way with a new steed.

Anderson rode on: ten miles to the Nueces River, another ten to Turkey Creek. At one point he noticed that a rough-looking fellow had been following him closely for several miles. Anderson moved off the trail and camped with several other tough characters who were acting less suspiciously. Another night he camped by himself, or so he thought. In the middle of the night he woke suddenly to see two glowing eyes staring at him from the edge of a thicket. After some time the jaguar moved on. Anderson was grateful that the cat was not as hungry as he was.

Anderson traveled the last thirty-four miles from the Chaco River to the Rio Grande through the bleakest landscape of the entire trek, with only two water holes on the way. As the border with Mexico came into view, Anderson must have been astonished at how little real trouble he had run into on his long exodus. Once he had crossed the river, he fell to his knees in his best thespian manner and kissed the ground, crying "Liberty!" Some Mexican soldiers observed this odd behavior and escorted him directly to their commander. Mexican general Jeronimo Trevino spoke to Anderson for a time in Spanish and then switched to English as they rode to his headquarters. "God bless you!" the general exclaimed when they arrived. He gave the refugee a warm handshake. Anderson did not know it at the time, but Trevino had been expecting him. He refused to allow Anderson to go to Matamoros as he had wished but insisted that the escapee travel 259 miles to Monterrey instead. Trevino suspected that if Anderson proceeded to Matamoros, he would be recaptured by Confederate agents.

Trevino gave Anderson a military escort for the long trek to Monterrey. They arrived at the home of Governor Santiago Vidaurri on Friday, November 1. Anderson had traveled more than four hundred miles in just eleven days. He was exhausted. He had a huge boil on his back side that would prevent him from riding again for a while. It took another eleven days for him to regain his strength. He finally set out in a guarded carriage with the governor's daughter, who was on her way to get married in Tampico. He still had a long journey ahead.

➤➤ ◄◄

CHAPTER TWELVE

Homeward

O N SUNDAY, NOVEMBER 3, Kitty wrote in her diary: "Escaped! And has he gone safe out of the hands of his enemies? Thank God!" It had taken twelve days for the news of her father's arrival in Monterrey to reach them in Brownsville, Texas. William G. Kingsbury urged the family to move to Matamoros for their own safety, but Colonel John S. Ford begged them to stay in Texas "for his sake." He suggested they go to the mouth of the Brazos River and await a steamer there. But Eliza suspected that the kindness of Ford, Francis W. Latham, Lieutenant Arthur K. Leigh, and other rebels was more than merely the civility of gentlemen. They were being used by the Confederates as bait for Anderson's recapture.[1]

The ladies packed on Monday. On Tuesday afternoon, they donned their bonnets and took a carriage down to the river. Rooms in Matamoros were hard to come by. While Eliza and her daughters sipped tea at Mrs. Sanforth Kidder's boardinghouse, Kingsbury scurried about town to find them suitable accommodations. He convinced Thomas Gilligan to let them stay in the home of his partner, William Malone, who had gone to Mexico City to be married. At first glance, their new lodgings were as close to Cincinnati as they imagined Mexico could be. Malone's mansion was the finest home in town. Since the war had shut down trade through Texas ports, Mexican officials had worked with Malone and other expatriates to smuggle European goods overland into Texas. They were making a killing. Malone's rooms were furnished with luxurious modern furniture and tastefully decorated. The sitting room boasted an extensive library and rare engravings. A balcony opened from this room to a fine view of the grassy, tree-lined plaza where bands entertained several times a week. Eliza hired an ex-slave from Mobile to serve them and settled in comfort to await her husband's arrival.

Two days before his departure from Monterrey, Anderson penned a letter to his wife, not knowing where she was or if she would ever receive the letter. He planned to catch a steamer sometime between November 28 and 30 if his funds held out; otherwise, he might be forced to embark on a slower but more economical sailing vessel from Vera Cruz. If his family was still in Matamoros or Brownsville, they might join him at Tampico and leave together. In any case, Anderson urged Eliza to get away as soon as possible and not to "trust Texas nor the Southern Confederacy at all." Eliza heeded his advice. Just as Anderson set out from Monterey with the governor's entourage, Matamoros erupted in revolution. Eliza and the girls looked out from their balcony at a scene that reminded Kitty of *Les Misérables*. The Criolinas had barricaded several key streets and were expecting the arrival of their enemies, the Rojos, any day. A battle might take place on the very plaza in front of their house. [2]

When a messenger came to the door announcing that the rival troops were nearing town, Eliza had a decision to make. Would it be safer to flee back into the arms of their Confederate "friends" in Brownsville, or stay and risk God-knew-what in the midst of an impending battle? Eliza decided to stay put. Most women and children were crossing the river as quickly as they could. Carts rattled all day on the cobblestone streets, piled high with the furniture of wealthy Americans anxious to save their possessions from plunder. Three days passed in such excitement, but no invasion came. Finally, on Thursday, a bugle from one of the church towers sounded the alarm. Mexican women ran through the streets shouting in Spanish, "Los Rojos vienen!" ("The Rojos are coming!"). Officers on horseback galloped across the plaza, barking orders. This continued for an hour or so. Eventually the excitement died down and the soldiers returned to the shade of the Customs House for a siesta. It was yet another false alarm.

After breakfast on Saturday, Gilligan arrived with a beautiful scarlet flower. As he was showing Kitty its description in his Spanish floral dictionary, a messenger knocked on the door. The boy delivered a note from Kingsbury. He had discovered a plot to capture Anderson as soon as he reached Matamoros. The family needed to be at the river in two hours. The *Ursulita*, captained by William M. Dalzell, was a ninety-four-ton steam schooner bound for Vera Cruz. Eliza and her daughters climbed aboard. The ship left the mouth of the river at eight at night for the three-day passage. She was barely under way when Eliza and Belle became seasick. Kitty managed better, but she felt apprehensive and alone. Hardly anyone aboard the vessel spoke a word of English.

Accommodations on the *Ursulita* were Spartan by any standard. Passengers slept on cane-bottom benches, when they could sleep at all, in the dirty, air-starved hold of the ship. The vessel rolled and pitched at the slightest wind or wave. Eliza and Belle took to sleeping on the floor with blankets in a vain attempt to quiet their angry stomachs. Kitty found that a sea chest was a more comfortable bed than her berth. She awoke one morning to a two-inch roach skittering across her hand. Their quarters were lighted by two small portholes, which was also the only source of fresh air in the humid, stinking hell on water. The sweet crackers they brought turned so musty that they fed them to their dog, Sumter. This gave him just enough energy to chase the tailless cat around the ship. To make matters worse, a sailor named Don Manuel Cruzado had taken an immediate interest in Kitty. All day long, she caught him leering at her. He turned away each time she intercepted his glance. Thank goodness they would only have to endure this for a few days . . . or so they thought.

Unknown to the passengers, Captain Dalzelle had miscalculated their route and veered far off course. After several days at sea, he had no idea where he was. Meanwhile, the weather was about to turn nasty. Eliza and Belle had begun to feel better and were even eating a little by Thursday. The moonlight danced on the water with an enchanting, phosphorescent glow. The old ship was five days out when the wind started blowing from the north. The breeze was refreshing and welcome at first, but as it grew in strength, the passengers bore the brunt of it. By Friday night, the *Ursulita* was enveloped in what locals called a full-blown "norther." Huge waves roiled the craft from side to side, first pitching and then heaving in a violent display of nature's fury. Crew members closed the portholes and the smothering heat became unbearable.

At one point, Kitty persuaded the sailors to open one of the small windows so she could stick her head out and breathe fresh air. She stood grasping the side of the spasmodic ship, her hair blowing wildly in the breeze and the lightning blinding her intermittently. It was both frightening and exhilarating. Suddenly, a big wave catapulted her backward into the darkness of the crowded cabin. The storm raged on through Saturday, blowing the ship past Vera Cruz and into the open waters of the Gulf. Kitty lay on the floor of the cabin, regretting the fact that she shared some of the same religious doubts as her father. "I vowed in my heart that I would try to love my God *more* and serve him better," she wrote. "How ungrateful and contemptible to seek so loving a Master in an hour of distress and darkness more than in days of joy and peace!"

When the storm finally ceased on Sunday, the ship was a long way from its destination. The *Ursulita* had exhausted her supply of fuel and had to rely solely on her sails to make it to Vera Cruz. The storm was followed by a dead calm, and the ship lolled languorously while the crew and passengers regained their bearings. Several days passed with occasional glimpses of shore, until finally on November 28, at about four in the afternoon, they reached the port of Vera Cruz. Eliza and her daughters had been at sea for more than eleven days. No one was there to greet them.

The Andersons found their way to the house of the U.S. consul, Mark H. Dunnell. From there, the party found rooms that looked quaint and foreign, even to such seasoned travelers. The single beds were quite high off the ground and the floor tiled with square bricks. A stout iron door was the only opening in the windowless room, and a set of narrow stairs led down to a surprisingly fine French restaurant. They had been settled less than a day when a well-dressed Don Marcos Cruzado called and boldly asked Kitty to accompany him to Mexico City. She politely refused. All that was left to do now was to wait for word from her father.

Charles Anderson was 140 miles out of Monterrey when he was greeted by a welcome and familiar face. Will Bayard had escaped the same day that Anderson had arrived at Governor Vidaurri's residence in Monterrey. Bayard joined Anderson near Victoria for the trip to Tampico. The two fugitives spent many happy hours on the road together on the way to their port of liberation. When they finally arrived at Tampico on November 28, the city had been under siege by the rebel forces of Don Luis de Carvajal for eight days. Not long afterward, half the town, including the U.S. consulate, would be burned down to mere ashes. The escapees were warmly received by U.S. consul Franklin Chase, who was preparing to abandon the city. Bayard took the schooner, *Sallie Gay*, bound for New York, while Anderson boarded the British Royal Mail Packet, *Clyde*, bound for Vera Cruz and Havana.

When Charles stepped ashore in Vera Cruz just days after his family's arrival, he was greeted by Consul Dunnell, who rushed Anderson to his wife and two daughters. Tears flowed in abundance at their reunion. The family had plenty of time to swap stories and reconnect on the voyage to Havana. Once there, the Andersons transferred to the U.S. steamship *Columbia* and sailed for New York, where they finally disembarked seventy-three days after their first attempt to leave Texas. Their arrival on December 11, 1861, created a sensation.[3]

⇥ ⇤

CHAPTER THIRTEEN

Hero

THE LAND WAR HAD BEEN going badly for the Union while Charles Anderson and his family were on the run. Since the embarrassing defeat at Manassas in July, federal armies had failed to make significant progress in Virginia. They had not yet established firm control in Kentucky. Lincoln realized that he was in for a long conflict. Despite successes on the seacoast, ultimately the war had to be won on the ground. He needed new leadership.

Robert Anderson had taken command of the Department of the Cumberland a short time after he surrendered Fort Sumter. Overwhelmed by the enormity of what he had already experienced in the war, and having never fully recovered from his old wounds in the Mexican War, he finally succumbed to nervous strain and resigned his commission. By early October 1861, William T. Sherman had replaced him in command of the department. Aging general Winfield Scott, a veteran of both the War of 1812 and the Mexican War, resigned on November 1. He was replaced by thirty-four-year-old general George McClellan. Lincoln's new top general led a force that exceeded seven hundred thousand men. With most of the fighting done for the winter, the Northern press was hungry for some good news. When Charles Anderson arrived in New York, they christened him a hero.

Anderson was the talk of the town. He and his family lodged in the finest hotels, dined at the best restaurants, and were visited by the cream of New York society. He gave numerous interviews and appeared at festivals and private dinners. His most prestigious invitation came from Peter Cooper, who asked him to speak at the heralded Cooper Institute on the night of December 21. This Anderson did in typical dramatic fashion, telling the story of Major General David E. Twiggs's treachery, the Alamo speech, and Anderson's subsequent escape. The *New York Times* described Anderson's story as "among the most moving and romantic episodes of the war." The capacity crowd loved it. Two days later, as Eliza and her daughters were traveling back to Ohio, Anderson and his brother Robert were feted at Astor House during a meeting of the New England Society. The dinner was lavish. The table included a scale model of Fort Sumter with toy cannons that fired and smoked. When the toasting was done, Robert's suddenly famous little brother boarded a train bound for Washington to meet with Winfield Scott. Scott and Anderson were attempting to arrange an exchange for Will Jones. After just a day in the capital, Anderson left for Ohio and arrived in Cincinnati, two days after Christmas.[1]

Back home in Dayton, Anderson began the New Year by seeking ways to contribute to the Union war effort. His son Latham was still fighting valiantly in New Mexico, where he was brevetted a major at Val Verde in February. Seven of Anderson's nephews were in U.S. Army service at various locations. Cousins, neighbors, and friends had rushed to the aid of his beloved Union. Anderson was now in his late forties and hardly the soldierly type. Surely he had other talents he could lend to the cause. His first priority was to assist more than three hundred Union troops, including the brave officers who had helped finance his escape, still held hostage back in Texas. On January 9, Anderson began a withering, two-month letter-writing campaign to military and administration officials in Washington. Writing to Edwin M. Stanton, Anderson mentioned that he had already appealed to generals Henry Halleck and Lorenzo Thomas, along with former New York governor Hamilton Fish, among others, to rescue his friends. His efforts and those of others would take months to succeed, but by the end of April all of the remaining prisoners had been exchanged.[2]

On January 10, Anderson addressed the Ohio General Assembly. His speech, in tone and content, established consistent themes that he repeated throughout the war. Political leaders and the general public needed to have an intimate understanding of the true nature of the terrible conflict and the causes that precipitated it. The war was the result of treason, pure and simple. It was planned by evil, ambitious politicians intent on establishing an oligarchy based on slavery. They had to be stopped and the Union restored at all costs before it was too late. Anderson felt it was his urgent duty to proceed to Washington and offer his services.[3]

He arrived in the capital on Thursday, January 16, and met with both President Lincoln and General McClellan the following day. "The president strikes me as one of the most unreserved, honest men I ever saw," Anderson wrote to his wife. "General McClellan impresses me exceedingly." Despite Eliza's worries that her husband would be made a brigadier general and Larz's latest scheme to get his younger brother the post of minister to Mexico, Anderson vowed not to seek any office. He trusted that the president would help him find a role in the effort to restore the Union. Lincoln did just that.[4]

The president asked Anderson to use his most powerful weapon—his speaking ability—to support the Union cause. The prelude was a brief tour of New England with the famed poet and editor of the *Atlantic Monthly*, James Russell Lowell. Lowell had admired Robert Anderson who, in Lowell's words, "served for a brief hour to typify the spirit of uncompromising fidelity to duty" during his ordeal at Fort Sumter. He saw similar qualities in Robert's youngest brother. When Lowell reflected back on their brief acquaintance years later, he remembered Charles Anderson as "the handsome, fair-haired Norseman who, with all his refinement, had a look as if he would cheerfully have gone out with a battle-axe to a holmgang." Anderson returned from his eastern tour excited and energized, for he was about to undertake an important mission: Lincoln was sending him to England.[5]

A critical foreign policy dilemma facing the Lincoln administration was the prospect of recognition or aid from England landing in the laps of the nascent rebel government. The Confederacy had sent commissioners to London in early May 1861, but the British were not eager to upset their delicate relationship with the United States. In October, Louisiana governor Thomas O' Moore banned the shipment of cotton to Europe in the hope that this action would pressure those nations to recognize the Confederate government. Opinion in England was split. The London *Times* supported the Union, while the *Post* expressed sympathy for the Confederacy. A Union naval blockade of Southern ports put additional pressure on European relations.

On October 12, the Confederate commissioners to France and Britain, John Slidell and James Mason, slipped past the Union blockade at Charleston on their way to Cuba. They intended to purchase arms for the Confederacy in Europe. As the commissioners sailed in the British packet ship *Trent* on November 8, they were intercepted by the USS *San Jacinto* and taken prisoner. The Trent affair, as it came to be called, created an international crisis, with talk of possible war between England and the United States over this alleged breach of international law and diplomatic protocol. The rebels could not have been more pleased with this turn of events. The crisis dragged on for months. Finally, on December 26, the United States agreed to release the two commissioners into the custody of Great Britain and admit that their actions were not legal. Serious damage had been done to relations between the two powerful nations, and embarrassed British politicians were lining up to support recognition of the Confederacy. Southern blockade runners using British ports created additional tension.

Lincoln's task was difficult yet straightforward. He needed to keep Great Britain and the other European powers neutral. To do this, he needed to employ deft diplomacy while shaping British public opinion. Charles Francis Adams was the kind of skilled diplomat that Anderson had always admired. The son of John Quincy Adams and grandson of John Adams, Adams was a distinguished politician in his own right. Lincoln pulled Adams from his congressional seat and appointed him Minister to the Court of St. James in May 1861. After the Trent affair had died down, the question of British recognition of the Confederate government persisted at the forefront of public discourse. Adams and Lincoln needed influential men to publish articles in the newspapers and give speeches supporting neutrality.[6]

Charles Anderson was a logical emissary and took on the job willingly. He left New York on March 29 aboard the *Glasgow*. He had waited more than a week for a letter of introduction from the president, which he never received. When Anderson dined with Winfield Scott a few days before his departure, Scott suggested that the U.S. government ought to pay his expenses. "I'll see them damned first," was Anderson's reply. He was going to England at Lincoln's request but would not be his hired man. Anderson would do what he did best: speak the truth and help restore the Union, no matter what the political implications might be.

The mission was short and fruitless, however. Anderson made some progress in social circles. During the month of April he introduced various English gentlemen who supported the Union to Minister Adams, but London newspapers declined to publish any of his articles. By May 2, he was already frustrated and felt he had little productive work to do. He stayed in London a few more weeks and made several speeches at the request of British politician John Bright. After a six-day holiday in France, Anderson returned home with bitter feelings toward the British. "They wish our nation ruined," he lamented. "The liberals sympathize with us, but mainly to end slavery. . . . They are all fools on this subject." He was sick of politics, fed up with diplomacy, and frustrated that he had wasted his efforts. It was time to make a tangible contribution toward saving the Union he so adored.[7]

⤜► ◄⤛

CHAPTER FOURTEEN

Rank Amateurs

WHEN CHARLES ANDERSON arrived back in Ohio, he had a job waiting for him. New governor David Tod began his term in January 1862. Three months later, the state suffered more than two thousand casualties at the horrific Battle of Shiloh, Tennessee. Faced with filling his federally mandated quota of seventy-four thousand troops, Tod needed leaders who could raise regiments. He guessed that Anderson, with so many family members involved in the fighting, could not resist this call to duty.

Tod was right. Anderson proved as effective a recruiter as he was a speaker. Recruiting posters painted a romantic picture of what was to come for Anderson's new Ninety-Third Ohio Volunteer Infantry: "An Anderson is at our head, We follow where he leads, And in our Paths of Glory, Will be traced most Noble Deeds." Neighbors and friends from Montgomery, Preble, and Butler Counties rushed to enlist. The regiment met its quota in just two weeks, with four companies coming from Dayton. Citizens there raised ten thousand dollars at one meeting to help equip the troops. Few of the volunteers had any military training.[1]

On August 9, Anderson himself enlisted and was awarded the rank of colonel. His previous military experience consisted of two years commanding a local militia called the Dayton Grays. He threw himself into his work, studying military tactics from the same manuals that his brother and son had used at West Point. Despite his intelligence and diligence, however, Anderson was woefully ill-prepared, like so many of his fellow officers, to lead an army into combat. What he did have were some of the intangibles that successful military leaders possess. His men loved, respected, and trusted him. In a war where so many thousands of ordinary citizens were being thrust into hellish conditions with inadequate training and support, this would have to be enough.[2]

The Union Army's situation in Kentucky and Tennessee in the summer of 1862 was perilous. Confederate John Hunt Morgan was wreaking havoc all over the region with his daring cavalry raids on federal positions. On July 13, general Nathan Bedford Forrest's rebel troops overwhelmed Union general Thomas Crittenden's force at Murfreesboro, capturing a startling number of men and supply wagons. While Confederate major general Edmund Kirby Smith menaced Union positions in Kentucky, fellow general Braxton Bragg pushed into Tennessee. Union major general Don Carlos Buell and his Army of the Ohio faced the important task of halting the Confederate advance well short of the Ohio River.[3]

Anderson established a camp within sight of his Dayton home and began training his regiment. After just a week of drilling, the call came. Buell's army needed all available men, ready or not. Anderson ordered all furloughed men to report to the regiment immediately. On August 20, the regiment mustered in to service. Three days later, the 39 officers and 929 enlisted men of the Ninety-Third Ohio finally received their arms and departed for Lexington, Kentucky. By the time Anderson's troops reached Cincinnati by train from Dayton, it was past eleven in the evening. The Ninety-Third Ohio stepped off the train, formed into some semblance of order, and marched to the river. The regiment took the ferry across to Covington, where the exhausted volunteers arrived about two o'clock in the morning. Having had no food since leaving Dayton, the soldiers simply collapsed on a pile of boards or on bare ground and slept until daybreak. It was a harsh beginning to their romantic dreams of glory. Most would look back on this first journey, however, as one of their easiest.[4]

The next day, the regiment boarded a train to Lexington, arrived in midafternoon, and marched to their assigned camp. They had not eaten since early that morning. Despite an alluring grove of trees just off the road, the men obeyed orders to lie down on either side of the turnpike. The previous morning's defeat of General Ormsby M. Mitchel's Union Army division about twenty miles from their present location had Anderson on high alert. The colonel lay down beside the road alongside his officers for a much needed rest. They slumbered for about an hour before they awoke to three rifle reports. One of the Union pickets had fired shots about fifty yards from where Anderson was sleeping. He jumped on his horse and galloped down the road as his officers ordered the men to fall in. Confusion reigned. When he returned a few minutes later, the colonel explained that some Union cavalry had ridden up the road toward the regiment, and failing to hear the command to "halt," had been fired upon. Fortunately, the only casualty was a hole in the cavalry lieutenant's coat. The regiment stood down into an uneasy rest and the officers wondered how their men would have reacted in a real emergency.

When they finally settled in at their fairground camp adjacent to Transylvania College in Lexington, the men were again in good spirits. Their baggage had finally arrived. The surrounding countryside was described by one soldier as "the garden spot of Kentucky" because of its attractive farmsteads. For five days, the soldiers enjoyed the first cooked food they had eaten since leaving Ohio. Anderson was appointed commander of the post at Lexington and camp life seemed pretty good. Late in the evening of August 30, however, General William "Bull" Nelson gave Anderson orders to move.[5]

The Ninety-Third Ohio, two other regiments, and nineteen wagons, all under Anderson's command, advanced toward Richmond, Kentucky, all night, arriving on the bluffs of the Kentucky River eleven miles from the town at about four o'clock in the morning. Anderson sent one company forward as pickets and they came back with terrible news: a rebel force of nearly seven thousand commanded by Major General Edmund Kirby Smith was on the opposite side of the river. Instead of falling back and joining Anderson's regiments as ordered by Nelson, U.S. brigadier general Mahlon D. Manson had engaged the enemy at Richmond and was routed. Nelson slashed at some of his troops with his saber when they began to retreat. The

Union Army suffered 5,353 casualties, while the Confederates lost just 451 men. Anderson's regiments were given three hours to rest before being marched back to Lexington. A thunder shower drenched the troops and they arrived back in camp at ten o'clock at night. The soggy men grumbled as they were immediately ordered to counter-march to the farm of James B. Clay, where they ate some hard bread and finally laid down on the bare earth at midnight. Captain Samuel B. Smith of Company K called these troops "the most woe-be-gone, demoralized force I ever saw."[6]

The sun shone the next morning, September 1, and for a few hours the mood of the troops brightened too. Then orders came to unload all of the baggage from the wagons except for food and cooking utensils. The troops formed a line of battle with one change of clothes in their haversacks, plus canteens, guns, and cartridge boxes. While they were drilling, some of the troops noticed smoke billowing about three hundred yards behind them. Captain Henry Richards of the Ninety-Third Ohio Infantry broke ranks and ran over the hill to see what was happening. To his dismay, he found that Union general Green Clay Smith had panicked and ordered all the baggage burnt, presumably to speed the retreat of his troops. Meanwhile, Confederate general Kirby Smith, fresh off his victory at Richmond, was advancing toward Lexington. Buell thought that if General Bragg captured Louisville, not only would Kentucky be lost but Cincinnati itself would be subject to invasion. Anderson's troops expected a battle. What they got was a footrace.

The evacuation of Lexington began around midnight. It took five days for ten thousand men to travel the fifty-two miles in oppressive heat. The scarcity of running water forced the soldiers to drink from whatever scum-topped stock ponds they could find. Ninety men fell by the wayside from exhaustion and thirst. Stragglers were captured by the enemy. Henry Richards did not mince words when describing the morale of the troops under General Nelson. "This march has been conducted in the most unchristian and inhuman manner," Richards wrote to his father from Louisville. He chastised Nelson for avoiding a fight and attributed his incompetence to "a great lack of courage or capacity." He worried that Colonel Anderson had taken ill; if he were to leave the regiment, Richards predicted, it would constitute its "death blow," as Anderson was "the only field officer having the confidence of the men."[7]

Anderson arrived in his native county in bad shape. The incessant movements of the past few weeks had left him exhausted. His asthma was back, accompanied by an even more dangerous condition: he had cholera. Forced to his bed, Anderson transferred command of his regiment to Colonel Hiram Strong. Of Anderson's insomnia, Dr. A. T. Babbitt said that "he marched every night in the effect of the quinine." He was not well enough to resume his duties for eighteen days. Eliza and the family went to visit their sick patriarch. Morale among the troops began to recover. While the Union generals waited a month for Bragg and Smith to mount an attack, Larz Anderson was given thirty thousand dollars to oversee the building of defenses on the north banks of the Ohio River. Ohio's citizens held their collective breaths.[8]

Colonel Strong had strong opinions concerning his current corps of leaders. General William Thomas Ward, the brigade commander, was "thick headed." Strong called division commander General James S. Jackson a "blustering, drinking, swearing bully." Strong and Anderson were elated when Buell's main force finally arrived at Louisville. The Ninety-Third was transferred to General Lovell H. Rousseau's acclaimed brigade in General Joshua W. Sill's division. Anderson returned to the regiment in late September.

Criticism of General Nelson was also widespread among officers and enlisted men. He made enemies easily, and one of these was fellow Union general Jefferson C. Davis. Nelson had suspended Davis over a recruiting issue, but General Horatio Gates ordered Davis returned to his command. They met at Galt House in Louisville, where Indiana governor Oliver P. Morton and others witnessed their brief reunion. Davis approached Nelson and accused him of exceeding his authority when the brigadier general suspended him. Nelson put his hand over his ear and refused to listen. At that point Davis repeated himself, drawing two slaps across the face from Nelson. "Did you hear that damned rascal insult me?" Davis cried as he stormed out of the room. He returned from the ladies parlor with a pistol and shot Nelson through the heart. It was the only instance in American history when one general had murdered another.[9]

Davis was arrested and set to be tried in Jefferson County court. Reaction to Nelson's death, however, was muted. On September 30, the day following the shooting, Anderson wrote to his wife about the affair. Although Nelson had always treated him with respect, Anderson felt that Davis was "entirely justified in killing him." Nelson had no right to "trample upon the rights or even the pride of others," Charles reasoned. He consoled Davis and told him that he "sympathized with the living as well as regretting the dead." Buell and other military authorities may have agreed, as Davis was never prosecuted for the murder.

Anderson hoped that his regiment would head back to Lexington, where they could learn their "new trade" as he called it, before being tested in battle. That plan was a fantasy. The relief that Union commanders felt by saving Louisville and Cincinnati soon turned to dread. Bragg had never intended to assault such a massive Union force. By threatening Louisville, Bragg had tricked Buell into leaving him an escape route open to the south. When Bragg started running, Buell was compelled to pursue. The chase was on.[10]

For five days Anderson's regiment marched until they reached the west side of the Kentucky River, opposite Frankfort, on October 6. Fleeing rebel troops had destroyed the bridges, forcing the Union soldiers to construct a pontoon bridge in order to cross the river. The next day, they had no sooner crossed the river when Colonel Anderson received word that Kirby Smith's forces had crossed to the west side. The Ninety-Third retraced its steps, crossed back to the west bank, and moved toward Lawrenceburg. Anderson's regiment was delayed by several brief skirmishes on the way. On October 7, he predicted a "big battle in Kentucky" in a letter to Kitty. He had no idea that it would happen the very next day.[11]

Confederate forces massed at the small town of Perryville, Kentucky, for several reasons. Perhaps the most important of these was access to fresh water. Kentucky had endured a terrible drought for months, and soldiers on both sides who were not completely dehydrated were sickened by drinking out of stagnant ponds. When the advance portion of Buell's army arrived on October 7, that water was almost reason enough to fight. The battle that ensued was terribly bloody, with about 20 percent of thirty-eight thousand troops engaged suffering as casualties. Bragg had pushed Union forces back nearly a mile but was forced to acknowledge that his poor strategic position was unchanged. He left that evening to rejoin Kirby Smith at Harrodsburg and continue their exodus.

Anderson's regiment and most of the division did not make it to Perryville in time for the fight. When they arrived three days later, the scene was horrific. Anderson had never seen the aftermath of battle, and it both shocked and fascinated him. He saw carcasses of horses with their legs straight up in the air. Anderson described hundreds of men lying "dead, swollen, bursting—some blackened literally as the blackest negroes." Other corpses still "white, pale, thin, beautiful," contrasted with those whose legs had been "torn in shreds of fibers and bones" and still others "with their entire skulls blown away, the cannon ball dragging out all the brains." After ten minutes of exposure to this hellish aftermath, many men were already desensitized. "How soon the most disgusting and appalling scenes become commonplace and dull sights," Anderson marveled. Before long, men were eating and even laughing in view of this catastrophe. Surely this laughter had a touch of nerves for the many soldiers who had not yet seen real combat.[12] Anderson felt that Buell's strategy of luring Bragg into the net was wise. How could he risk letting him out again? Buell was viewed by his own troops "with universal contempt and suspicion," Anderson wrote to Kitty. Their anger increased when Smith and Bragg slipped the noose and made their escape through the Cumberland Gap into middle Tennessee.[13]

President Lincoln had seen enough. He replaced Buell with Major General William Rosecrans. On October 24, Rosecrans arrived after a successful campaign in northern Mississippi. The soldiers rejoiced.

Perhaps now they would end these incessant, debilitating marches and meet the enemy in a decisive and successful battle. They were on their way to Nashville to rest, regroup, and prepare for the next engagement. Despite two or three days without rations due to a commissary officer's mistake, Anderson's troops remained in good form and spirits. The soldiers of the Army of the Cumberland finally had a leader they could stake their lives on.[14]

The weather changed drastically from summer drought to late October snow. Rosecrans made sure that his troops had tents, their first since leaving Louisville. The general held an officer's reception on November 2 near Bowling Green, Kentucky. Anderson was impressed by Rosecrans's "simple, good-natured urbanity and sense" in contrast with the "affected hauteur and self-sufficiency" of Buell. There was talk at the gathering of making Anderson a brigadier general, but Anderson doubted that would ever come to pass. "I am not a Democrat with a following to be bribed," he asserted, "and the Administration can't forgive the offence of being for the Union outside of the Republican Party." He would never ask Lincoln directly for this or any favor. He wished that his friends would not waste their time on such efforts and instead concentrate on helping the army win the war. If Anderson had his way, Rosecrans's army would not go into winter quarters at Nashville but would push aggressively to the south, not stopping until they drove the Confederates into the Gulf of Mexico.[15]

The Ninety-Third Ohio arrived at Nashville on November 7. The garrison there had been cut off from all communications for nearly two months, so they were overjoyed when they saw the massive army march into town. Anderson's regiment settled in for a month of drilling, guard, and fatigue duty. They were on picket duty for twenty-four hours every fourth day. A month of normal camp life was the first opportunity for sustained military instruction that the men had seen since they had enlisted back in August. The men were now well-fed, rested, and hungry for a fight. On December 6, they got their wish.

Anderson's regiment left camp at 7:30 on a Saturday morning on a foraging expedition. They were accompanied by men from the Fifth Kentucky Infantry, the First Ohio Infantry, and the Ninety-Seventh Ohio Infantry regiments, in addition to four companies of artillery.

These units escorted a wagon train some two miles in length down a minor road south toward Murfreesboro. After about seven miles, the train was halted by the sounds of cannon fire, and the Ninety-Third, which had been guarding the rear of the train, moved forward to form in line of battle. Not long after some minor skirmishing had taken place, Anderson received word that the rebels had maneuvered between the train and their camp and had captured five of their wagons. Brigade commander Colonel Harvey M. Buckley then ordered the Ninety-Third to relieve the Fifth Kentucky, who had been skirmishing with the enemy in the rear, turn the wagons around, and return to camp.

The train was long and not easy to turn. By 3:30 p.m., they were finally headed back when reports reached Anderson of rebels approaching on his right. Anderson and Hiram Strong rode up a small hill to witness a large number of Confederate soldiers running from the woods into a deep valley, shouting at the top of their lungs. The rebels thought they were attacking the center of the long train, not the rear of the same train now moving in the opposite direction. Anderson's men raced along the side of the road, placing themselves between the train and the oncoming enemy assailants. As the Ninety-Third passed through a barnyard and reached a shed, they were greeted by a hail of bullets such as none of them had ever seen.

Anderson and his men were enveloped in a cacophony of whistling projectiles that made an awful sound like a hundred hammers battering the barn walls in rapid succession. Men shouted in confusion as the center of the Union column fell back several yards. Colonel Strong thought that the regiment might be lost right there. He was relieved when Company H emerged from under the shed, formed a battle line in the center, and commenced rapid return fire at the rebels less than two hundred yards away. Strong hid his horse behind the barn and rushed forward to find Anderson. He could not locate him.

One soldier said that Anderson's horse had bolted away, taking its rider with it. Others said that he had been shot. Still others maintained that the colonel's horse had run off without him. With their nearest support, the Ninety-Seventh Ohio, two miles distant, Anderson's Ninety-Third Ohio was isolated and vulnerable. Strong became concerned. He finally saw Anderson running toward him over an open field 150 yards away, where he had gone with his regiment's Company F. The engagement lasted just thirty minutes longer. When it was over, the Ninety-Third Ohio had driven off the enemy with a loss of only one killed and three wounded. Anderson praised the men for their "gallantry and firmness in this, their first fight." The short but intense skirmish could hardly prepare them for what was to come just a few weeks later.[16]

On Christmas Eve 1862, Anderson's fervent wish was granted. Rosecrans was moving south to confront Bragg and force a decisive battle. What should have ended in Kentucky in the defeat of a much smaller Confederate force was now a huge challenge. Bragg's troops had joined General John C. Breckenridge's army to form a formidable force of thirty-five thousand men. Anderson respected Major General Alexander McCook but claimed that his new brigade commander, Colonel Philemon P. Baldwin, "would not be trusted in civil life with the guidance on a smooth pike with a gentle ox-team." Still, Anderson had confidence that his men, though inexperienced in warfare, were of good character and would perform well in battle. The huge army marched in three columns, with McCook's right wing traveling the Nolensville Pike south to Triune.[17]

Two of Anderson's nephews were among the forty-one thousand Union troops moving toward Murfreesboro. Colonel Nicholas L. Anderson, son of Charles's brother Larz, commanded the Sixth Ohio Infantry. Nicholas's younger brother, Edward L. Anderson, was a captain in the Fifty-Second Ohio. Edward's regiment had been formed about the same time as had his uncle's. Edward and Nicholas had escaped from the battle at Perryville unscathed. Nicholas's troops were a seasoned, frontline fighting force. During the advance southeast from Nashville, Edward's regiment was charged with maintaining the supply train with provisions. The three Andersons were slowly converging on a momentous event.

While Charles Anderson was excited to finally engage Bragg's forces, he was less confident of his own leadership. "The tangled team does not feel the reins," he admitted. "Indeed the driver does not feel very sure that he holds any." Of the coming march to battle, Charles offered a haunting foreshadowing: "Some of our best hearts and minds will be called to their long account," he predicted, "while a brigade of like heroes are gobbled up or cut to pieces in that sublime enterprise of robbing widows and orphan babies of their winter food, which we call foraging."[18]

The Ninety-Third Ohio's journey to Murfreesboro was slow and uneventful. Rain all day and heavy fog the next meant that Anderson's men marched in mud that sometimes reached their knees. At times they could not see the road in front of them. Some soldiers' shoes were so wet after four days of rain that they simply disintegrated, forcing them to march barefoot. A few minor skirmishes along the way held no promise of a big fight. Bragg's cavalry was famous for harassing its enemies to slow their progress. Anderson's troops joined the rest of the division at three o'clock in the afternoon of December 30, three miles northwest of Murfreesboro, near the division headquarters of Brigadier General Richard W. Johnson. Colonel Baldwin's Third Brigade was placed in reserve behind the First and Second Brigades, which formed in a line of battle to the southeast, west of Stones River.

In some sections of the long line of opposition, the two armies were so close to each other that conversations between enemies took place. Conditions were so miserable that the bands of each army began playing not long after sundown to provide their forces with a small amount of pleasure. "Yankee Doodle" competed with "Dixie" as rival bands tried to outdo each other up and down the lines. At some point one of the bands launched into the poignant melody "Home Sweet Home." In an instant all bands on both sides played the touching tune, while Confederate and Union soldiers sang in unison.

Anderson's men finally fell into an uneasy sleep in a cedar thicket on that cold night. Their clothes and blankets were soaked and the ground just as wet. Most were hungry. It was pitch black darkness, as no fires were allowed. About midnight, another heavy rain set in. Some soldiers were so exhausted they just slept through the downpour, which continued all night. Bragg and Rosecrans slept little if at all. Each planned a morning attack on their enemy's right wing. Bragg would strike first.[19]

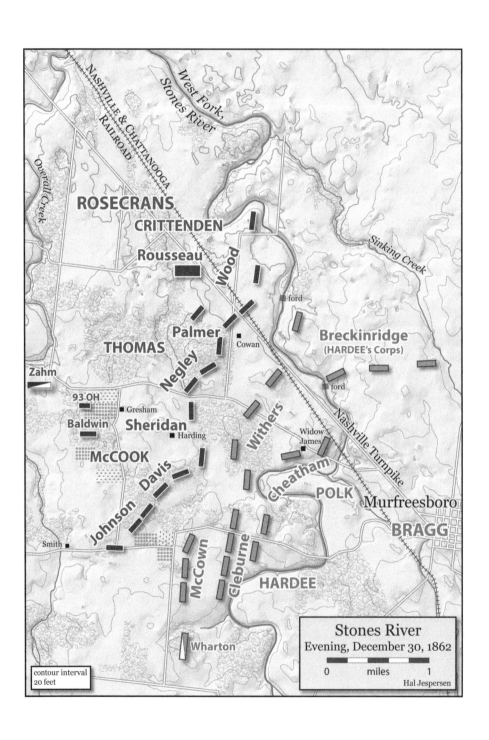

NASHVILLE & CHATTANOOGA RAILROAD

West Fork, Stones River

Overall Creek

Sinking Creek

ROSECRANS

CRITTENDEN

Rousseau

Wood

ford

Palmer

Cowan

Breckinridge
(HARDEE's Corps)

THOMAS

Negley

ford

Zahm

93 OH

Gresham

Withers

Nashville Turnpike

Baldwin

Sheridan

Harding

Widow
James

McCOOK

Davis

Cheatham

POLK

Murfreesboro

Johnson

BRAGG

Smith

McCown

Cleburne

HARDEE

Wharton

Stones River
Evening, December 30, 1862

contour interval
20 feet

0   miles   1

Hal Jespersen

➤ ◄

CHAPTER FIFTEEN

Blood and Buttons

NEW YEAR'S EVE DAY dawned cold and dreary. A fine mist made the air seem heavy. The brigades of August Willich and Edward Kirk awoke about five o'clock in the morning, anticipating a warm fire and a hot breakfast. These men had a first look at their position and were pleased by what they saw. Most had an open line of fire in front, sufficient cover in the form of cedar breaks in their rear, and a potential escape path to the north ending at the Gresham house. Brigadier General August Willich, one of the most experienced officers in Major General Rosecrans's army, protected the Army of the Cumberland's exposed right flank. General Edward N. Kirk, a veteran of the Battle of Shiloh, commanded the brigade to the left of Willich, just across a small path called Gresham Lane.[1]

Colonel Philemon Baldwin, commanding the Third Brigade in the division of Richard Johnson, was with his men about a mile behind the other two brigades. Baldwin had four regiments at his disposal: the First Ohio, the Fifth Kentucky, the Sixth Indiana, and Charles Anderson's Ninety-Third Ohio. These men were in reserve, positioned far enough back to respond to any threat to the Army of the Cumberland's right flank. Most of the men of the Ninety-Third Ohio had been out scouting with cavalry half the night, after a tiring march the previous day. Since Anderson's men had been late in arriving, Baldwin ordered them to take a position a few hundred yards behind Willich and Kirk. Anderson complied, but the night was so cold that his troops could not sleep. Feeling that they might rest easier in a cedar break, he moved them back behind the other reserve regiments of Baldwin's brigade. This was against orders, but Baldwin was already asleep. The mere happenstance of this move would save many of Anderson's men, as the very spot where the Ninety-Third Ohio first camped became the focal point of the Confederate attack just hours later.

On that cold and dreary day, the Army of the Cumberland was deployed in a long north-south line paralleling the west fork of Stones River to its east. Rosecrans had more than forty-one thousand men at his disposal. Their immediate objective was the town of Murfreesboro two miles southeast of the river. More than thirty-five thousand men from the Confederate Army of Tennessee, under the command of General Braxton Bragg, stood between Rosecrans and his objective. Bragg had chosen Murfreesboro as a defensive position to block what he believed to be Rosecrans's ultimate goal of capturing Chattanooga, Tennessee.

Rosecrans deployed his army in three sections in a line of battle four miles long. Major General Thomas L. Crittenden commanded the army's left wing. The center was led by Major General George H. Thomas. On the right wing, Major General Alexander McCook deployed his men in a long line with no natural obstacle to serve as an anchor protecting his right flank. This would prove to be a vulnerable position for the Union forces. Early that morning, General McCook enjoyed a shave at his camp on the Gresham farm. As coffee boiled and bacon simmered, the captain of one of his artillery batteries took half of the unit's horses five hundred yards to the rear for watering. Elsewhere, the men in each of the three divisions under McCook began to rouse themselves.

On the far right, at a salient angle where the north-south Union line made an abrupt turn to the right, or west, the men of Richard Johnson's division rose from their bedrolls. August Willich of the First Brigade received an order from General Johnson to have his troops armed and ready by daybreak, but the silence convinced Willich that the enemy had departed. Edward Kirk had left three of his Second Brigade regiments in a dense cedar break, rather than move them to a clearing in front that would have afforded better visibility for firing. After breakfast, Willich rode slowly north to confer with Johnson, giving one of his colonels instructions should anything happen while he was away. This lack of preparation would cost both brigades dearly.

Meanwhile, Charles Anderson's regiment and the rest of Philemon Baldwin's Third Brigade were in the reserve camp about a mile behind the Union front lines, just within the bounds of a large stand of cedar trees. Anderson and his second-in-command, Colonel Hiram Strong, had spent the night at Johnson's camp, returning to their brigade at about six in the morning. Twenty minutes later, they heard musket fire and before long the booming sounds of artillery from the south, indicating that the battle had begun. Hours before, while the Union brigades were eating a leisurely breakfast, Confederates led by Brigadier Generals Matthew D. Ector of Texas and Evander McNair of Arkansas had formed their troops in ranks. With no sustenance other than a small ration of whisky, the rebels smashed into the Union right wing. McCook's troops were caught completely by surprise.

Sergeant Major Lyman Widney of the Thirty-Fourth Illinois walked casually out toward the picket lines of Kirk's brigade when one of the soldiers ran toward Widney. As he passed, the soldier exclaimed, "They're coming!" Widney heard no firing, so he was skeptical and moved further forward until he could see the enemy's breastworks. What he saw frightened him. A tide of men in gray uniforms was pouring out of the defenses and onto the open field in front of him. Widney hurried back to his regiment. In just minutes they were under a tremendous attack. "They came down on us like a tornado," Widney remembered. His comrade, Sergeant Arnold Harrington, was shot through the knee joint. The men threw themselves flat on the ground and commenced firing, while their six cannons threw shells and grape shot over their heads into the onrushing rebels. "It reminded me of the passage of a swarm of bees," Widney later wrote of the battle. In ten minutes, twenty-one men of the regiment were killed and more than one hundred wounded.

The soldiers of the Thirty-Fourth Illinois fired only three rounds each before they were forced to retreat. They began running through an open corn field, but the tops of the stalks had been cut off, so cover was limited. The turf exploded around them as bullets made little furrows that looked to one soldier as if a mouse had been ploughing the ground. Other projectiles hit the corn stalks with a splattering sound. The worst sound of all was the thud of a Minié ball lodging in flesh. Kirk himself was struck in the thigh and later died from this wound. The retreat soon degenerated into a full-speed run.

The men of Willich's brigade first heard skirmishing and then heavy firing on their left flank as Kirk's brigade came under attack. Men from Ector's Texas brigade overwhelmed Willich's front line, driving the Yankees into their own camp, where some Union troops were killed while lying in their tents. Robert Stewart of the Fifteenth Ohio Infantry saw his pickets running back to camp, followed closely by a swarm of yelling and screaming Confederates. "Dropping our pots and pans, leaving our haversacks and blankets, we snatched up our cartridge boxes and rushed for our guns," Stewart recalled, "only to find ourselves with our backs to the foe." They too could do nothing but run. One dead Union soldier was found still clinging to his coffee pot.

Bragg's strategy was working perfectly. Kirk and Willich's front-line brigades were swept from the field. Confederate General J. P. McCown's forces, including his crack cavalry troops, were turning the Union right in on itself and driving it back to the northeast. In the meantime, battle-hardened troops from the Arkansas and Tennessee brigades of Brigadier Generals St. John Liddell and Bushrod Johnson had run over McCook's left flank and were advancing toward Baldwin's reserves. Fewer than thirty minutes after the battle began, Charles Anderson ordered his regiment out of the cedar break to form a line of battle to the left of the Fifth Kentucky.

Baldwin immediately countermanded Anderson's orders and the Ninety-Third Ohio moved back into the woods. The men watched in earnest as their comrades from the First Ohio and the Fifth Kentucky

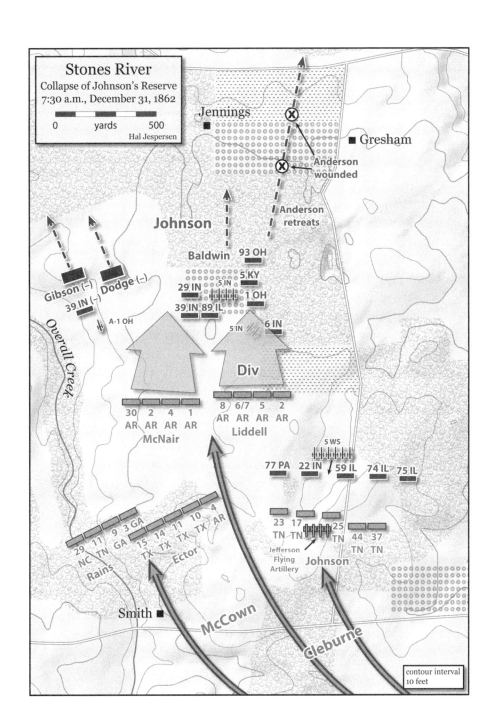

Stones River
Collapse of Johnson's Reserve
7:30 a.m., December 31, 1862

0   yards   500

Hal Jespersen

Jennings

Gresham

Anderson
wounded

Anderson
retreats

Johnson

Baldwin   93 OH

5 KY

29 IN   5 IN   1 OH

39 IN   89 IL

5 IN   6 IN

Gibson (–)   Dodge (–)

39 IN (–)   A-1 OH

Overall Creek

Div

30   2   4   1
AR AR AR AR

8   6/7   5   2
AR AR   AR AR

McNair

Liddell

5 WS

77 PA   22 IN   59 IL   74 IL   75 IL

29 11   9 3 GA
NC TN GA

15 14 11 10 4
TX TX TX TX AR

Ector

23 17   25
TN TN   TN   44 37
                TN TN

Jefferson
Flying
Artillery

Johnson

Rains

Smith

McCown

Cleburne

contour interval
10 feet

marched into the cornfield, settling behind a rail fence and scattered limestone boulders. It was now 7:30 in the morning. The First Ohio took the brunt of the assault and responded admirably, keeping the rebels from advancing for about twenty minutes. Bullets and artillery from both sides claimed many lives in one of the fiercest engagements some of the experienced soldiers had ever seen. When Confederate Brigadier General McNair's Third Brigade finished mopping up the remnants of Kirk's forces, he pivoted right to support Liddell.

At that point Major Jacob Stafford, commanding the First Ohio, knew that further resistance would be suicide. He shouted orders to retreat, but the constant artillery barrages drowned him out. He repeated the command and still was not heard. The third time he yelled at the top of his lungs. The Ohioans fell back into the Fifth Kentucky, became confused, and broke into a dead run. The Kentuckians, left alone in the cornfield, also skedaddled. The Ninety-Third Ohio Infantry was now the only Union regiment facing the enemy from the edge of the woods.

Anderson was losing his patience. He asked for orders. No response came. He asked again. No reply. Anxious to do something, he deployed skirmishers across the line of the woods from the left flank of the two retreating regiments east to Gresham Lane. While this movement was under way, Baldwin finally appeared on the scene and ordered Anderson to form his regiment in a line of battle on the left flank. Just as the Ninety-Third Ohio was preparing for what would have been certain annihilation against two brigades of adrenalin-fueled rebel killing machines, Baldwin shouted, "Colonel Anderson! For God's sake, retreat!"

Anderson ordered his men to about-face and they marched north through the woods in slow time. When the rebels entered the trees, Anderson's men increased their speed. By the time the Ohioans exited the forest, they were in an all-out run. Anderson's horse was hit three times, twice by bullets glancing off trees and once by another spent ball that did little damage. As Anderson turned to see how rapidly the enemy was advancing, he was hit in the pit of his stomach by a ball at a range of seventy-five yards. He thought he was mortally wounded, but the ball hit the second button of his coat, then glanced off the third vest button, passing through the back of his coat. A stinging sensation seconds later confirmed that the bullet had torn away flesh on the outside of one left rib. It was not a serious wound. Then Anderson's horse was struck above the root of its tail near the spine and dropped like a stone. Anderson jumped off, but the animal unexpectedly rose again. When the colonel attempted to grab the reins, his horse knocked the drawn sword from his hands and ran away. Kicking and bucking through the lines, the horse fell again, presumably dead.

Anderson joined his troops in their scamper, entering a cotton field, where the real slaughter began. He was a surprisingly fast runner. Despite his age, his long legs allowed him to overtake the much younger Captain William Birch. As Anderson passed Birch, he was hit again and experienced another miraculous escape from serious injury. The ball hit the middle button of his left sleeve and glanced off his hip joint, creating a flesh wound fewer than two inches deep. Several days later, Anderson found the actual bullet had lodged harmlessly in his boot. Meanwhile, the booming artillery was so distracting that some soldiers stuffed cotton into their ears to avoid the concussions. In the cotton field the remnants of the Ninety-Third Ohio reformed briefly with elements of other retreating regiments and attempted to make a stand. It was brief, bloody, and unsuccessful. Anderson's regiment lost many of its killed and wounded in this area. The retreat finally ended as soldiers from Horatio Van Cleve's division arrived. Anderson's troops had been pushed back more than two miles. Their backs were to the Nashville Pike.

Anderson went to the hospital surgeon to have his wounds examined and dressed. When he removed his coat, he saw that it had five bullet holes. Anderson returned to his regiment. Remnants of Johnson's shattered Second Division assumed a reserve position at the far northwest end of the battlefield. In front of them, rival cavalry brigades battled to gain control of the turnpike. Should the rebels cross the pike, capture the supply wagons, and cut off a northern escape route, the Union army might be pushed into the river. The

Union cavalry held. The fighting was essentially over for Anderson and the Ninety-Third Ohio, though prospects for a Union victory looked bleak at best.[2]

What Anderson did not know was that while he and the entire right wing of the army had been swept from the field, two of his favorite officers were gallantly buying Rosecrans the time he needed to redeploy his forces and prevent a crushing defeat. Generals Philip H. Sheridan and Joshua W. Sill had been mutual friends since their days at West Point. Sill had been Anderson's division commander until shortly before the army left Nashville, when he opted for command of a brigade under Sheridan. An Ohio native, Sill was revered by his men for his intelligence and his fine character. Unlike the rest of McCook's divisional commanders, Sheridan had his men up and ready at four o'clock in the morning. He and Sill had met McCook two hours earlier and warned him of an early morning attack. McCook had appeared unconcerned.

About 7:30 a.m. the South Carolina and Alabama brigade of Colonel Arthur M. Manigault attacked Sill's position with typical fury, pushing back the Thirty-Sixth Illinois and the Eighty-Eighth Illinois. As General Sill rode up to rally his troops for a counter-attack, a bullet tore through his brain, killing him in an instant. After several hours of intense fighting, hordes of Confederate infantry were closing on the divisions of Sheridan and Brigadier General James S. Negley like a vise, surrounding them on three sides. Sheridan's and Negley's brave stands came at a terrible cost until finally the brigades of Major General Lovell H. Rousseau arrived to relieve them. The rebel onslaught was reaching its peak, and victory for the Butternuts appeared close at hand.

Rousseau's reinforcements filed past the brigades of Colonel William Grose to his right, when they were met with a furious assault and their left flank thrown back. Grose ordered the Sixth Ohio, commanded by Anderson's nephew Nicholas, along with the Thirty-Fourth Indiana, to his front right, while other regiments faced southeast in V-shaped formations to defend the Nashville Pike. Colonel Nicholas Anderson's troops and the Hoosiers watched as crazed and confused Union soldiers from Sheridan's and Negley's divisions fled by in haste. When they finally cleared their ranks, the oncoming rebels were a mere one hundred yards distant. A desperate firestorm erupted. The Thirty-Fourth Indiana was overwhelmed almost before the men could fire a shot. Nicholas Anderson's troops withstood the first volley with considerable loss but responded bravely, exchanging fire for about twenty minutes.

The Confederates were so close that Nicholas ordered his men to fix bayonets and prepare for hand-to-hand combat. Before he could give the command to charge, however, he found himself outflanked on both sides and was forced to retreat. Nineteen men, including his adjutant and five color-bearers, died there. In all, 112 were wounded. The Sixth Ohio had held its ground for forty minutes and prevented a breakthrough to the pike. Unlike that of his uncle, Nicholas's battle was far from over. He had been wounded in the thigh but refused to leave the field. The Sixth Ohio replenished its ammunition and formed a line of battle astride the Nashville Pike. More men of Nicholas's regiment died while holding that position just west of a landmark known as the Round Forest, where Colonel William B. Hazen was making a determined defense of the Union left. Hazen held his position all day in the most contested section of the battlefield.[3]

General Rosecrans, who seemed to be everywhere during the battle, cheering on his forces and adjusting his strategy, was riding to the Round Forest in the early afternoon. Without warning, a twelve-pound shell cut through the air and decapitated chief-of-staff Julius Garesche, splattering Rosecrans with the blood and brains of his best friend. Rosecrans appeared shaken for a moment then turned to Sheridan and told him that good men must die in battle.

By nightfall the Union Army still held the Nashville Pike. Both armies had sustained horrendous casualties in what was fast becoming one of the bloodiest major battles of the Civil War. Confederate commander Bragg was encouraged following the first day of battle. Although he had not achieved his ultimate goal, his men had demolished nearly a third of the Union Army and captured more than three thousand prisoners. His telegram to Richmond implied victory. "God has granted us a Happy New Year," he boasted. Rosecrans spent the first part of the evening riding through the lines, consulting with his division commanders, and encouraging the rank and file. He then assembled a council of war. The shell-shocked McCook had seen enough slaughter and wanted to head back to Nashville. Generals George Thomas and Thomas Crittenden wanted to remain in position and fight. Rosecrans decided to stay.[4]

On New Year's Day both armies rested. Most of the adversaries respected an informal truce so that they could tend to the wounded and bury their dead. Nicholas Anderson had time on his hands as he rested his wounded leg and wondered what the next day would bring. The Harvard graduate and lover of literature composed a poem that day that revealed his feelings about the gallant men lost in the terrible battle:

STONE RIVER, JAN 1, 1863

The day had sped. The night winds wildly moan
Their wintry chorus o'er the prairie West;
Weird wandering shadows, lengthening, floating, on
To angels' realms find refuge in their breast.
Hark to the sound! The engine's rushing blast
Thrills the hamlet as it rattles past.

An aged father totters to the door.
"Great battle fought!" He trembles at the cry;
The dim-eyed mother breathes a broken prayer
For souls now hushed in death and victory.
Resounds the shout,— "the battle surely won!"
Ah! Where their boy who to the war has gone?

The prattler, standing by his mother's knee,
Lists to the shout, and eager clasps her hand:
"Oh tell me, mamma, where in Tennessee
Is papa now, and where his patriot band?"
He hears the sob; he startles at the tear,
And quivering lips which faintly murmur, "Where?"

Sleep silently, brother, husband, son, and sire,
Where violet blooms bedeck thy heather bed!
There let us raise the monumental spire
To mark the tomb of brave unnumbered dead.
Rear high the shaft above the sweeping river,
Of martyrdom and love, a sign forever![5]

The foes dug trenches and repositioned their troops for the next phase of the battle. Rosecrans tightened his formation and sent Van Cleve's division to the far left, across the Stones River to an eminence on the east bank. This was a shrewd move, as the hill commanded a view of the open fields in front of his army. It was the perfect location to place artillery batteries. Bragg received no report of this movement until the following morning, when his own plan was already decided. It proved to be a critical missing piece of information.

Former Kentucky senator and presidential candidate John C. Breckenridge commanded a division in the corps of Confederate Lieutenant General William J. Hardee. Breckenridge's troops were massed on the east side of Stones River, facing the Union left wing. Frustrated by inaccurate reports of enemy troop movements on the first day of the battle, the Kentuckian inspected the Union positions personally on the morning of January 2. When he saw Union troops dug in on a hill near McFadden's Ford, he became concerned. Dozens of artillery pieces aimed on an attacking force from this position meant that his planned attack would be sure suicide. Breckenridge reported his findings to Bragg, whose response was curt. He ordered Breckenridge to take the hill. By sending the victory telegram to Richmond two days earlier, Bragg had committed himself to another attack. He could not back down now.

Breckenridge returned to his command and related the orders to his brigade commanders. One of these brigades was an eclectic mix of volunteer units from Kentucky. These men were volunteers who formed the First Kentucky Brigade, more popularly known as the Orphan Brigade. They had been thus named due to the fact that Kentucky was initially neutral, forcing supporters of the Confederacy to enlist in nearby Tennessee. General Roger W. Hanson, commander of the Orphan Brigade, exploded with rage when he heard the orders from Breckenridge. If Bragg insisted on murdering his own troops, he threatened, Hanson would kill him first. Breckenridge and another officer had to physically restrain Hanson until he calmed down. The men were instructed to advance rapidly to within a hundred yards of the enemy, fire, then claw their way through the underbrush, and finally attack their opponents with bayonets. The Union gunners were ready with fifty-seven cannons in position by four in the afternoon to meet the expected onslaught.

Nicholas Anderson and his Sixth Ohio stood in the rear of four lines of battle when Breckenridge's attack began. The Confederates ran across the fields and hurled themselves into the Union lines. Sergeant Samuel Welch of the Fifty-First Ohio described the simultaneous first volleys. "It seemed to me that both lines . . . were annihilated," Welch observed, as dozens of men from either side fell. The Union soldiers fled "like blackbirds," according to Jervis D. Grainger of the Sixth Kentucky Infantry. The men had to cross the icy river sixty feet wide and two feet deep, then scale a twenty-foot limestone bluff with enemy bullets striking the rocks as they climbed. "My idea was that the Army of the Cumberland was rapidly passing out of existence," Welch recalled. When the beleaguered bluecoats finally crested the riverbank, they found Negley's reinforcements waiting there to aid them.[6]

Major General Thomas L. Crittenden, commander of the Union left wing, relied on his chief of artillery, Major John Mendenhall, to time the firing of the cannons. They waited until as many of the Confederates were exposed in the open field as possible before all fifty-seven guns fired at once. The result, according to Colonel Charles Anderson, was "the most stupendous and continuous fire of artillery . . . in a small space ever heard on this continent." In just a few minutes the rebels lost an astounding eighteen hundred men.[7]

Negley's and Hazen's brigades then crossed the river and began a counterattack against Breckenridge's decimated division. Grose's brigade, including Nicholas Anderson's Sixth Ohio, also moved forward against Breckenridge's right flank. For the first time in the Battle of Stones River, a large portion of the Confederate army was in retreat under withering fire. Just two hours after Breckenridge's attack, the Union Army had advanced to the enemy's original breastworks. Two more hours of sharp fighting finally dislodged the rebels from their trenches, forcing them to retire. Rosecrans's left wing pulled back into a defensive position before nightfall. It was a stunning turn of events.

The Battle of Stones River was over. The Northern press was ecstatic at the result. The editor of the *Louisville Journal* wrote that the Rosecrans name was famous before but "had now become immortal." The timing could not have been better for the Lincoln administration. The president's signing of the Emancipation Proclamation on New Year's Day had transformed the conflict into a virtual holy war. Although it angered many in Ohio and other northern states, Lincoln's groundbreaking executive order effectively ended Confederate hopes for assistance from Britain or France. The military victory also opened the door to an eventual invasion of the South from Nashville through Chattanooga and into Georgia. "God bless you and all with you," Lincoln gushed. He later told Rosecrans, "You gave us a hard-earned victory, which, had there been a defeat instead, the nation could scarcely have lived over." For the soldiers the end of the battle was hardly a cause for celebration. Close to nineteen thousand men in blue and gray lay dead or wounded. Heaps of body parts piled up outside field hospitals and unburied corpses stiffened on the battlefield. Both armies felt eviscerated and needed time to recover physically and mentally from the terrible experience.[8]

Anderson wrote to his eldest daughter from the newly named Camp Sill, on the east side of Stones River, that evening. Although his wounds were minor, the pain was real and kept him awake at night. His persistent fever caused his doctor to fear that he might have contracted typhoid fever. He sent his suit of clothes to his daughters "marred as you see by the traitors," but the torn and bloody uniform was later stolen from a holding area at Nashville. Rumors swirled around the camp that the enemy had retreated south more than fifty miles to Fayetteville, Tennessee. Others speculated that Bragg had been reinforced by Major General James Longstreet and was preparing for another great battle. In reality, Bragg was making yet another escape to lick his wounds and ponder how such a promising tactical triumph had devolved into a bloody strategic defeat.

For the next ten days, as Anderson recovered in camp two miles south of Murfreesboro, the press and other pundits were busy critiquing the performance of the principal leaders of both armies. Anderson was not as critical of McCook as others. The attack had been a complete surprise after all, he reasoned. "What more could he do?" Anderson asked. Bragg's plan was excellent, he admitted, but the rebels "unaccountably failed in vigor in following it up." What Anderson did admit, and what McCook's critics were quick in pointing out, was the fact that the Union right wing was spread too wide and too thin, with no real reserves and no natural shields on its right flank. But Anderson was being too kind to his friend. If Sheridan had been in McCook's place, the entire right wing of the Army of the Cumberland would have been up and ready at four in the morning. Countless lives might have been saved.[9]

On January 7, Rosecrans approached Anderson about the reorganization of the army. He suggested that Anderson might consider commanding a brigade. Anderson put him off. Nothing would be happening any time soon, Anderson figured, so he requested leave to go home and recuperate. He made a brief speech to his old comrades at the Ohio State House on January 13, but the effort only fatigued him further. Unsure of his ability to return to the field, Anderson resigned his commission on February 21, 1863. He left the job of leading the Ninety-Third Ohio Infantry to his capable second-in-command, thirty-four-year-old Hiram Strong. Strong was anxious to prove himself worthy of the challenge, as he had missed the Battle of Stones River due to pressing family business back home. Anderson's retirement may have saved his own life, but Strong would fall just a few months later, mortally wounded while commanding the Ninety-Third Ohio at Chickamauga.[10]

Richard Clough Anderson (1750–1826)
possibly by Matthew Harris Jouett

Eliza Brown Anderson
(1816–1901)

Private Collection

Kitty Anderson
(1842–1928)

Private Collection

Silhouette of
Charles Anderson 1830

Miami University Libraries,
Oxford, OH

Henry Clay
(1777–1852)

Library of Congress

Robert Anderson
(1805–1871)

Library of Congress

Lt. Col. Robert E. Lee,
(1807–1870)

Library of Congress

John Sherman
(1823–1900)

Library of Congress

William T. Sherman
(1820–1891)

Library of Congress

Paroled officers of the U.S. 8th Infantry at San Antonio, Texas, 1861. From left, Lt. James Judson Van Horn; Lt. Royal Thaxter Frank (seated); Brevet Lt. Col. James Voty Bomford (6th Infantry); Lt. Zenas Randall Bliss (seated); Lt. William Graham Jones. Jones, the fiancé of Kitty Anderson, was killed at Chickamauga in 1863.

Charles Anderson home, now the Argyle Club, San Antonio, Texas in 1936

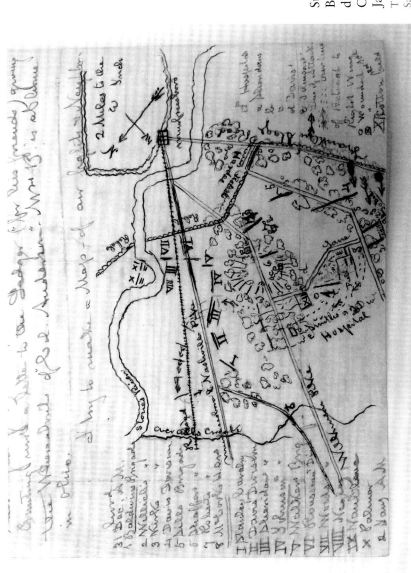

Stones River
Battlefield Map
drawn by
Charles Anderson,
January 7, 1863

Clement L. Vallandigham
(1820–1871)
Library of Congress

Charles Anderson,
Colonel 93rd Ohio Infantry
Author Collection

Cartoon protesting General Burnside's arrest
of Vallandigham, June, 1863
Library of Congress

Draft manuscript of Anderson's Gettysburg oration,
November 19, 1863

Private Collection

John Burns "The hero of Gettysburg"

Gravestone of Charles and Eliza Anderson,
Kuttawa Cemetery, Kentucky

→→ ←←

CHAPTER SIXTEEN

A Dangerous Man

A S SPRING 1863 APPROACHED, Charles Anderson's health took another turn for the worse. A severe case of bronchitis ebbed, but his constant adversary (asthma) returned with a vengeance. As Anderson lay in his bed back home in Dayton, an old friend and political rival was planning his next move after losing his seat in Congress that fall. The brilliant and handsome Clement L. Vallandigham had many of the same talents as Anderson, combined with one quality that his fellow attorney lacked: limitless ambition.

Val, as nearly everyone called him, had known Anderson on the judicial circuit and later in the Ohio state legislature. He had worked harder than Anderson and had become one of the leading attorneys in Dayton. He had also become an immensely popular leader among Ohio Democrats. Although Anderson was a devoted Henry Clay Whig, the political differences between the two charismatic men did not prevent them from becoming close friends. When Vallandigham's son Willie died suddenly in 1848, he was overwhelmed with grief. He marveled at the support he received from the local community. "Mr. Anderson was an especial comfort to us," Vallandigham wrote to his brother, "He is an extraordinary man."[1]

Unlike Anderson, however, Vallandigham was a man of humble birth and few resources. The cemetery plot where his son lay was the only piece of ground on earth that he owned when he buried the boy. Edwin M. Stanton, who later became Lincoln's secretary of war, recognized the potential in the young attorney and lent him five hundred dollars to open a law practice. Like Anderson, Vallandigham possessed a superior intellect and was well-read and fervently self-righteous. He and Anderson reviled the abolitionist extremists for playing their part in driving the country toward disunion; but Vallandigham lacked the perspective that Anderson had gained from his intimate experiences with the Southern conspirators. As war neared, their differences grew and the friendship ended.

Vallandigham was ever conscious of an opportunity to steal the spotlight in order to promote himself and his political opinions. When he learned of John Brown's raid at Harpers Ferry in October 1859, he rushed to the scene. One of his colleagues in Congress heard of the visit and called Vallandigham a "pettifogging inquisitor." The *Cincinnati Commercial* derided Vallandigham's questioning that "probed among Brown's wounds for material with which to manufacture political capital." Vallandigham made the convincing argument that Brown was a terrorist who deserved to hang. He chastised abolition enthusiasts such as Ralph Waldo Emerson, who attempted to canonize Brown. Society is based on the rule of law, Vallandigham insisted. No high moral principles could justify outright murder.

If Brown's raid was the spark that might light the fire of disunion and civil war, then Vallandigham was determined to extinguish it. In the lively discussions that followed in the Thirty-Fifth Congress, he made a landmark speech that defined his position as the leader of the antiwar movement, while exacerbating sectional rivalries in a unique way. It was an intensely partisan oration. Vallandigham blamed the Republicans for forming a party along sectional lines to further agitate the differences between North and South. Northern radicals, he argued, were trampling the Constitution and its purposeful balance between the interests of free and slave states. Making Brown into a martyr, Vallandigham reasoned, meant placing abolitionist doctrine above the sacred law of the land. This was an odious notion on its face. It was certainly no reason to break up the Union and risk commencing a devastating civil war.

While Vallandigham preached unity on the one hand, the focus of his speech was the special interests of the West. He took advantage of the increased sectional tensions by pressing his own sectional agenda in Congress. Members should exercise care, Vallandigham advised, not to ignore the interest of his part of the Union. He boasted that he was "as good a Western fire eater as the hottest salamander in this House." He would advocate for the welfare of the West, Vallandigham vowed, to his dying day. His bold proclamation of a third political section put a stake in the ground that he stood by stubbornly for the rest of his public life. Vallandigham's Western factionalism led to unusual and dangerous proposals. By tirelessly promoting such radical ideas, he would become one of the most controversial figures of the Civil War era.

With war on the doorstep, Vallandigham and Anderson shared some common ground. Both supported the last-ditch efforts of Larz Anderson and John J. Crittenden to save the Union by extending the Missouri Compromise line westward. When those efforts failed and seven states had seceded, Vallandigham became morose. As the Union dissolved before his eyes, he compared his helpless feelings with "one who watches over the couch of his beloved mother slowly dying," with no power to save her. When the news of Robert Anderson's surrender of Fort Sumter reached Ohio, most citizens clamored for war. Vallandigham dug in his heels. President Lincoln and his abolition friends had brought on this war through coercion, Vallandigham maintained. Democrats should oppose the war on those grounds. Many of his friends were too busy volunteering for service to stop and listen. Vallandigham, who commanded Dayton's militia, left his uniform hanging in his closet and stayed home while his neighbors marched off to defend their country. One local newspaper called Vallandigham "invincible in peace, invisible in war."

The *Dayton Journal* urged Vallandigham to resign at once, on account of his "treasonable sentiments." The *Journal*'s editor asked, "Could Jeff Davis desire a more faithful emissary than C. L. Vallandigham? Shame where is thy blush?" Vallandigham was left standing nearly alone among such well-known Ohio Democrats as Samuel S. Cox, William Allen, David Tod, and John Brough. They all rallied behind the flag. Party loyalties took a back seat to patriotism. Vallandigham stood his ground under a withering verbal assault.

Lincoln's suspension of the right of habeas corpus, his naval block-ade of the Confederate States, and the raising of a huge army were extralegal measures that were not sanctioned by the Constitution, Vallandigham reasoned. The usurpation of power from the Congress was unprecedented, and Vallandigham feared that the civil liberties at the very heart of the republican ideal were therefore at risk. When Congress was asked to validate the president's actions, the Ohio congressman vowed, "I will not vote to sustain or ratify—never." Vallandigham promised that he would vote "millions for defense, not a dollar or a man for aggressive and offensive civil war." The line be-tween dissent and treason is often blurry in wartime. Vallandigham was walking a political and legal tightrope.[2]

Lincoln took a personal interest in ending the congressional career of Clement L. Vallandigham. Brigadier General Robert C. Schenck was also a Dayton resident, former Whig congressman, and a life-long friend of Anderson. The day after Anderson arrived from his Texas escape, Schenck wrote the president, suggesting that he give Anderson an equivalent commission. Wounded at the Second Battle of Bull Run on the last day of August 1862, Schenck was recuperating at Willard's Hotel in Washington City when Edwin M. Stanton and Salmon P. Chase paid him a visit. "You are the only man who can beat that traitor Vallandigham," Chase pleaded. When Lincoln also visited and suggested that Schenck could do his country a greater ser-vice at the ballot box than on the battlefield, Schenck agreed to run.[3]

The war had lasted beyond most people's worst dreams by the fall of 1862. Morale in the North and the West ebbed as the body count piled up with no final Union victory in sight. Not only had Braxton Bragg forced Don Carlos Buell all the way back from Alabama to Louisville, but the rebels had installed a secessionist governor in Kentucky. Vallandigham's star was again on the ascent as the Lincoln administration took a battering in the Democratic press. A reces-sion stoked the race-baiting techniques so commonly used by western Democrats during the previous thirty years. "If the laboring men of this state do not desire their places occupied by Negroes," the editor of the *Cincinnati Enquirer* wrote on August 4, "they will vote for the nominees of the Democratic ticket." Vallandigham acolyte Thomas O. Lowe was even cruder. "The Constitution as it is, the Union as it was, *and the Niggers where they are*," he wrote. The threat of a tide of cheap labor released by a future emancipation of slaves combined with war weariness to create distrust of the Lincoln administration. Dissenters, many of whom were recent Irish immigrants, also resented what they saw as moral condescension on the part of New England Puritan abolitionists and temperance crusaders. They formed the base of an informal protest group that became known as Copperheads, and Vallandigham became their political champion.

The Republican press was just as yellow as its rivals. Scurrilous rumors about Vallandigham's supposed "treasonable plots" circulated widely in newspapers and pamphlets. Just weeks before the election, Lincoln played the war hero card by extolling Schenck's bravery at Second Bull Run and promoting him to major general. Vallandigham lost in a rout, but Democrats throughout the Western states gained strength, winning fourteen of Ohio's nineteen congressional seats. Anderson's troops rejoiced when they heard the news of Vallandigham's defeat. A straw poll of the regiment gave Schenck in excess of four hundred votes, while Vallandigham garnered fewer than a hundred. Vallandigham was not discouraged. He attributed the defeat to political shenanigans. The setback only made him more determined to get his message out and stop what he felt was a horrible mistake of a war. He could think of no better podium than the governor's chair.[4]

In March 1863, Vallandigham went public with his desire to run for chief executive of his native state, an office then occupied by David Tod. Custom dictated that the nomination be given to Hugh J. Jewett, who had run unsuccessfully against Tod in the last gubernatorial contest. When Vallandigham sought the support of party leaders that spring, he was rebuffed. No matter, he told his friends, the people would support him. He published a collection of his former speeches in a campaign manifesto titled *The Record of Hon. C. L. Vallandigham on Abolition, the Union, and the Civil War*. Anderson, another influential man without current employment, was one of Vallandigham's avid readers.

What Anderson read made him both angry and concerned. Vallandigham's epistle promised to explain "why negrophilistic fanaticism includes . . . an intense hatred of Vallandigham." The author repeated his claim that the North was the sole aggressor in the conflict. Vallandigham reasoned that the slavery question, a purely political issue in the South, had motivated moral and religious zealots in the North to overstep their bounds. Slavery was the South's problem to deal with. This was the same state sovereignty argument asserted by many Southerners. Vallandigham professed a "serene indifference" to the peculiar institution. The most important object, he preached, was to return the Union and the Constitution to where it was prior to the rebellion. Vallandigham's conservative verbiage at the beginning of his tome eventually gave way to radical proposals to reform the Union into a confederation of three coequal sections.

Vallandigham reprinted a speech he gave in Congress in February 1861 titled "How Shall the Union Be Preserved?" In it, he proposed that any measure introduced in the U.S. Senate require the concurrence of a majority of the senators from each section: North, South, and West. He further recommended that the president and vice president be elected to six-year terms by a concurrent majority of state electors or by a special election if no popular majority was reached, as had been the case in 1860. In January 1863, Vallandigham predicted that, in the case of permanent disunion, "the whole North-West will go with the South," citing evidence of "political revolution" in the fall 1862 elections. "The day which divides the North from the South," Vallandigham argued, "the self-same day decrees the eternal divorce between the West and the East." This was hardly the talk of the conservative Union man whom Val had professed to be. This was the naked ambition of a man who viewed the Ohio governor's race as just another stepping-stone to a much greater destiny. Someone had to stop him.[5]

Charles Anderson found himself in a familiar position. He was seriously ill, with no prospects for the future. He focused on ways that he could once again try to rebuild a career for himself and his family, but all he could think about was the health of his beloved country.

Like a man hopelessly in love, Anderson was obsessed with finding ways to lend support to the great cause of his life. His service in the army had been brief. His diplomatic mission had ended in failure. He possessed one set of tools, however, that appeared useful in this titanic struggle—a keen mind, a silver tongue, and a powerful voice. As soon as he was well enough to stand, Anderson hit the road with a message designed to shore up support for the war effort. The threat of Vallandigham's dangerous ideas moved him to action.

Anderson began to assemble support for a Union Party effort that would transcend the incessant bickering between Democrats and Republicans and focus on uniting behind the army and the Lincoln administration. He rallied the officers of the Ohio regiments at Murfreesboro to draft a set of resolutions that denounced Peace Democrats in the North as traitors and demanded a mass meeting to be held in Cincinnati on February 23. Current and former governors of both Ohio and Indiana attended, along with General Lew Wallace and other key leaders of both major political parties. Anderson was too ill to attend the meeting at Pike's Opera House but sent a letter instead that was later published. It spoke for the troops and their feelings of rage against their former friends, who were creating a "fire in the rear," while they fought and died for their country.[6]

Anderson argued strenuously against the so-called Peace Party. Reunion with the present Confederate government was impossible, he stressed, as the regime was "a despotism the most absolute and unmitigated upon the globe." The North could not place their trust in the same conspirators who had plotted and carried out abject treason and dominated a formerly free people by the power of a slaveholding oligarchy. This is a war between two opposite ideals of government, Anderson declared. The South, by continuing to breed and hold slaves, had committed to a Spartan-like society of rule by brute force. Their thirst for more lands to accommodate their increasing numbers of slave captives promised an inevitable war of conquest against the free states, Anderson predicted. The threat of a hostile, adjacent neighbor state would turn the North into a military republic.

To Vallandigham's prediction that an imagined West section might unite with the Southern Confederacy, Anderson did not hide his disgust. In like fashion, he decried, any Christian gentleman could "strangle or poison his beautiful, diligent, virtuous, intelligent, amiable, and lawful wife, and then unite his destinies with the most filthy, diseased, abandoned harlot he can find." The Southern oligarchy was, to Anderson's view, the Delilah to his Union Samson. Was secession not horrible enough that Vallandigham wanted it to happen all over again? History had proven that the "let us alone" argument of the South was a canard. After all that had transpired and amid declarations from both sides to such conflicting ideas of social organization, these two sections could not coexist as separate nations. One idea had to prevail. Anderson emphasized that he did not want to prosecute the war and crush the rebellion out of feelings of revenge for the injuries that the South had caused him. On the contrary, it pained him to contemplate the ruin of his native land. He still loved the Southern people. He just hated their treason.[7]

A similar meeting took place in Columbus, Ohio, on March 3. Governor Andrew Johnson of Tennessee was the keynote speaker. He was still a Democrat, Johnson explained, but any Democrat who talked of compromise was a traitor to his country. He did not believe in fighting a war to free the slaves, but if their emancipation was necessary to put down the rebellion, he would do what needed to be done in order to save the Union. As Anderson's health improved, he joined a bandwagon of like-minded speakers that fanned out across the state. Public opinion was turning back toward a more vigorous prosecution of the war, Governor Tod wrote to General William T. Sherman in early March. The new Union Party, formed to bridge the gap between abolition-leaning Republicans and conservative Democrats who also supported the war, was a force to be reckoned with. Anderson could wave the bloody shirt with the best of them.

Vallandigham was every bit Anderson's equal as a speaker and drew huge crowds of Copperheads in his bid to claim the governor's chair. His rhetoric became more and more incendiary, as he tested the limits of free speech in wartime. When General Ambrose E. Burnside, commander of the Department of the Ohio, issued Order Number 38, which made it illegal to criticize the Union war effort, he took aim at Peace Democrats like Vallandigham, who were actively undermining support for the army. Anyone convicted of aiding the enemy, Burnside declared, was a spy and a traitor and would suffer death. The mere act of "declaring sympathies for the enemy," Burnside decreed in his order, "will no longer be tolerated in this department." Vallandigham's supporters relished the thought of their champion being painted as David, clad in a garment of civil liberties, and doing battle with one of King Lincoln's Goliaths. A campaign song was born:

> O brothers don't forget the time when Burnside was our fate,
> And the laws were superseded by order 38.
> Then, like a free-born western man,
> Our Val spoke brave and true,
> O when he's chosen governor,
> What will poor Burnside do?
> Won't he skedaddle,
> As he's well used to do?[8]

Burnside did not skedaddle or even wait for the election. He took action. The general cited quotations from Vallandigham's speeches in which the Democrat accused Lincoln of prosecuting the war not for the preservation of the Union but for "the purpose of crushing out liberty and erecting a despotism." Vallandigham further suggested that the president should have accepted the mediation efforts of France, restored the Constitution as it was, and ended the war honorably. By suggesting that Lincoln and his military authorities had acted with "a base usurpation of arbitrary authority," Vallandigham encouraged resistance, discouraged enlistment, and therefore aided the enemy. Burnside arrested Vallandigham at home in his nightclothes on May 5. In his zeal to silence a traitor, the general created a martyr.

A military tribunal took just two days to convict Vallandigham and sentence him to prison at Fort Warren in Boston Harbor. Four days later, former Ohio senator George E. Pugh applied for a writ of habeas corpus on Vallandigham's behalf. The U.S. District Court judge denied it. Congress, after all, had conferred the right to suspend habeas corpus, among other war powers, to President Lincoln two months earlier. Reaction to Vallandigham's conviction was immediate. The governors of New York and New Jersey howled in protest, suggesting that the arrest was not only illegal but amounted to "military despotism." Lincoln was angry too, as he felt that Burnside should have consulted him before he overreached. In an effort to save face and mollify some of his sharpest critics, the president altered Vallandigham's sentence and ordered him to be deported to the Confederate States.

Vallandigham's supporters in Dayton were incensed. They took out their hostility on the city's Republican newspaper, burning the offices of the *Dayton Journal* to the ground, along with half a city block. Martial law was declared. Vallandigham was the former editor of the rival *Dayton Empire*, whose editor had been shot and killed by local Republican Henry M. Brown the previous November. In that event a melee had followed in which the prison guards holding Brown fired on a crowd of angry Democrats who had assaulted them with stones. Vallandigham's sudden martyrdom created a public relations nightmare for Lincoln. Burnside's rash action had spurred a Democratic Party revival, not just in Ohio but throughout the North and the West. National unity was threatened and the war effort potentially compromised.

Unless Lincoln acted quickly to control popular opinion, his party and his presidency would be in big trouble. In a stroke of public relations genius, the president employed logic to help him out of this predicament. Vallandigham had not been arrested because he was a threat to the administration or the commanding general, Lincoln emphasized. He was prosecuted "because he was damaging the army, upon the existence of which, the life of the nation depends," Lincoln asked, "Must I shoot a simple-minded soldier boy who deserts, while I must not touch a hair of the wily agitator who induces him to desert?" The Democrats could hardly reply.

Another problem was that Vallandigham did not *want* to join the rebels, and the Confederate government did not want him either. "I am a citizen of Ohio and of the United States," he declared when he crossed rebel lines. "I am here within your lines by force and against my will," he continued. "I therefore surrender myself to you as a prisoner of war." Jefferson Davis did not know quite what to do with this odd character, so he invoked the same law as he had used with Anderson two years earlier. Vallandigham was declared an "alien enemy" and transported under guard to Wilmington, North Carolina. As soon as he could arrange his own exodus from the South, Vallandigham hopped aboard a blockade-runner to Bermuda and made his way to Canada. Having become the most famous American exile, he relished the attention. Visitors frequented his new campaign headquarters at a hotel in Windsor, Ontario, where he formally declared his intention to run for Ohio's governorship in absentia. As Republicans vilified Vallandigham, Ohio Democrats rose to defend his honor.[9]

→→ ←←

CHAPTER SEVENTEEN

Severing the Head
of the Snake

THE OHIO DEMOCRATIC CONVENTION opened on June 11, 1863, to a buzz like few meetings in the history of the Buckeye State. Everyone was talking about Clement Vallandigham. Party leaders like Samuel S. Cox and George W. Maypenny were convinced that Vallandigham's nomination would be the death knell for the Democrats. The rank and file, however, worshipped him. When it came time to decide the nomination, the result was never in doubt. Vallandigham carried the convention by a vote of 411 to 11. One of his disciples published a long poem in the *Hamilton True Telegraph* a few days after the convention. Titled "Vallandigham: The Bastiled Hero," the rhyme began and ended with verses that, although not models of literary achievement, were heartfelt expressions of affection for their newly beatified champion:

> They bore him to a gloomy cell,
> And barred him from the light,
> Because he dared to tell
> The people what was right.

> Lift up thy head, O martyred brave,
> Thy chains shall broken be,
> The people come their friend to save—
> Look up, thou shall be free.[1]

Anderson and his Union Party allies were concerned. They had recently witnessed public opinion turn on a dime, producing catastrophic results. Key Southern states such as Georgia were split evenly on the eve of secession just two years earlier. Voters there experienced a tide of emotion that led to overwhelming majorities for disunion. What Union supporters needed was a solid coalition of Republicans and "War Democrats" to keep Ohio voters focused on defeating the Confederacy and reuniting the country. They found their new leader in a most unexpected place.

John Brough was a lifelong Democrat who had opposed Lincoln's election in 1860 and had indicated that he would likely do so again in 1864. Brough was the president of the Bellefontaine and Indianapolis Railroad. He spent most of his time in Indiana but maintained his former home in Cleveland. On June 10, he gave an address in Ohio urging his fellow Democrats to support the administration's war for the good of the country. Lincoln was the commander in chief. Brough reasoned, "Like a soldier in the ranks I hold it to be my duty to obey him . . . without questioning his policy in this great contest." It was just the kind of simple and sincere profession of faith for which the Ohio press had been waiting for. Two Cincinnati dailies, the *Commercial* and the *Enquirer*, printed the speech and took up the call for Brough's nomination. Even radicals in the Union Leagues jumped on the Brough bandwagon, as they did not stand a chance of having one of their true believers win in the fractious environment. Brough secured the nomination over incumbent governor David Tod on the first ballot.[2]

Although Brough was an accomplished orator and respected businessman, prosperity had greatly enlarged his waistline. He cut a rather portly figure when compared to the tall, handsome Vallandigham. The new Union Party candidate needed a running mate who could compete on the stump with Vallandigham and the Democrat's candidate for lieutenant governor, George E. Pugh. The attractive forty-one-year-old Pugh was a decorated veteran of the Mexican war, a former U.S. senator, and a well-respected attorney. With the very future of national unity seeming to rest on the fall elections, Union

Party leaders desired a candidate whose own record of support for the Union cause was exemplary. They selected Charles Anderson.[3]

Anderson did not attend the convention in Columbus. The day after the meeting closed on June 17, 1863, party leader John Caldwell wrote to the candidate to inform him of his nomination to run for lieutenant governor. The following day, Anderson received another letter from an old friend, newly elected U.S. congressman William Johnston. The congressman congratulated Anderson on his achievement and proposed a tongue-in-cheek campaign slogan: "Charlie is lean and Jack's not that. A steak of lean and a steak of fat." There would be few such humorous moments in this campaign, which has been remembered by many historians as one of the nastiest gubernatorial races in U.S. history.[4]

One man who was not pleased about Anderson's nomination was his brother and mentor, Larz. On June 26, Larz expressed displeasure at the thought of his youngest brother reentering politics. Politics was for the wealthy, Larz insisted. His brother appeared consistently on the verge of financial ruin. After Charles explained his rationale, however, his older brother gave him his blessing. Charles accepted the nomination on July 1. In his acceptance letter, he claimed that the election of Vallandigham to the governor's chair would be "a greater calamity than the defeat and capture of any army we have in the field." On July 4, Larz wrote a letter pledging his support. "I am glad that you have accepted the nomination," Larz admitted, "not on your own account, but for the sake of the country." His younger brother was making "a great sacrifice," Larz realized, "against all personal predilections and objections, to duty and patriotism." He advised Charles not to focus on the legality of Vallandigham's arrest. Concentrate instead on the war as the way to save the Union, Larz pleaded. Knowing that his brother could not afford to make the run, Larz sent him five hundred dollars to use toward campaign expenses.[5]

The Ohio gubernatorial election became a referendum on Lincoln's war policies. The same day that Larz gave his blessing to Anderson's candidacy, Lincoln's generals were concluding two key battles that turned the tide of the war. Confederate defeats at Vicksburg and Gettysburg meant that a Union triumph was inevitable. Confederate general John H. Morgan's alarming but ill-advised raid through Indiana and Ohio during July 8–26 also helped rally voters behind the Union cause. The biggest question was whether the public had the stomach for the additional young lives and treasure it would take to finish the job. Brough and Anderson entered the race as the favorites when only weeks before the Democrats had held sway with public opinion.[6]

The campaign was fierce, ugly, and violent. The pace was relentless. The candidates themselves retained an air of civility, but their minions were crass and even vulgar. One of Salmon P. Chase's flunkies contacted Anderson, advising him to tone down his refined image on the stump. "Smoke and throw away your cigarettes," Joseph Geiger wrote to the candidate on July 10. "Use a horse cock," Geiger bleated, and "look like a man, not a female baby." Anderson did not reply. The *Dayton Empire*, reborn after being temporarily censored by Burnside, lashed out at Anderson, branding him an "abolitionist" in the same vein as Joshua Giddings and Salmon Chase. "We cannot conceive how any man can long remain in such company," the *Empire* sneered, "without becoming black." In fact, Anderson despised the abolitionists nearly as much as he reviled the Copperheads.[7]

Ohio senator John Sherman and his brother, General William T. Sherman, were personal friends of Anderson and lent their support. Senator Sherman hit the road delivering countless speeches in support of the Brough-Anderson ticket. He ridiculed Copperhead complaints about Vallandigham's arrest and exile. If Democrats really must vote for someone they felt was wronged, then vote for Anderson, Sherman reasoned, "who suffered ten thousand times more at the hands of traitors" than had Vallandigham in his civilized banishment. General Sherman was typically blunt. Vallandigham's supporters were cowards, the general insisted in an August letter to Anderson. "They try to cover up their cowardice with a plan of peace." "I have seen such men in battle," Sherman continued. "When bursting shells and hissing bullets made things uncomfortable, they would suddenly discover that they were sick or had left something back in camp. I am no voter but I have some 20 lb. rifles that have more sense than 4,100 of the voters of Ohio," the general exclaimed. "If you want them say so."

This election was the first in which Ohio soldiers in the field could cast a legal vote. Joseph Leeds of the Seventy-Ninth Ohio Infantry wrote that there was not much excitement in camp as all but a dozen soldiers in his regiment were voting for Brough. He described a "frolick" that the men had a few days before the election. "We hung old Val in effigy," Leeds related, "and if we had the old boy himself we would serve him the same way." Numerous officers, like Colonel Stephen McGroarty of the Sixty-First Ohio Infantry, were given furloughs so they could hit the meeting circuit and stump for the Union candidates.[8]

The candidates barnstormed all over the state. From mid-August through mid-September, Anderson gave nineteen speeches in thirty-four days. Pugh's voice gave out during an exhausting campaign schedule as he stood in for his exiled running mate. As victory for Brough and Anderson neared, the election rhetoric grew more personal. Vallandigham gained a coup of sorts on August 21, when Anderson's brother Marshall declared for the Democrats. Marshall's logic was simple. Whoever supports the war effort, by virtue of the Emancipation Proclamation, supports abolitionism. "Abolitionism," Anderson's brother declared, "is the sire and dam of disunion." Marshall had worked hard early in the war to enlist troops and willingly sent two sons into Union service. His nephew died at Vicksburg. What he could not abide, however, was the loss of civil liberties that Lincoln's wartime actions foreshadowed. He supported Vallandigham, he declared, because he preferred "the principle of Liberty to the price of blood."

Marshall went on to compare the Union ticket to a jockey and his horse. "Smiling Jack" Brough left Anderson carrying the heavy speaking load during the campaign. If not kept to a focused message, Marshall claimed, "just as sure as the glowing hide of the fat knight emits the odors of Africa, so surely will Charley fly the track, and then 'farewell, a long farewell to all your hopes and glory.'" Vallandigham sent the same message about Anderson in a less brotherly tone: "Charles is a very uncertain quantity—a filthy gentleman whose brain is not very securely anchored in his skull cap." Political independence was not something that many politicians or even brothers understood or respected.[9]

On September 18, Anderson gave the last of his campaign speeches in Mount Vernon, Ohio. A day later, the bloody Battle of Chickamauga began. Anderson's former regiment suffered severely, among nearly thirty-five thousand casualties. Its commanding officer, Colonel Hiram Strong, was mortally wounded. Other friends and family were casualties of this epic battle. Colonel Nicholas Anderson of the Sixth Ohio suffered grave injuries. Kitty Anderson's fiancé, the loyal and brave Will Jones, died on the field. Charles Anderson went home to grieve with his daughter, hoping that this military defeat would not turn the tide of the election. He need not have worried.

Brough and Anderson won the day by more than one hundred thousand votes amid the largest turnout in Ohio electoral history. They won the soldier vote by a majority of nearly forty thousand, while winning both Vallandigham's home county and the city of Dayton. Officials in the Lincoln administration celebrated. Treasury secretary Salmon P. Chase said that the Union could "count every ballot a bullet fairly aimed at the heart of the rebellion." Lincoln himself admitted that he was more anxious about the Brough-Vallandigham contest than he had been over his own election in 1860. When Ohio governor David Tod wired the good news to the president, Lincoln reportedly responded, "Glory to God in the highest; Ohio has saved the Union."[10]

➤➤ ◂◂

CHAPTER EIGHTEEN

The Pit Bull
and the President

THE OHIO ELECTION RESULTS WERE widely publicized, thrusting Anderson back into the national spotlight. When New York's Union Party faced a tough battle with Democrats for control of the state legislature, party leader William P. Wellen reached out to Anderson, asking him to speak before the November 3 contest. He declined. Anderson had made it clear to anyone listening during his own campaign that he was in the race for one purpose only: to win the war and save the Union. "I am and expect to be neither a Republican nor a Democrat," he declared. "The one is not better than the other." In later years he looked back on this opportunity, calling himself a "fool." Anderson believed that his stubborn independence and refusal to go fishing for higher office may have ultimately cost him a shot at the vice presidency.[1]

David Tod identified with Anderson's unfettered stance. The governor, a radical Democrat before the war, had governed under the Union banner. Tod placed the welfare of the country above party loyalties. As his administration wound down, the governor, who had demonstrated so much commitment and patriotism in raising volunteers for the war, searched for ways to secure his legacy. He looked to Anderson to help his cause by staying the course. The governors of the various states that had suffered casualties at the epic Battle of Gettysburg were asked to send delegations to a ceremony in November 1863. The consecration of a new national cemetery within the borders of the battlefield prompted this great gathering. President Lincoln, Secretary of State William Seward, and countless other government officials planned to attend. Tod embraced the idea with more enthusiasm than any of his peers. He assembled a large delegation of state officials, including former governor William Dennison, Brough, and Anderson, to represent Ohio at a mass meeting the evening following the dedication. When it came to a featured speaker for the event, Tod's choice was obvious. He asked the lieutenant governor-elect to prepare suitable remarks for the occasion. Anderson eagerly accepted.[2]

The governor and most of the Ohio delegation departed on Monday, November 16. They expected to stop for the night in Altoona, Pennsylvania, but fate intervened. Two freight engines collided on the tracks near Coshocton, Ohio, so the dignitaries were delayed after a trip of fewer than eighty miles. Tod was already under attack from Democratic newspapers for funding the transportation from the state treasury. He and his fellow passengers added fuel to the fire when they spent the next four hours enjoying libations at a local distillery called Hay's Fountain. "High Times on the Way to Gettysburg," jeered the headline in the *Daily Ohio Statesman*. The *Cincinnati Enquirer* hooted that Ohio's public officials "should be ashamed of themselves."[3]

Brough and Anderson missed the party at Hay's Fountain, joining the delegation in Harrisburg, Pennsylvania, on Tuesday. The railroad added as many extra trains as they could as the assemblage swelled to more than fifteen thousand. Governors from at least eight states arrived in the tiny town of Gettysburg with their entourages. The Presidential Guard, multiple detachments of infantry, eight companies of artillery, and a cavalry unit converged on the scene. Shortly after sundown, President Lincoln, three cabinet secretaries, foreign diplomats, and distinguished citizens disembarked for the next day's festivities. When the immense crowd pleaded with the president to speak, he made his apologies. Lincoln was ill and fatigued.[4]

One man who seldom appeared tired was legendary Massachusetts politician and educator Edward Everett. David Willis, who helped finance the cemetery project and organized the event, chose Everett for the dedication's principal speech. He so coveted the famous orator that he was willing to delay the consecration a month to give Everett adequate time to prepare. Everett's pedigree was impressive. He was a former governor who had served in both houses of Congress. He held the post of ambassador to the United Kingdom and later became the twentieth U.S. secretary of state. Everett was once a Unitarian preacher and a former president of Harvard College. His unsuccessful candidacy for vice president on the John Bell ticket in 1860 closed out his political career, and he became a full-time orator. His words were much anticipated by the throngs attending the memorial ceremonies.

November 19 dawned cold, and a heavy fog reinforced the solemnity of the occasion. At ten o'clock the long retinue of dignitaries began a slow march through the streets of Gettysburg to the cemetery. The head of the procession arrived at the speaker's platform at a quarter past eleven, when the soldiers honored the president with a military salute and the dedication program began. Lincoln sat between Seward and Everett on the packed stand. The crowd listened as the band played a funeral dirge composed by Adolph Birgfeld called "Homage d'un Heros." The Reverend Thomas H. Stockton, chaplain of the U.S. House of Representatives, then gave a long and soulful prayer, which left most people in the audience, including Lincoln and Everett, in tears. Another musical interlude followed before Everett rose to deliver the keynote address.

Everett's speaking style was classical in every sense. He prepared meticulously for each major oration and usually memorized his speeches. He had poured over maps of the battlefield and interviewed participants. His purpose was not only to honor the dead but also to inform and inspire the living. Battlefield memorials were his specialty. He had given memorial speeches at Lexington, Concord, and Bunker Hill. Everett was world renowned for his dramatic flair, his sweet, almost musical voice, and his commanding stage presence. He rivaled the great actors of his day in his ability to hold an audience spellbound for hours. But the Massachusetts icon was also a sick old man who would be dead in a little more than a year. This was to be one of his last important moments.

Everett's oration did not disappoint. He opened his address by demonstrating his intimate knowledge of Greek culture and military history, comparing the present consecration to the funerary customs of ancient Athens. Referencing the funerary speech of the great Pericles before him, Everett relished his unusual opportunity to eulogize the recently slain on the very soil they died defending. One observer appreciated the intelligence of the speaker, as he placed the epic battle into the broader context of world history. This same witness remarked that, despite Everett's regal bearing, he appeared somewhat aloof, like a Greek statue. Others listened with "breathless silence" as tears streamed down their cheeks.

Everett delivered a long discourse on the history of both the Gettysburg battle and the war. He laid blame for the conflict squarely on the shoulders of ambitious politicians from the cotton states. Everett made his case in the dignified and learned manner he felt was appropriate to such an occasion. The famous orator did not need to use incendiary language to repeat well-worn charges against the enemies of the Union. Yet he appeared naïve in his conciliatory call for reunion at the close of his speech. The great masses of Southerners, he claimed, held "no bitterness" against the government in the North. On the contrary, they were "yearning to see the dear old flag floating upon their capitols, and they sigh for the return of peace, prosperity and happiness, which they enjoyed under a government whose power was felt only in its blessings." History would prove him wrong on this point. Recrimination was lodged deep in the hearts of most citizens of both sections, the North and the South, after nearly three years of bloody slaughter.[5]

Lincoln's famous address was intended to be little more than the brief "dedicatory remarks" mentioned in the event programs. His two-minute masterpiece stood in sharp contrast to Everett's two-hour dissertation. Unlike Everett, Lincoln had not mastered Greek and was hardly an expert on classical history. His simple, direct language came from the heart. The president's words transcended the battle itself, imparting lasting meaning to the immense sacrifice and tying the results of the war to a new vision of America's future. In the last third of his remarks, Lincoln referred to an "unfinished work" and "great task" without specifically mentioning either the war or the South. The great cause of reunion was in the hands of the people, as the president so elegantly stated. Under his leadership they would win the war and save the republic.

The dedication ceremony broke up around two in the afternoon. Governor Tod announced that the Ohio delegation's meeting would be held at the Gettysburg Presbyterian Church on Baltimore Street early that evening. The building had been used as a hospital for cavalry troops during the battle but was restored in time for the event. Tod urged Lincoln, Seward, and other important personages to attend the gathering so they could hear Anderson speak. They readily accepted the invitation. This was supposed to be Anderson's show, but an ordinary seventy-year-old tradesman ended up stealing the headlines.[6] Old John Burns was a grizzled veteran of the War of 1812. When the rebels appeared near the doorstep of his farm in sleepy Gettysburg, the old shoemaker grabbed his ancient rifle and begged Union commanders to enlist his aid as a sharpshooter to help defend the town. California writer and poet Bret Harte composed a ballad about him:

> The only man who didn't back down
> When the rebels rode through his native town;
> But held his own in the fight next day,
> When all his town folk ran away.[7]

Burns mustered in with the 105th Pennsylvania Volunteers on the spot. It was said that he brought down three Confederate soldiers. Lincoln had heard the tale and made Burns his special guest for the evening. The aged hero and the president walked arm in arm in an informal procession to the Presbyterian Church. Before the president arrived, an overflowing assembly had been seated.

Governor Tod called the meeting to order. Tod appointed ex-governor William Dennison chairman of the meeting and instructed journalist I. P. Allen to function as secretary. Tod hoped that the meeting would comfort the families of fallen soldiers to know that Ohio not only appreciated their sacrifice but also understood what it meant to the great cause of reunion. Some attendees urged General Robert C. Schenck to say a few words, but the "Hero of Vienna" declined to upstage his old friend Anderson. With the formalities concluded about a quarter past five, Lincoln, Seward, and the secretary of the interior James P. Usher made their entrance to the enthusiastic applause of the capacity crowd. Burns, wearing the simple costume of a country farmer, sat in a pew between Lincoln and Seward. Dennison rose and introduced the featured speaker, who was treated to "rousing cheers" by the large audience. Anderson was in his element.[8]

Anderson's oration was, in comparison to the words of Everett and Lincoln, as a revival meeting is to a formal homily and a benediction. Everett was erudite and subdued. Anderson was fiery and provocative. Whereas Lincoln promised a restoration of freedom and republican ideals, Anderson vowed to crush the rebellion at any cost. Fresh off a vitriolic campaign where defeat foretold unimaginable political consequences, the lieutenant governor–elect had a message to deliver: The memorial is over. This is a rally. Let's go forth and finish the job at hand. He began with an admonition, so that the crowd would not misunderstand the purpose of the convocation. Even though Ohio was the only state to hold its own meeting in conjunction with the dedication ceremonies, this was "no narrow and exclusive prejudice of state pride." Theirs was a meeting to promote the national interest. Ohio had sacrificed her fathers and sons for the Union cause. All of the loyal states had a solemn duty to uphold: repay the national sacrifice and restore peace and prosperity to the country.[9]

Anderson had credibility when it came to speaking about personal sacrifice to the Union cause. His border-state upbringing and long residence in a free state gave him a broad perspective on the key issues of the war. His legendary political independence assured listeners that his words were not merely propaganda emanating from an administration true-believer. His differences with Lincoln were well known, but on the one overriding issue, he and Lincoln were on exactly the same page. He stood in the church at Gettysburg as an unyielding apostle of Unionism. The audience listened with interest and respect.

The speaker dispensed with Everett's conciliatory tone and spoke in a more direct manner. In memorial gatherings it was customary to tread cautiously so as not to offend the living, Anderson admitted, but "the dead must have justice at their own graves." One should not be overly concerned with refinement or charity in such dire circumstances, Anderson insisted. Instead, he said, "We should speak and judge . . . without the cowardice of fearing that our catholic truths shall be miscalled politics." This was the proper way to respect the dead and their ultimate sacrifice. The retired colonel then launched into a withering attack on the invaders with images of brutal honesty that were the hallmarks of his verbose yet engaging style. "That host of rebels, deluded and sent hither by conspirators and traitors, were vanquished and fled cowering in dismay from this land of Penn and Franklin—of Peace and Freedom—across the Potomac into the domain of Calhoun and Davis—of oligarchic rule and despotic oppressions." Anderson defined treason as "the bottom sin" and used biblical passages from Luke, excerpts from Shakespeare, and the poetry of Byron and Shelley to illustrate his points.

But his choicest missiles were launched straight from the heart. Anderson mocked the Southern conspirators as debased aristocrats who "were born into the inheritance of unjust power; nurtured by the milk of slaves and slavery, rocked in their cradle by servile hands." Southern planters were "schooled in their lessons and their sports, into the indulgences of unrestrained passions," only to be "indulged, persuaded and flattered by Northern Allies and Panderers." These privileged despots, "cultured into morbid activities and pampered, at last, into insane, parricidal, suicidal arrogance," plotted against and eventually betrayed "our very Civilization as a people." Anderson was getting carried away by his own passion and recrimination. The crowd ate it up.

The very dead that lay just yards away were not sleeping the peaceful sleep of honored heroes that Everett spoke of so calmly and eloquently. "Their blood cries out from all this beloved ground," Anderson exclaimed, "to all these wide heavens above, for God has heard that cry." He warned that "a yet bloodier retribution awaits— nay now falls upon—those wretched men, whose crime neither Earth can hide nor the seas can cleanse." The speaker was careful to absolve the majority of his Southern brethren and even military leaders like the noble Lee from his excoriating characterizations. "The wicked purposes of vile and desperate politician traitors," Anderson explained, "have overruled the good dispositions and infatuated and misguided the honest impulses" of the people.

At stake in the terrible conflict, Anderson insisted, was a cause much greater than a particular political or military leader. This was a people's war fought for sacred principles. With characteristic audacity, the excited speaker faced Lincoln and presented a chilling scenario. "Let them seize and destroy our National City—its wood into ashes and its marble into sand. Let them imprison—hang—burn our President with all the heads and hands of the departments. . . . Yet we are still a nation. Foreign monarchy must understand—Domestic Oligarchy must re-learn, that our National Being flows on forever in a stream of moral principles and not through any chain of printed deeds or written charters." This was a macabre scene painted by an excited partisan. It was certainly an Anderson original. Lincoln and his cabinet members may have squirmed in their pews, but the audience cheered "wildly."

Survival of the republican ideal, Anderson claimed, was the nation's God-given destiny. The course of nature will not change "to please a junta of insane slavery oligarchs," the speaker assured the crowd. Society cannot go backward "into the chaos of black barbarism and of red despotism, at the bidding of these puny and palsied Canutes of South Carolina and Mississippi," Anderson roared. The assembly broke into immense cheering in response to this creative insult to their arch enemies. Applause and shouting continued for several minutes. When he resumed, Anderson sketched a convincing picture of the everyday soldier. They died, not for political purposes, nor to free the slaves, but "to save the nation's life." Their homespun honesty and humble nobility made an effective contrast with the monstrous personalities that Anderson had just finished inventing.[10]

Once he had gained his audience's attention, Anderson repeated a familiar refrain, lauding America as an original and exceptional new creation of civil government. Disunion by the traitors destroyed not only the best government ever created by man but also disrupted commerce and threatened to end what had been unprecedented prosperity. The mere suggestion that the two sections could exist as separate nations with common borders and not end up as two warring, military regimes was preposterous. The ensuing military republic in the North would be only slightly less evil than the military oligarchy that already existed in the Confederate States. The defeat of Vallandigham should have put that issue to rest, but Anderson had an inkling that the fantasy of a peaceable separation might resurface. The lion could only lie down with the lamb if the lion became like a lamb, not the other way around. The cheers from the audience resumed.

As the address was winding down, Anderson could not resist the impulse to offer his opinion on the most controversial topic of the day: the emancipation of the slaves. He had committed political suicide in public so many times that he had lost all fear of retribution. Lincoln and especially the radical abolitionist Seward must have braced themselves at the broaching of the subject. The Democrats had been playing the race card for many years. As long as the opposition press tried to claim that the war's sole purpose was abolition, the Peace Party would be a force to reckon with.

The Copperheads argued that general emancipation would release a flood of black barbarism and cheap labor and create a huge dependent pauper class in the North. These predictions were valid, according to Anderson, only if a separate slave nation were to be established alongside the free North. If slavery were to be abolished throughout the South, on the other hand, the freedmen would have little incentive to pick up and move. The speaker said that he was willing to "tolerate the master-disease and crime within the Union" for a time until it gradually ran its course. This was the position favored by Lincoln earlier in his political career. The key was reunion, with or without slavery, according to Anderson. That said, he shared the fears of the vast majority of his fellow Ohio citizens. They could not abide a sudden influx of black faces taking up residence in the house next door.

"So seriously do I estimate those evils," Anderson stated, "that if all other causes of war against the establishment and recognition of the Southern Confederacy of slave states could be obviated and removed, I do really think that these dangers from having our land converted into a vast Cloaca Maxima [sewer] for their overflowing filth, would constitute a just and sufficient cause to war, to the end of the century." Many people thought the same way but precious few Union or Republican politicians dared to speak such words in a public forum. Anderson was a powerful orator and could be as vicious as a pit bull when the occasion demanded such vitriol. In politics, however, he was loose cannon.

Anderson's speech lasted less than an hour. Despite its controversial ending, he received universal praise from those in attendance. Lincoln shook Anderson's hand and congratulated him on his fine effort. Seward agreed. Brough and Anderson left with the presidential party on the 6:30 p.m. train to Washington. The Ohio delegation passed a resolution of thanks for the colonel's "able and eloquent" address and requested that he publish it for posterity. Excerpts of the speech appeared in a few newspapers, such as the *Cincinnati Commercial* and the *Springfield Republican*, but the entire speech was never printed. The explanation of S. A. Hines, editor of the *Cincinnati Gazette*, was typical. The Everett speech had taken up so much space that it left little room for Anderson's words. When Anderson looked for the manuscript thirty years later, he could not find it.

The three addresses at Gettysburg were not a random collection of individual orations. They were a carefully planned and constructed ensemble designed to accomplish different yet complimentary purposes. Each speaker intended to eulogize to some degree. Everett's style was deliberate. He sought to educate his audience. Lincoln was inspirational. He intended to elevate the war to a higher moral plane. Anderson was provocative. His address was designed to motivate, even agitate the crowd to support a vigorous prosecution of the war. Lincoln's words entered the canon of American scripture where they remained, timeless and permanent. Everett's speech was printed and then largely forgotten. Anderson's oration had an even shorter exposure, disappearing from sight immediately and remaining buried for nearly 150 years.

➤➤ ◄◄

Unfortunate Misstep

O N THE TRAIN FROM DAYTON to Columbus in January 1864, just two months after his speech at Gettysburg, Charles Anderson reflected on his future. He was about to assume one of the most meaningless jobs in government. The lieu-tenant governor–elect had responded to the call of duty in yet an-other critical hour of his beloved, fragile Union. He planned to serve his term, assist the new governor in sustaining the war effort, and enjoy time with old friends and rivals in the state legislature. A Union military victory appeared inevitable. Anderson wanted to use this interlude to prepare for the next chapter in his life. He had no idea where that road might lead.

Anderson gave a brief, reserved address to the Ohio state legisla-ture at the inaugural ceremonies, occupied his new office, and went to work. He found the administrative workload stifling. His lack of any real authority made the job mundane and trivial. John Brough was busy raising an additional thirty thousand volunteers in reply to President Lincoln's request for more troops. Anderson was relegated to menial tasks. He relieved his boredom frequently at his brother Larz's house in Cincinnati. He spent an entire day there dressed in full theatrical costume, channeling the lead character for a local pro-duction of Macbeth. After several agonizing months in a job he de-tested, Anderson wondered what he was supposed to do next. Union Party bosses had their own ideas.[1]

Despite his previous pronouncements, Governor Brough fell in line to support Lincoln's reelection bid. He had expressed differences with the president for many years, but the war persisted, and he was determined to stand behind the commander in chief. His lieutenant governor, on the other hand, had a long record of political independence and would not kowtow to the leader of any party. Anderson was aghast when the radical abolitionists co-opted the president's agenda and turned a war for the salvation of the Union into a war to free the slaves. The ramifications of this growing crusade were vast. Many working-class Americans recoiled at the thought that their sons and brothers were dying to free the Negro. Once the war was over, many feared that a veritable flood of newly freed slaves would leave the devastated South and invade the industrial North, bringing with them a debased standard of morality and competing with whites for work. Americans had also grown weary of a war where the result seemed decided, but there was no immediate end in sight.[2]

Anderson worried about what the postwar nation would be like. Divisions in the country and even in his own party made Lincoln's reelection, perhaps even his renomination, appear doubtful. Radicals like New York newspaper editor Horace Greeley were not satisfied with the president's moderate stances on abolition and reconstruction and called for an alternate Republican candidate. Lincoln's own secretary of the treasury, Salmon P. Chase, plotted to become the nominee. In April the U.S. Senate passed the Thirteenth Amendment abolishing slavery in the United States and areas under its control. Lincoln was eventually nominated in early June. The Democrats responded in August by selecting General George McClellan, who had been relieved of his command by Lincoln earlier in the war. Resurfacing at the Democratic convention in Chicago was none other than Clement Vallandigham, who gave the keynote address and drafted the party platform. Lincoln ignored Vallandigham's illegal repatriation rather than stir up the expelled Democrat's most ardent supporters.[3]

Indiana governor Oliver P. Morton and Ohio Union Party leader Godwin V. Dorsey reached out to Anderson in August, asking him to join Governor Brough in stumping for Lincoln in their states. Anderson refused. He was not satisfied with either candidate. "As for Mr. Lincoln," he predicted, "he might well attempt to row up the Niagara Chute in a particularly frail birch bark canoe, with a particularly weak feather for a paddle, as to talk about abolishing slavery as a condition for reunion." Lincoln's "personal facility in changing course to every last wind" was troubling to Anderson. "It is a cruel duty to declare against my own political friends," the lieutenant governor declared, "but it is my duty."[4]

Anderson underestimated Lincoln's political genius and paddling ability. McClellan unwittingly helped the president's cause by refusing to accept the portion of the Democratic platform that represented the war as a failure, thus splitting with the Copperhead faction of the party. But Northern morale was sinking. Lincoln himself told a soldier in late August: "I am going to be beaten, and unless some great change takes place, *badly* beaten." While Lincoln and his cabinet laid plans to cooperate with the incoming administration, great news arrived on the telegraph. General Sherman had taken Atlanta on September 2. Everyone on both sides of the great conflict knew what that meant. The way was now clear for the Union Army to march virtually unmolested to Savannah and eventually to South Carolina. Sherman was feted in cities across the North as the greatest general of the century. Even the *Richmond Examiner* admitted that the fall of Atlanta had come just in time to "save the party of Lincoln from irretrievable ruin." Two months later. Lincoln won in a landslide.[5]

Anderson was in an awkward position. Peace Democrats despised him. War Democrats merely tolerated him. Republicans felt betrayed by him. His legendary political independence was wearing thin with all but a few loyal friends. Anderson was still respected for his intellectual prowess, his oratorical skills, and his unimpeachable integrity. On the other hand, he was increasingly seen as inflexible and dogmatic in his own extreme brand of Unionism. He was a political liability. Anderson was certain that he was right. Surely the political power brokers and the people of Ohio would see the truth of his opinions and come to think as he did. In case they did not, however, Anderson began to lay plans for a possible retirement elsewhere.

In January 1865, Larz's eldest son, Richard Clough Anderson, negotiated the purchase of a large tract of iron mining lands in Lyon County, Kentucky. Charles Anderson imagined he could eventually enjoy a quiet life filled with "intelligent society, books, and agricultural pursuits," back home in his native state. He needed to defer this dream for at least another year, as his term did not expire until early 1866. Besides, there might be other opportunities coming his way. If he could just get the right people to sponsor him for that long coveted foreign ministry assignment, or even high political office, he might still have a career in politics. Ohio's lieutenant governor was an unusual talent and still had dozens of powerful allies.[6]

A gracious way to escape the tedium of the lieutenant governorship and fulfill a lifelong ambition was to make yet another attempt to secure a foreign diplomatic post. Anderson went after this goal in earnest. One position that he especially desired was minister to Spain, which had been open since Gustav Koerner had resigned in July 1864. Koerner could not reconcile his minuscule salary with the heavy financial obligations at the Spanish court. Anderson conducted a furious letter-writing campaign, enlisting postmaster general William Dennison, a former governor of Ohio, as well as Thomas Corwin, late minister to Mexico, in the effort. Attorney general James Speed, a boyhood pal, and judge advocate general Joseph Holt jumped on the bandwagon. Speed wrote that he had seen Secretary of State Seward on Anderson's behalf, but that the few available positions were already spoken for. Ohio congressman Rutherford B. Hayes told Anderson that he would urge Lincoln to find a post for him. A last ditch effort by another faithful friend, Ohio senator John Sherman, took the matter directly to the president, but Lincoln refused to countermand Seward's intentions. Three days later, Lincoln appointed Senator John Parker Hale of New Hampshire to the post. Anderson could hardly argue that selection, as Hale was an accomplished politician and former Free Soil candidate for president. He was also the father of the beautiful Lucy Lambert Hale, who was secretly engaged to a famous actor named John Wilkes Booth. Dennison and Sherman went to see Seward together three days after the Hale appointment, but the secretary claimed there were no vacancies. Anderson, in his zeal for a plum foreign assignment, just could not take a hint.[7]

Four days after General Lee's surrender on April 9, 1865, Anderson and his brother Robert attended a ceremony to restore the American flag at Fort Sumter, where Robert had surrendered his command after a gallant stand exactly four years earlier. The event was planned shortly after Sherman had captured Charleston in February. Hundreds of ebullient dignitaries were on scene. With the war over, there were several reasons to celebrate. Robert raised the banner that one of his sergeants had risked his life to keep flying during the bombardment. It was hard to tell what was most battered: the cherished flag, torn and tattered by shrapnel, or Robert Anderson himself, broken and worn-out from defending his country in numerous wars. As the remnant flag stiffened in the breeze, cheers arose from the spectators while cannons on island and shore boomed a victory salute. The crowd had no way of knowing that back in Washington, shortly after the Sumter flag was restored, the man who bore the weight of more than six hundred thousand dead on his conscience had entered Ford's Theatre for his own appointment with bloody destiny.[8]

The stunned North collapsed into mourning at the news of Lincoln's assassination. Governors and municipal leaders planned the largest funeral train in U.S. history, passing through seven states to Lincoln's final resting place in Springfield, Illinois. Governors Brough, Morton of Indiana, and Stone of Iowa accompanied the body on its twelve-day, 1,654-mile journey. William G. Deschler, chairman of the ceremonies at Columbus, offered Anderson the honor of delivering the eulogy to the slain president. He declined. Although he and Lincoln had not always been on the best of terms, Anderson would soon realize that the untimely death of Abraham Lincoln was a great tragedy for the South, as Lincoln's own scheme for conciliatory reconstruction died with him.[9]

It was business as usual at first. President Andrew Johnson delivered an amnesty proclamation on May 29, signaling his intention to honor Lincoln's plans and place control of Southern political affairs back in the hands of those who had wielded power before the war. With the conflict over, Republicans and Democrats had much less to squabble about. Even Vallandigham suggested that the Democrats should get behind the new president's reconstruction plans to help heal the nation's gaping wounds. He accepted the fact that slavery was dead. The issue climbing to the forefront of political debate, however, was the political status of black Americans, in both the North and the South. Should they be allowed to vote and become full citizens? This issue, Vallandigham declared, should be settled by each state. He was speaking not only for the Democrats but for an overwhelming majority of whites, including Anderson, who held that same opinion.

Anderson had first gone public on the issue of black suffrage in June 1864, in a speech to the Montgomery County Republican Party nominating convention. The lieutenant governor's resolutions did not mince words. "We are utterly opposed to the enfranchisement of this class," the resolution read, "neither because they are black, nor because they have been slaves merely, but solely because, that having been so recently slaves, we know that as a mass, and upon the average, they are not capable and worthy of this exalted function." Some remembered Anderson's celebrated 1849 speech declaring Anglo-Saxon supremacy a myth and cried foul. How could he assert that blacks were not inherently inferior to whites and then deny them the vote? These critics had not read the speech carefully. One of the central tenets of Anderson's argument was that any people, given the proper conditions and circumstances, could rise to dominance over a less fortunate population. Slaves had been denied basic rights and education for generations. They were not yet ready for such an important responsibility.

Anderson had grown up with slavery, but since he had gone on record early as an opponent of Ohio's Black Laws, his opinions on the so-called "Negro question" carried some credibility. Denying the franchise to newly freed slaves was a nuanced position for abolitionists. They deplored the moral depravity of slavery but recognized the dangers inherent in such radical change. Anderson predicted that giving the vote to blacks immediately would "Africanize—yes, worse still, Mexicanize our people and institutions, which would, in consequence, pass through wildest anarchy into a settled despotism." He urged the party to end this radical agitation or risk ruining both the party and the Union itself.[10]

The topic remained in the forefront of political debate, and everyone seemed to have an opinion. Anderson's close friend General William T. Sherman shared his views on the Negro and other moderate measures of reconstructing the Union. Sherman's opinions, expressed in a social situation, had been published without his consent, thus violating the custom that soldiers should stay out of politics. Anderson was vocal in defending the general. In a private letter to Anderson, Sherman maintained that he had done and was prepared to "do as much toward ameliorating the condition of the negro as anyone," but to give them the franchise would lead to "the utter ruin of their race," or to the damage of the "national character." Giving blacks the franchise was a political ploy by the radicals to manufacture votes, Sherman argued. "Our country needs repose," the general counseled. To place newly freed slaves on the same political and social footing as whites would create new troubles. These attempts were, in Sherman's words, "mischievous and dangerous." Sherman wanted the president to stop wasting his time pardoning individuals, declare a general amnesty for the South, and get on with the business of an orderly and peaceful reunion. Anderson shared these hopes. Both men suffered disappointment as reunion devolved into partisanship.[11]

Early in 1865, Brough had turned down Lincoln's offer to succeed Salmon P. Chase as treasury secretary. Now that his term as governor was winding down, Brough had to decide whether to run again or go back to his business career. It was an easy decision. The governor had grown unpopular with military officers when he insisted on awarding promotions strictly on seniority rather than merit. The public had become accustomed to the refined manners and dignified bearing of previous chief executives. They did not love the hard-working but gruff "Fat Jack." On June 16, Brough announced that he would not stand for reelection. He had taken the job only out of a sense of duty, he declared, and he had done his work honestly and conscientiously. Just days after the announcement, Brough was walking across the State House yard when he stumbled and fell, bruising his hand and badly spraining his ankle. This seemingly innocuous event had significant consequences for Anderson.[12]

While Brough nursed his ankle, Anderson continued to campaign for a diplomatic assignment. The United States minister to the Kingdom of Italy, George Perkins Marsh, had been appointed to the post by Lincoln in 1861. Marsh was already an accomplished diplomat, having served under President Zachary Taylor as minister to the Ottoman Empire. In 1864 he wrote a book titled *Man and Nature* that would establish his fame as the father of the U.S. conservation movement. In 1865, however, Marsh's son was dying, so he was granted leave to return home and care for him. The word on the street was that Marsh would soon resign his post. Anderson trotted out a series of big names to support his candidacy to succeed Marsh, but Secretary Seward was still recovering from a near fatal encounter with one of Booth's co-conspirators. In the meantime, the indefatigable Brough was trying to move his immense frame around with a cane, which inflamed his injuries. Gangrene set in. On July 19, Sidney Maxwell, Brough's aide de camp, reported that the governor was hemorrhaging and had developed a "congestive chill." He did not believe that Brough would recover.[13]

While Charles Anderson was filling in for the bedridden governor, Ohio senator Robert C. Schenck had made some headway with President Johnson. "Andy wants a note calling attention to your case," Schenck wrote. The senator sat down and wrote the note in front of the president, who endorsed it, instructing Seward to give it special attention. Seward acted as if he had never met Anderson, despite having greeted him just eighteen months earlier at Gettysburg. In the meantime, Governor Morton of Indiana was sponsoring his own candidate for the expected vacancy—a poet and artist named Thomas Brennan Read. Morton had even convinced General William T. Sherman to endorse the recommendation. Sherman sheepishly admitted that he did not know that Anderson was seeking the post. Ohio senator Benjamin Franklin Wade also saw the president, who made it clear that he would defer to Seward. "It passes my comprehension," John Sherman wrote on August 2, "that Seward says he did not know of your application." It was all a big waste of energy, as Marsh decided to return to his post. He ended up holding the position for twenty-one years, the longest such service in U.S. history.[14]

General Benjamin Rush Cowen wrote Anderson on August 26 to tell him that Brough had again taken a turn for the worse. "Friends have given up all hope of his recovery," Cowen lamented, "and the governor himself has ceased to hope." Two days later, Brough died and Anderson became governor. One of his first official acts was to declare a day of mourning on September 1. He asked that businesses close their doors from ten a.m. to three p.m. in remembrance of their departed leader. Those who knew Anderson well wondered if this unexpected honor would be a blessing or a curse to a man so utterly fed up with politics. George Henshaw, a Cincinnati furniture dealer and family friend, was unsure if he should offer "congratulations or condolences." Noting that Anderson's name would now go down in Ohio history, Henshaw remarked to his friend "Whether this is a source of gratification to yourself you alone know."[15]

Anderson began his four-month gubernatorial tenure by lobbying Secretary of War Stanton to allow Ohio's volunteer army units to muster out of service. The war was over, Anderson reminded the secretary. The brave men who volunteered their service in that cause should be discharged immediately. In September, Governor Anderson ordered the books of the state treasury audited. He discovered that Ohio treasurer Godwin Volney Dorsey had been embezzling state funds during wartime. This revelation turned Anderson's stomach. He ordered the popular Dorsey arrested. When critics accused the governor of exceeding his authority by exercising judicial powers without a trial, Anderson's reply was straight from Lincoln's own playbook. "Powers legally wanting must be forcibly usurped," he argued, "to meet an exigency and danger to the public." Ohio attorney general Chauncey Olds backed the governor's decision.[16]

Anderson spent the balance of his lame duck term networking with old friends and planning his future. Being elected governor was never a consideration. He did not want the job and, besides, party leaders had already made their choice. Union general Jacob Dolson Cox, a former Whig state senator and ardent abolitionist, had helped found Ohio's Republican Party in 1855. He was an advocate for President

Johnson's reconstruction policies. Cox hated slavery but did not think that freedmen had demonstrated that they were ready to assume all of the privileges of citizenship. They should certainly not be allowed to vote. Other former abolitionists, such as Henry B. Payne, shared the same moderate views on black suffrage. They courted Anderson as a potential dark horse for the U.S. Senate race in 1866. It was another false hope, as both John Sherman and Robert Schenck, whom Payne expected to align with radicals like Massachusetts senator Charles Sumner, refused to show their hands on the controversial issue.[17]

When it came time to deliver the traditional annual state message for the year 1866, Anderson saw an opportunity to give his political views their widest airing to date. While he did not address the issue of full black citizenship directly, he did weigh in obliquely. The now fractious Union Party and Governor-elect Cox had been unable to agree on a unified platform and deferred the matter to the incoming legislature. Radical senators from the the northeast corner of Ohio introduced a resolution to strike the word "white" from the state constitution. Anderson took a firm stand against the proposal and pointed out that any amendments to the constitution in such times were probably unwise and would need to be considered in the election of 1867. The issue was not settled until the ratification of the Fifteenth Amendment in 1870, which prohibited states from denying the franchise to men on the basis of race. The Ohio legislature approved the Fifteenth Amendment by just one vote in the senate and by a mere two votes in the house.

Besides the typical reporting on public works, finance, railroad, and pending legislation, Governor Anderson felt compelled to offer his opinion on what the press was calling the "Mexican Imbroglio." Mexico's domestic affairs had been a mess for years. The French had taken advantage of this internal strife and America's preoccupation with its own civil war by invading Mexico. They had established a Catholic-sponsored government headed by Maximillian Ferdinand, a Hapsburg archduke from Austria. The United States had been vocal in sponsoring republican movements to oust European colonial gov-

ernments throughout Latin America, and the thought of a permanent French colony on its southern doorstep was unsettling to say the
least. Now that the war was over and the Union controlled a huge
army, some were invoking the Monroe Doctrine and suggesting that
the United States conquer Mexico as part of its manifest destiny.

Anderson bristled at the very prospect of another bloody war
based on what he believed were false principles. The governor invoked Washington's farewell address, which warned against "entangling alliances," arguing that the Monroe Doctrine proscribed that
the United States assume "guardianship over all the imbeciles of
the continent or globe." Mexico could never be a true republic after
forty years of anarchy, Anderson maintained. He called Mexicans
a "population of fanatics and barbarians" and wished "they could
only go back into Aztecs." He could not help but revisit the annexation of Texas that he had so strongly opposed. "Without that fatal
golden apple of discord," Anderson audaciously claimed, "we should
not have had our War of Rebellion." Anderson equated the aim to
"propagandize Liberty" to Mexicans with past efforts to promote
Christianity to the "Saracens of Jerusalem or the Chinese at Peking."
He closed by again invoking Washington's "eleventh commandment":
mind your own business.[18]

Anderson's state of the state message created a sensation. Dozens
of letters poured in from all over the country requesting copies of the
speech. The *New York Times* published a long article on the address,
with fully half of the text devoted to the governor's position on the
Mexican question. General William T. Sherman weighed in immediately with his complete endorsement of Anderson's position. The
general was convinced that it would be "suicide . . . as a nation to
engage in a new war with an old one yet smoldering." Sherman was
aware that some of his peers, including General Ulysses S. Grant,
were pushing for action against France in Mexico. "I don't care,"
declared Sherman, "and will assert my own convictions regardless
of their popularity." Little wonder Sherman and Anderson were such
close friends.[19]

War hawks attacked Anderson's New Year message. Famed archeologist and U.S. commissioner to Peru, Ephraim George Squier,

described the reaction in New York. Anderson's address was greeted by "mingled groans and hisses," according to Squier. Cries of "Turn him out!" came presumably from less informed listeners who did not realize that the governor had only a few days left to serve. "When you come to New York," Squier advised, "be sure to register yourself under another name." Anderson rewrote the speech in French so that even the colonists in Mexico would know exactly where he stood. In the end, however, Seward rattled the saber, France backed down, and Benito Juarez established a Mexican republic.[20]

Anderson's four months back in the national spotlight were over. He had few plans and essentially no political capital. He had always stood resolute on principle in the face of whatever forceful winds might be blowing against him, but he had never encountered a gale as strong as that being produced by Sumner and his Radical Republican acolytes. The changes they wrought were certain to wipe Anderson clean off the political map and transform his beloved country in ways he had barely begun to imagine.

→→ ←←

CHAPTER TWENTY

Dreams Lost
and Fulfilled

I T DID NOT TAKE CHARLES ANDERSON long to realize that the country that he had loved since boyhood was gone forever. The great republican Union of free and slave states had been tenuously stitched together like a garment that was beautiful in its outward appearance but flawed in its construction. It had literally come apart at the seams. Anderson had dedicated his very soul to preventing disunion, predicted its disastrous consequences, and risked his own life to hold it together. Now the war had been won, not to preserve the Union that his father had fought to create but to usher in a radical new government construct that departed from the practical vision of the Founding Fathers.

Anderson spoke a few words early in the 1866 election canvas at Dayton for which he was roundly condemned, thus signaling the abrupt end of his political career. He called the U.S. Congress "traitors to their principles." They fought a war while denying that there was ever any secession, then passed laws and amendments while eleven of the thirty-six states were disqualified from participating. "I must tell the North," Anderson predicted, "that in following the lead of Congress, they are plunging into another civil war." He warned that radical measures create "national and social destruction . . . through anarchies and despotism." Anderson was revolted by "petty, paltry politicians filling the olden places of our departed statesmen." Republicans howled in protest at his brazen attacks.[1]

President Johnson's moderate reconstruction policies suffered a death blow in the midterm elections of 1866, when Americans elected huge Republican majorities of more than two-thirds in both houses of Congress. Radical Republicans like Senator Charles Sumner and Representative Thaddeus Stevens were unhappy with what they saw as measures by Southern white leaders to restore their own political rights while squelching economic and political opportunities for freedmen. They demanded universal manhood suffrage and finally had the political power to attain that goal. Ignoring Johnson's veto of both the Freedman's Bureau and Civil Rights bills, Congress approved the Fourteenth Amendment to the Constitution, which guaranteed birthright citizenship and equal protection under the law. To enforce the new statutes, the Military Reconstruction Act of 1867 split the former Confederate States into five militia districts administered by the U.S. Army. The South became a police state.[2]

Anderson was heartbroken. He moved his family to Eddyville, Kentucky, near the Lyon County iron lands he had purchased previously where he could divert his mind from his "ruined, lost country (a wreck of prosperities and liberties)." He tried to express his grief at the aftermath of the war but struggled to find the proper words. "Suffice it to say," he lamented, "this is no longer a free country." Anderson drafted a letter to Senator John Sherman, admitting "an inextinguishable desire to leave this Country" and suggested that the vacant mission to Vienna would be appropriate. But he knew that he had killed that dream by his own irresistible impulse to alienate former political allies. He never posted the letter.[3]

Abraham Rencher, a former U.S. congressman from North Carolina and former governor of the New Mexico Territory (whose daughter had married Anderson's son), was less remorseful and more defiant. "Almost any alternative would be preferable," Rencher exclaimed, "to that of having your property and character and even life itself depend on stupid Negroes recently emerged from a state of slavery . . . directed and controlled by those who would feel nothing for us but bitter hatred." Reconstruction was not reconciliation, as Lincoln, Johnson, and Anderson had hoped it would be. It was retribution.[4]

When Governor A. G. Curtin of Kentucky invited Anderson to a convention of Union war veterans in Philadelphia in 1869, he could not bring himself to attend. "I certainly do sympathize with the cause for which we fought," Anderson explained, but he could not abide "the present motives of a majority of [his] associates in that war." He found himself in a "strange position between the two parties," and his conscience would not allow him to align with either. Anderson believed that the Republicans intended to create a partisan, sectional dynasty that would be just as evil as the slavery-based Confederate oligarchy they had so recently defeated. Despite the deep despair Anderson felt in separating from his former comrades, his conviction that the Republican Party had further "debased into a vast, organized faction to secure personal plunder and power" disgusted him. He would rather abandon politics altogether than throw in with his old allies or certain Southern Democrats, who looked the other way as groups like the Ku Klux Klan used violence and intimidation in an attempt to preserve the old social order.[5]

The political landscape that Anderson had known was inverted, as black legislators entered the hallowed halls of Congress while many of the South's former white leaders were denied the franchise. In a time of political extremism, Anderson retired to his rural surroundings, determined to start a new life for himself and his family. The long-deferred boyhood dream of becoming a gentleman farmer had become a reality, only this time Anderson's ambitions were much grander. He aimed to create a model community from scratch. His new home would incorporate all the beauty, economic prosperity, and high-toned social intercourse that he so loved. The project continued for the rest of his life and never came to full fruition, but it gave Anderson a chance to fill a void in his soul. At his new paradise he called Kuttawa, Anderson finally became the man he had always wanted to be.

He chose his retirement place carefully. Much of the land was part of a failed iron mining speculation. He was certain that it still held great promise with the proper application of capital. Anderson's experience with railroads in the Ohio legislature helped him foresee that a need to build new rail lines meant a postwar boom in iron production. But such growth was slow to develop in the economically devastated South. The property incorporated great scenic vistas of the Cumberland River, mineral hot springs, and plenty of pasturage for his stock. It was an ideal location for the country lifestyle that the younger Anderson had envisioned. It also suited his goal of founding an entire community based on his own elaborate plans, since it had natural beauty, abundant resources, and the potential for easy access to the Illinois Central Railroad. Such ambitions required significant investment, however. In 1873, Anderson's description of his finances boiled down to three words: "poverty, debt, and hopelessness." Despite these challenges, he laid out the new town of Kuttawa in 1874 and solicited residents and investors.

Anderson produced extensive plans and drawings of his model community in his own hand. He took care to name each feature in the same sort of romantic language that Frederick Law Olmsted had used decades earlier in enticing Anderson to settle in Texas. Vista Ridge overlooked the river on one side and the town on the other. Mineral springs named Mint, Diamond, Opal, and Wild Rose promised youth-renewing waters capable of curing various diseases and afflictions. The thirty-acre artificial Loch Clough was perfectly situated for visitors traveling to a planned resort to enjoy boating, swimming, and other recreational pursuits. Silver Cliffs was a lovely park that stood hundreds of feet above the languid Cumberland. Anderson envisioned a world-class university perched atop these cliffs, if he could only get Leland Stanford, John D. Rockefeller, or Cornelius Vanderbilt to fund the project. When a friend asked Anderson why he had planned the streets and avenues to be unusually wide, he responded that someday a new method of conveyance would grace the streets of his beautiful Kuttawa. He just did not know what that new vehicle might look like.[6]

Anderson walked his property daily, meticulously planning each landscape feature. He also took time to write letters to old friends and family. There was much to correspond about, especially with old Texas friends whom he had left behind. Foremost among those friends was his "deliverer, that noblest of all the heroines of this dreadful, yet glorious war, Mrs. Ludlum." Anderson found her reasonably well, despite her harsh treatment at the hands of the Texas rebels. He petitioned for Ludlum's appointment as postmistress in San Antonio, but the job was given to someone else. Will Bayard, the young man who had joined Anderson in his escape from Camp Dorn, was attempting to advance a stalled military career. He reported being shunned by Texas relatives who felt betrayed by him. J. C. Houzeau, who had also risked his life to free Anderson, was living in New Orleans, editing the bilingual *New Orleans Tribune*.

George Paschall reported that Governor Pendleton Murrah had robbed the Texas treasury and had drunk himself to death in Monterrey, Mexico, where a number of ex-Confederates had settled. Paschall called it a "buffalo stampede." Anderson's jailor, Henry E. McCulloch, "had the temerity to remain," but Texas chief justice Royal T. Wheeler, who had boasted of his part in Anderson's arrest, proved himself "a coward even in suicide." Paschall described Wheeler "shooting at himself a year before he took his shameless life." One of Anderson's closest Texas friends was Presley Edwards, who had stayed on and cooperated with the rebels. "I think you do injustice to many of your old friends," Edwards wrote in 1870. "There was a discrimination to be made between Unionists and Anti-Secessionists," Edwards claimed. Hard-core, unconditional Southern Union men like Anderson were a rare breed. Most men stood by Anderson until the war began, Edwards explained, but then accepted the sectional reality of the conflict. The war had been over five years, and even Anderson admitted that he still loved old neighbors like his cousin Florida Tunstall, "even if she is a rebel."[7]

There was one relationship in Anderson's life that needed repairing most of all. His brother Marshall had been shunned by many Ohioans on account of his Copperhead sympathies. Marshall was estranged from his family due to his strident Catholicism and his attacks on Charles during the 1863 gubernatorial election. Marshall elected to move to Mexico in 1865, ostensibly to join an archeological expedition. His primary aim was to assist Matthew Maury in establishing the New Virginia Colony as a refuge for former Confederates.

The scheme was a failure and Marshall returned home the following year. His sons and sister were not speaking to him by this time. Charles, on the other hand, reached out to his older brother immediately upon his return and made a generous overture to resume their brotherly affection. Their brother John had died after contracting dysentery while visiting a Union Army camp in August 1863. Robert was failing steadily, and Larz had become chronically ill. This was no time to let past political or religious differences diminish the importance of family.

In December 1872, Charles Anderson began an extended correspondence with Marshall and revealed an intimate secret that he had never shared with anyone outside of his immediate family. Charles was an atheist. "I have long struggled to conceal this want of faith from others as well as myself," the younger brother admitted. It was a lonely situation for Anderson, seeing his brothers and sisters "safe and happy in a Christian faith," while he remained an outsider in "a mere prescribed negation, a vacuity in faith." It had been this way his whole life, he said, despite the positive examples set by his brothers. Once he had read the Bible, Charles suffered "a chronic doubt of its truth," its "strange statements," and its scheme of redemption. Marshall pleaded with his brother to make an attempt at salvation, but Charles could not accept Jesus as savior even to save himself, as that would betray his conscience. He poured his heart out in an attempt to lift this "weighty restraint" that had existed so long between the two brothers. "I have gone beyond my warrant I am sure," Charles admitted, "but when did I ever do otherwise?" His confession of disbelief was an admission that very few politicians or licensed attorneys could afford to make. Now that he was out of the public eye, Charles no longer pretended that he believed. He needed Marshall to know the truth while they both still lived.[8]

The 1870s was an uncertain time for Anderson and his Kentucky neighbors. A financial panic in 1873 caused a loss of confidence and general deflation that lasted nearly six years. Despite these challenges, Anderson's interests in iron mining and the rapid growth of the railroads meant that he fared better than most. The political winds changed direction in the 1876 presidential election. As Anderson watched from the sidelines, a seismic shift was taking place that would change the South dramatically. Southern states were back in the Union and President Grant's administration was suffering from a corruption scandal. Southern Democrats were eager to expel the carpetbaggers and restore their agricultural economy to a system that more closely resembled the prewar period. They nominated New York governor Samuel J. Tilden as their candidate. Anderson was "grieved, shocked and stunned" at this result. It was not Tilden or the Democrats whom he opposed, but rather the way that the nominee's henchmen bribed editors in Kentucky and purchased delegates at the convention. Now Tilden was pandering to the base prejudices of Southerners who wanted to divide the country once again "by the old slavery line." He could not abide what he considered "the gangrene" of politics.[9]

Three days before the election, Anderson published articles supporting Ohio governor Rutherford B. Hayes for the presidency. His friends were shocked. Hayes supported Radical Reconstruction and black suffrage policies that Anderson had opposed. Hayes, however, was a man of spotless integrity, a fellow Union war veteran, and a longtime friend. The election was one of the closest and most controversial in the nation's history. Hayes claimed that if he were beaten, it could only be through bribery and corruption in the North and violence and intimidation in the South. The result was a constitutional crisis. Tilden finished with a 250,000 vote plurality but was one vote short of victory in the electoral college. Irregularities in four states meant that both parties claimed their votes. Republicans had hard evidence of voter intimidation in the South, where Tilden had posted large wins. Congress created a commission to decide the election and Anderson worried. "I almost subside into the chilly darkness of despair," he wrote to his daughter Kitty. "The future is black with hopeless portents," he moaned.[10]

Hayes and the Democrats finally arranged a deal whereby Hayes would be awarded the disputed states, thus winning the election by a single electoral vote. In return, the new president agreed to withdraw troops from the South, with the condition that the voting rights of all citizens, black and white, would be respected. Reconstruction was over. It would not take long before Democrats throughout the South would use home rule to reassert white dominance and effectively disfranchise blacks for nearly one hundred years.

Anderson resisted further attempts by others to rekindle his interest in politics. The occasional overtures for a judgeship or other patronage job wafted his way, but these schemes were mere tokens of respect for the ex-governor. When Larz died after years of failing health, Charles's attention turned inward. He focused on ensuring a sound future for his children and securing his father's family legacy. He tackled both tasks with ardor and energy.

Despite a lifetime of financial booms and busts, Anderson had several ventures that finally yielded steady returns. His model town of Kuttawa was now more than a dream. It was a self-sustaining and moderately prosperous little village. In 1880 he opened the Kuttawa Mineral Springs resort, which became a well-known vacation destination in the region. Visitors stayed at the resort's hotel near a spring-fed swimming pool, food stands, and mineral springs. Anderson's Kuttawa Iron Ore Company was also successful. Lyon County had fewer than seven thousand residents in 1880, but the future looked bright. Anderson had designed his own pastoral playground. He published papers on a wide variety of subjects, including proposed techniques for the profitable extraction of natural gas. When it came time to cash in his excess property in 1890, Anderson sold all but one thousand acres for $160,000. Larz would have been proud.

Anderson always had a passion for history. As he entered the twilight of a long and eventful life, he became obsessed with the responsibility of cementing his family's place for posterity. He wrote and spoke tirelessly for the final fifteen years of his life, producing a wealth of insight into the great events of the American experience. He wrote a long account of his childhood on the family's Kentucky plantation. He wanted to ensure that the world would not forget his patriot father. It pained Anderson to visit his father's overgrown grave. "All memory of that heroic patriot and of his once noted home, Soldier's Retreat," bemoaned Anderson, "is utterly lost." In a twenty-three-page letter to his nephew, Anderson proposed that they raise funds to move his father's body to Cave Hill Cemetery in Louisville and erect a monument similar to Zachary Taylor's. Larz had written the simple epitaph but had placed the monument in "a secret hidden away spot of forgotten ground." This was no place to "elevate father's family name as high in the national sphere as is warranted," claimed Anderson. His appeal drew little interest until years after his own death.[11]

Anderson was prolific in his correspondence and much in demand for speaking engagements in his later years. He was asked on countless occasions to reprise his experiences in the Texas secession treachery, the bloody battlefield of Stones River, the contentious gubernatorial election of 1863, and many other events. He responded with both generosity and frankness. While most Southerners adopted a mythical, Lost Cause version of Civil War history, many Northerners tried to heal old wounds by glossing over past sectional differences. Anderson ignored both camps and spoke the unchangeable truth as he saw it then and still believed it.

His talented son, Latham, had been brevetted a brigadier general after the end of the Civil War. Latham went on to modest success as a civil engineer. Tuberculosis forced Latham to move in with his cousin, Dr. Charles Anderson of Santa Barbara, California, where he died on June 9, 1910. Daughter Kitty never married after losing her fiancé, Will Jones, at Chickamauga. She founded the first Sunday school in Eddyville, Kentucky, later moving to her sister Belle's home in Phoenix, Arizona, where she died in 1928. Belle, the youngest child, married former Confederate officer Thomas C. Skinner. She also died in 1928. Kitty and Belle were responsible for saving nearly all of Charles Anderson's important papers. Eliza Brown Anderson outlived Charles as well, dying at their home in Kuttawa, Kentucky, in 1901 at age eighty-five. She was a devout Christian, quietly devoted to her husband. Her letters reveal a traditional woman whose sole focus was the physical and spiritual well-being of her family. Eliza was buried beside her husband in Kuttawa Cemetery.

Anderson wrote that when his own time came, he wanted his family to "hide his corpse away in the nearest fence corner, in preference to parading the disagreeable object above ten miles for sepulture." Perhaps he felt that he could never live up to what he saw as his father's more significant legacy. He personally designed his own gravestone. It was "a mere slab, containing naked names with three events: births, marriage and death." "It has a double white pine tree," Anderson elaborated, "with a double bed at its base, for us two, in our last long sleep, after sleeping together, so peacefully, in all these 50 years." A prolonged illness in the summer of 1895 had given Anderson time to get his affairs in order. He wrote a new will devising his property to his children and grandchildren, as their need was greater than Eliza's. The will read like a promotional piece for the planned sale of Kuttawa as a unit to railroad interests. The document exceeded sixty pages but was never completed or probated. Anderson died September 2, 1895. For one of the few times in his eighty-one years, Charles Anderson's energy ran out before his ink did.[12]

✦ ✦

American Sacred Scripture
Reconsidered

PRESIDENT LINCOLN'S 272 words at Gettysburg may be the most famous speech in the English language. Generations of American schoolchildren have memorized it. Legions of historians have waded through a 150-year accretion of myth and legend in order to derive truth and meaning from the brief text. Celebrated scholars have conducted tireless studies of extant versions of the manuscript, tracking Lincoln's every move in the days and hours leading up to the address. Has any secular speech ever been subject to this degree of forensic examination? Yet new sources continue to come to light in both photographs and documents, hinting at answers to the persistent fog of mystery surrounding Lincoln's iconic address.

The recent discovery of Charles Anderson's Gettysburg speech manuscript may not seem so significant in the shadow of Lincoln's masterpiece. After all, Anderson's speech was not part of the formal battlefield program. Neither Lincoln nor any of his cabinet members had direct input into Anderson's oration before it was delivered. Widening the camera aperture from a granular analysis of the text itself to the broader context of the event reveals an important perspective of the speeches of Edward Everett, Abraham Lincoln, and Charles Anderson as a rhetorical ensemble.

The dedication of the Gettysburg Soldier's Cemetery was not merely a way to honor fallen heroes at the most famous battle of the war. It was the administration's most important political event since Lincoln's election three years earlier. The timing of the consecration could not have been better. Union Party election victories in Ohio, Pennsylvania, and New York had blunted the efforts of so-called Peace Democrats to rally support for an armistice with the Confederacy. A large assembly of loyal governors, military heroes, foreign dignitaries, and other influential people regarded the dedication as a must-see event. In this unusual setting, Lincoln began his bid for reelection in earnest.[1]

Lincoln believed that only a decisive military victory cemented by his own reelection would save the Union. To achieve both, he constructed a tenuous coalition of constituents from across the Northern political spectrum. Only a masterful leader could get abolitionists, conservatives, border state Unionists, and "War Democrats" to join his political acolytes and pull, more or less, in one direction. The war to preserve the Union had to be won, not only on the battlefield and at the polling place but also in the hearts and minds of a diverse group of citizens. Gettysburg was an opportunity to move that process forward.

Besides an abundant assemblage of dignitaries, grieving families of soldiers, and throngs of curious onlookers, Lincoln's political operatives were everywhere. His two personal secretaries, John Hay and John G. Nicolay, were joined by Pennsylvania newspaper editor John Wein Forney. Forney was such an outspoken administration advocate that some Democrats called him "Lincoln's dog." Loyal governors packed train cars with important Republican editors who would supply the appropriate spin to the dedication. Democratic editors howled in protest, suggesting that Lincoln and his minions had turned a sacred event into an "insensate carnival." Those denunciations rang hollow. Many Democrats who had lost sons and fathers in the war appreciated the president's efforts to memorialize them.[2]

Lincoln's speech was political genius. Not only did the language rise above partisanship, it actually transcended sectional animosity. The speech bridged divisions emerging within his own party between conservatives who favored gradual emancipation and conciliatory terms for the South, and those who argued for Radical Reconstruction. As historian Martin P. Johnson has suggested, Lincoln was "talking moderate but leaning radical." However clever and calculating the president was in crafting his speech, two to three minutes was not enough time to properly honor the dead and make the case for aggressively prosecuting the war. Lincoln needed two traditional orations to bookend his remarks. Everett and Anderson performed that task admirably.[3]

Lincoln played no active part in the selection of either featured orator. He knew both men personally, though he was much better acquainted with Everett. The president, Secretary Seward, and the rest of Lincoln's inner circle had read numerous speeches by both men and knew what to expect. Anderson had supported Bell and Everett, not Lincoln, for president in 1860. Neither Anderson nor Everett had always been in lockstep with Lincoln, but this was also the case with many in the president's own cabinet. All three featured speakers shared a devotion to the Union that could not be rivaled. Lincoln's mastery of the art of political consensus-building suggests that he was comfortable in such an ensemble. It suited his purposes.

Everett's opening speech was classic in every sense. He had given many memorial orations throughout the East. As a part of the consecration ceremonies, Everett's speech was strictly circumscribed to fit the traditional boundaries of eulogy on the battlefield. By the time Lincoln was composing his address, he had seen an advance copy of the opening oration. The rhetorical heavy lifting done by Everett in his two-hour dissertation freed Lincoln to speak from inspiration. When Lincoln sat down following his brief address, stunned listeners must have wondered how such an optimistic vision could be achieved under such dire circumstances. Lincoln's restrained elegance compelled his audience to read between the lines of "unfinished work" and to divine the meaning of "the great task remaining." To blatantly call for an acceleration of an immense and bloody war effort would have been ghastly in the context of a cemetery dedication. So Lincoln suggested that his hearers "take increased devotion to that cause," and left it for Anderson to spell it out for them.

The choice of the day's concluding speaker was critical to the success of the event. Ohio governor David Tod made the decision, as he told Anderson, "upon consultation with several of our mutual friends." The historical record stands silent as to their identity. Tod, however, was a stalwart Lincoln supporter. He was intimately involved in recruiting thousands of volunteers for the Union Army. Lincoln eventually offered the job of secretary of the treasury to Tod, who declined due to poor health. Tod's predecessor as Ohio governor, William Dennison, chaired the Ohio rally at Gettysburg. Lincoln later appointed him postmaster general. Ohio's importance in the upcoming presidential election could hardly be overemphasized. It was in Lincoln's best interest to court favor with Ohioans and to rally their most influential leaders behind the administration's war effort. Anderson held impeccable credentials in this respect. Where else could Lincoln find a former slave owner and border state Union man who had escaped from a Confederate prison, been wounded on the battlefield, and helped defeat the most notorious Copperhead in the North? Anderson completed the work that Everett began, framing the president's remarks and concluding with a call to action.[4]

Anderson's résumé made him the logical choice to conclude the day's events. His recent speeches and letters made him even more attractive to the president's political allies. He shunned all party affiliation. No one familiar with his many published orations could mistake Anderson for a Lincoln acolyte. In his *Letter to the Opera House Meeting* from February 1863, Anderson held the Democrats responsible for secession but found the Republicans guilty of "making that ruin utterly remediless and hopeless." While he did not approve of Republican policies, he refused to do anything to obstruct them, since they wielded the power of his nation "in a struggle for its very life." In his May 1863 speech to the Xenia, Ohio, Union Club, Anderson downplayed Lincoln's suspension of habeas corpus, calling the order a "mild restraint of a few dangerous traitors for a brief period." Bold executive action was warranted in a time of civil war. Anderson remained an unyielding Union man and urged his listeners to rise above the "low level of party passions and purposes, and up to that exalted summit of patriotism and wisdom" to a place where the national interest was paramount. Just as Lincoln kept an active rival like Salmon P. Chase in his cabinet for most of his first term, Tod and the president's other Ohio friends knew that Anderson could be used most effectively to broaden the appeal of Lincoln's message and buttress his military leadership among political opponents. What Anderson actually said at Gettysburg broke little new ground, but the fact that he spoke in concert with Everett and Lincoln spoke volumes.[5]

Anderson made as strong a case for continuing to prosecute the war as had been heard by the many dignitaries assembled in Gettysburg Presbyterian Church. Lincoln and Seward were pleased that the concluding speaker at such an important event had performed his duty so well. They also heard a man who, in his zeal to save the Union at any cost, clung to the same conservative views that Lincoln had once held on emancipation. Lincoln had moved on to a new, more radical vision of the postwar Union. He knew that most of America's citizens were not there yet. Even so, leaders like Anderson were useful to the administration. "I am willing to receive any man," Lincoln explained, "or class of men, who will help us even a *little*." Although Anderson was a self-proclaimed "fossil Whig" and had all but stopped evolving politically, he was a brave patriot. People who differed with him often loved him. Nearly everyone respected him.[6]

Anderson's ability to electrify an audience was so highly valued that Republicans abided his independent nature. Anderson chastised the motives behind emancipation as "ends of doubtful, perhaps vain benevolence." His suggestion that a "middle course" was still open to tolerate slavery within the Union demonstrates how love for his country had blinded him to the political realities of the day. The president was not threatened by Anderson's naïve remark. Lincoln understood that he had opened the door to freedom with his proclamation and the arming of black troops. There was no going back to the old order. When Anderson used the phrase "of a government of the people, for the people, ever made on earth," he may have elicited a grin from the chief executive. Anderson unwittingly borrowed the same, well-used transcendentalist preacher's powerful phrasing that the president had used to close his own address just hours earlier. These words might have embarrassed the president had Everett spoken them. For Lincoln, however, it likely reassured him that despite their political differences, he and Anderson shared similar core values. Months before the Gettysburg dedication, Anderson described himself as "a man having no other religion than a love of Union." Lincoln's own religious beliefs were mysterious and private, yet he and Anderson held the same great obsession deep in their hearts. Lincoln had the political talent to will that dream into reality.[7]

Politics in the nineteenth century was played out in the newspapers. The average citizen interpreted the Gettysburg dedication event through the lens of partisan press reports. Reaction to Lincoln's address ran the gamut. The *Daily Republican* from Springfield, Massachusetts, gushed that the president's address was "a perfect gem; deep in feeling, compact in thought and expression, and tasteful and elegant in every word and comma." Ohio's *Crisis*, on the other hand, called Lincoln's brief speech a "mawkish harangue." To many, it was clear that the solemn ceremony also served as the start of Lincoln's reelection campaign. Diarist Adam Gurowski suggested that Lincoln's speech served as a preview of his party's platform for 1864. The *Wabash Express* published a banner headline the day before the ceremony that read: "MR. LINCOLN FOR THE NEXT PRESIDENT." Numerous reports of the ceremony placed the reporting of the event next to a column endorsing Lincoln's reelection. Newspapers spilled most of their ink, however, on Everett's long speech.[8]

Many Republican newspapers devoted their entire front page to the featured oration at Gettysburg. Such coverage of the event was no accident. It was carefully orchestrated political propaganda. Everett had distributed proof sheets of his speech in advance to newspapers throughout the North. Some Democratic papers and even the occasional Southern reporter gave Everett's long oration valuable column inches at a time when war news took precedence. Everett was cast as the strong Union man who once opposed Lincoln but now made an academic argument fully supporting Lincoln's war measures. Forney's *Washington Daily Chronicle* called Everett's effort "magnificent" and so "vivid as though written on a sunbeam." The *Cincinnati Enquirer* ridiculed it as "a collection of disjointed drivel and platitudes; barren in sentiment." Although Everett waited until the following year to declare for Lincoln, readers could see that he was firmly in the president's camp.[9]

A frequent criticism of Everett's speech from all sides intimated that his oration, however eloquent, was missing something. *Harper's Weekly* echoed most Democratic organs, suggesting that the featured speech lacked heart. One witness described the speaker's effort as "beautiful but cold as ice." Everett himself did not see his role as one to incite the passions of his audience, especially in such a somber setting. For his model funeral oration in the vein of the great Greek statesman Pericles, Everett would not "rise above plain good sense." As to the notion of playing to the heartstrings of his audience, Everett wrote, "I must humbly dissent." The fire that was lacking in Everett's speech appeared in ample measure during Anderson's concluding oration. Unfortunately, Everett's words took up so much space in the newspapers that there was often little room left for Anderson's major speech.[10]

The omission of Anderson's text from most Republican papers was one of the few missed opportunities in an event that was a political triumph for the president. The relatively few that did critique his effort demonstrated that Anderson was successful in his role as cheerleader for Lincoln's aggressive war measures. Ohio's *Springfield Republic* noted that the greatest applause came in the "passages which did not accord with the extremely conciliatory tone of Mr. Everett's oration." After reading Everett's speech, Abraham Stagg of the *Columbus Gazette* recalled that the lieutenant governor–elect's speech was "the best one made on that occasion." The *Portage County Democrat* called Anderson's oration "the great production of the day." Even hostile presses such as the *Crisis* helped serve Lincoln's purposes by connecting Anderson to Seward and "their rhetoric [of] hate and Abolition." No one who knew Anderson could call him an abolitionist with a straight face. Lincoln and his political friends had the Peace Democrats on the defensive.[11]

Although Anderson served as Lincoln's faithful ally in the war effort, he refused to support the president's reelection bid. Lincoln's more progressive vision had simply passed him by. Anderson's national star fizzled out just a few years later. For a brief moment at Gettysburg, however, he was a powerful tool of the administration—sharp and pointed but not dulled from overuse. Lincoln ignored him soon after the event, as there were plenty of such loyal implements at his immediate disposal. Anderson's incendiary speech, combined with the erudite effort of Everett, allowed Lincoln to ascend to that higher plane to which Anderson wished all politicians would aspire. In this instance Lincoln the statesman inspired a nation while Lincoln the politician assembled a winning coalition.

Charles Anderson's Gettysburg Address

Fellow Countrymen,

We are standing over many Dead. Nor were they gathered here, in the still successions of passing generations. They have been laid thus low, neither by the regular gradations of natural diseases, nor by the chances of accidental calamities. Death has here made one of his greatest harvests—and all at one fell blow. And the occasion of their destruction is as memorable as their numbers and its suddenness. They all fell fighting side by side, heart with heart, as if the multitudes were one, for their native land and their native institutions of equal laws and free government. And that Country sends us all hither, as its representatives, to "take note of their departure"; to honor their memories, and, from their example, to instruct and to inspire their surviving co-patriots. And the State of Ohio, impelled by no narrow and exclusive prejudice of State pride, but as an integral part of that Nation, with her great full heart, throbbing in deep sympathy with our National Cause, as the Ocean beats his Giant pulses in solemn harmony with general Nature, has deputed us to contribute her evergreen chaplets of amaranth and laurel to the tombs of her own fallen. For here rest in death her own beloved of the 5th, 7th, 29th, 66th, of the 25th, 55th, 72d, 75th, 82d & 102d Ohio Infantry and of the 6th and 1st Ohio Cavalry. These were contributions of our State to the National Sacrifice. Let us therefore, in all simplicity of truth and with due modesty of manner, so speak and hear, that we may best discharge our grave duties to the Dead, to the Living and to the Posterity of our Country and our Kind.

The aptest of all the innumerable tributes to departed worth, ever cut in marble or flowing through traditions, is that brief sentence, inscribed beneath the dome of St. Paul's Cathedral, over the remains of its great architect. "Si quaeris monumentum;—circumspica"!

Standing here and now, upon this great Battle-field, we must be impressed, by this idea, with a new force and a wider and deeper significancy. I feel it indeed, as a sublime truth. A few weeks ago, a vast army, well organized; completely equipped; skillfully drilled; thoroughly disciplined; most ably commanded, inspired, all by the highest courage and confidence of easy victory and ardent, with a fanatic zeal of insane delusion against your prosperity, your peace, your liberties and our common National Unity;—their arms all flashing gleams of light athwart the startled landscape—their banners and battle flags all flaunting against the perturbed Air,—marched hither to this very spot,—to invade, to conquer and to destroy. *But they were confronted. Our* men, the lovers of their Country; the friends of equal rights and rational liberty and the enemies only of oppression, injustice and despotism; leaving their own sweet homes and their dear Kindred; marching by day and night; through sun and dust; in thirst and hunger and fatigues; with lesser numbers, but with equal courage; confronted that proud foe on the very field on which we stand. How the battle began, how it raged and how it closed, you now full well know. These things are now recorded history. Suffice it to say; the Army of Patriotism and Liberty was victorious. The Army of Treason and Despotism was decisively beaten. That Host of rebels, deluded and sent hither by conspirators and traitors, were vanquished and fled cowering in dismay from this land of Penn and Franklin,—of Peace and Freedom,—across the Potomac into the domain of Calhoun and Davis,—of Oligarchic rule and Despotic oppressions.

But where are they, who with such patriotic labors, patience and courage, and with no stronger shields than their own brittle breast-bones, opposed their manly hearts to the deadly missiles of those wide lines of volleyed thunder? *Alas! my friends, there they lie.* Mute and still and cold, fallen, "with their backs to the Earth & their feet to the Foe" there they rest, in that long dark sleep, which can be awakened only by the last trumpet.

And now my friends let us for a short while, attempt to transfer our meditations backward, from this hour, to the crisis of that battle. From the standpoint of its decisive blow, let us speculate upon results; if the victory had been on the other side. In that case, this lovely scene—this fair face of Nature would have been scarred and disfigured through all time. This goodly town, with its accessions of Bridge and Market and Church; these happy homesteads, with all their pertaining parts—all these products and developments of Peace, Industry and Art,—in one word, all this *Civilization*—would have disappeared from hillside and valley and left, instead, a void of empty desolation, or, else, the more dismal spectacle of the charred skeletons of their black and ashy ruins. For; we must not deceive ourselves, with the charitable faith, that the conspirators, who coolly plotted the extinguishment of the Nation and the perpetual extirpation of all these various and grand interests and principles, which made and is our Nation, would fail to order, or that the hordes of dupes and zealots, who blindly follow such leaders, would pause to execute, the destruction of these infinitely lesser things of fence and barn, of Home and School and Church—of Village and City. As Treason is the bottom sin, whether of Earth or Hell, you must reflect, that Traitors are actually elevating themselves in perpetuating any lesser crimes. Nothing would deter these bold, bad men, except the want of opportunity and power, or perhaps the fear of retaliation.

How is it then, my fellow countrymen, that those saddening spectacles do not, at this time and place, oppress with dismay, the heart of some lonely traveler in a wilderness of ruin? *Why* is it that this face of Nature is now all radiant with the smile of peace and that these happy homes of farm and village are yet instinct with human lives and their loves and hopes? The answer must come from the mute lips beneath us. Our reasons and consciences shall interpret their dumb replies.

"We have died, that you may live. We have
toiled and fought—have been wounded and
suffered in keenest agonies even unto death, that
you might live;—live in quietude, prosperity
and in freedom. Oh! Let not such sufferings and
deaths be endured in vain. Oh! Let not such
lives and privileges be enjoyed in ungrateful
apathy towards their benefactors! Remember us, in
our fresh and bloody graves,—as you are standing
upon them. And let your latest posterity learn
the value of the issues in that Battlefield and the
cost of this sacrifice beneath its sod!"

But now, my friends, (speaking again with ourselves, the alive to
the living,) as you once more turn your eyes and thoughts upon the
surrounding scene in its present real condition of Nature un-marred
and Art undestroyed, do you, like the curious traveler in St. Paul's,
inquire, for the monuments of *these* fallen heroes; *Look around you.
Behold this smiling landscape! See these happy homes*!

It would be, however, a very imperfect estimate of the services and
the victory of these Dead, if we should limit our contemplations to
their local and visible results. It will be a delicate task, I know, fitting
to expose on this occasion, the causes and ends of this Rebellion.
This is a *civil War, in present progress*. And the usage in like cer-
emonials is so to speak of the Dead, as not to wound, or even to
offend the Living. Nevertheless, my fellow Countrymen, the *Dead
must have justice, at their own graves as in all history*, even though
the living actors may seem to lack our charity, and ourselves to be
wanting in an over-refinement of taste. Our true course, therefore,
will be first of all things, to speak the truth and the whole truth. We
should speak and adjudge, indeed, wholly without partisanship. But,
we must perform these duties without the cowardice, of fearing that
our Catholic truths shall be miscalled, politics. In order, rightly, to
read and record the merits of these Dead, we are compelled, truly and
fully to consider the nature and the ends of that great War, of which
this Battle and these Deaths, were the incidents and consequences. If

we are capable of this simple duty, then shall we all, with the mind's eyes, see in the results of that sacrifice, monuments to their memories, as much grander and more enduring than all these living scenes, which Treason has been compelled thus to leave standing, or than any future structures of marble, or bronze, which Patriotism may freely rear, as great moral principles are more worthy and more durable than any material things are, or ever can be.

This great War then—let it never be forgotten—is that original, first, human conflict between Freedom and Despotism. It may be called, by what lesser name or quality you choose, of those many and changeful causes and agencies, which lie, or arise more nearly to ourselves, its actors and sufferers: but, be assured, notwithstanding these partial truths, that the great, fundamental cause of this, our, War, is that olden contest between these antagonistic principles, which can never cease, so long as Mankind shall inhabit this Earth, or shall include the Few, whose ambition loves power and the Many, whose blindness, or weakness invites oppression. Nor will it ever end, until that Millennial day of perfect liberty, when

"every man shall eat in safety
under his own vine, what he plants; and sing
The merry songs of peace to all his neighbors"

We know well enough, my friends, that there are many minds, so charitable or so perverse, as not to perceive this great, glaring, luminary—truth. They cannot believe, that, at this era of the World's Civilization, Christianity and Freedom, upon this Continent, and in this Republic, there could be found, numbers of men, so wrongheaded or else so falsehearted, as to love Despotism rather than Liberty,—as actually and vigorously to conspire, betray, rebel and to wage vast war against these essential, fundamental, vital principles of our Government and Society. Are these men—let me ask—unconscious and blind to the unceasing workings of general Human Nature? Do they not believe, those century-bequeathed lessons, that "Power is ever stealing, from the many to the few" and that "The Habit of Tyranny makes tyranny a Necessity." Have they never read History, nor studied its Philosophy? Do they not know that it is the maxim of pure philosophy from uniform history, that there never has existed a Republic, which did not always contain these parties, the Democratic, the Oligarchic, and the Monarchic? And, have they not been observing and reflective on what, of our own Nation's history, has been passing under their own eyes? And which, now, of the Sections of this nominal democracy, has uniformly controlled its National Government? Its *majority* Section? Every man of you knows better, You all know,—the most unthinking and ignorant amongst you,—that the Minority—*these same conspirators and their predecessors in Oligarchic Revolutionism*, have by the aid of Foreign and Native blind impulses and prejudices, actually monopolized all the functions of our Nation. And what class of men has controlled the governing party? Real Democrats? Men trained in, and addicted to, the principles and practices of equal rights; of justice, mercy and of freedom to all mankind, or even to all their own race? No—indeed! And, let us all, in this solemn presence of the Spirit of that God, who overlooks and we trust, overrules all things, in the immediate, nearest, presence of those departed spirits, who must *yet* linger around these, their late tenements of clay,—who float in the very Air here enclosing us,—solemnized by this fellowship,—elevated by that presence,—let us all, both recognize and declare the undeniable truth of our own observation in our own history; that *not* democrats or republicans, but oligarchs and despots have alone "done this deed without a name." Men, who, as private individuals, were born to the inheritance of unjust power; nurtured by the milk of slaves and slavery; rocked in their cradles by servile hands; schooled in their lessons and their sports, into the indulgences of unrestrained passions; and confirmed by the routine duties of daily business and the enjoyments of daily society, in a spirit of unbridled willfulness and, who, in their public and official capacities, have been even yet more indulged, persuaded and flattered, by Northern Allies panders of both the leading parties into an arrogance as boundless as the Sea and as insatiate as the Grave;—*this* is the class of men and of Americans,—which has alone contrived and perpetuated this blackest crime of history. Yes. We know, that it is the spirit of Oligarchy, born in the purple of Despotism, cultured into morbid activities and pampered, at last, into insane, parricidal, suicidal arrogance, that has contrived, plotted, betrayed, rebelled and at length, warred against our National existence, as a Government and against our Liberty, Education, Morality, our very Civilization, as a people. It is Oligarchy (the privileged few, if you prefer the word) which, having already, like a thief in the night, stolen so much power from the many, with the mask, now thrown aside and turned highway robber, *openly* battles, to usurp not merely all political powers, but all their shows and symbols. For, nothing alas! can be more evident than that with the same incongruous alliance of partizan ignorance with cunning aristocracy, the Southern minority might have continued to rule us to the end of the century, if they could have been content with the *substance* of supremacy. It was only the morbid insanity of their overblown arrogance and lust of dominion, which impelled them to the Charlestown-conspiracy against the integrity of their own faction, as an agency in dissolving the Union. And, so it is, that having slowly and slyly corrupted our unconscious democracy into a secret but actual Oligarchy in the Past, they have now, "with a high hand and outstretched arm," in open, flagrant, formal, bloody and persistent *war* assailed and *now* endeavor, in its very strongholds, to overthrow Human Freedom, as a form of government and as a spirit of good! And, my dear fellow countrymen, here lie in their bloody graves, the slain victims of that treachery and cruelty! Their blood cries out from all this ground below us, to all these wide heavens above for God has heard that cry. And a yet bloodier retribution awaits,—nay now falls upon,—those wretched men, whose crime neither the Earth can hide nor the Seas can cleanse.

I know that many will also disbelieve all these truths. Multitudes of men of all countries and ages live and die under unbroken delusions to names and appearances. They will ever think that a particular man is a democrat or republican, because he bears the name and wears the garb. They can never imagine a Nobleman, or a Queen, unless they always see them with stars and garters, or a crowned head? Do they not know that the Duke of Devonshire wears plainer and cheaper clothes than his own footman? Could they suppose that a simple, modest little woman, daily clad in a black worsted gown, with a plain linen collar and a widow's cap, is *Victoria*? And yet, for all that, he is the highest and proudest of the World's Nobility and born legislator and judge and she,

"A Queen and daughter to a King."

And they do not, in like manner, remember, that the name and appearances of a *Christian*, cloaked, to all eyes save one,—Judas Iscariot? And so, my countrymen, throughout all Nature and all Art, whatsoever,—just in the proportion as these are genuine and valuable things, there will always be the counterfeit and worthless. And of all the manifold shams and counterfeits of this cunning, wicked world, none have ever been so base and bald, nor yet so successful as the counterfeited democracy of our own Southern States. Not merely has this name been, *not the thing itself.* It has been actually and all the while, the exactly opposite incompatibility and antagonism of that true thing. It has ever been a positive oligarchy. And their ruinous heresy of "States Rights" has been from the beginning merely an oligarchic mask for the conservation and propagandism of slavery black and white. These things being so;—and as surely as we live, or as these still forms below us are dead—*they are so*—this battle, in which they died, was one of a War between Freedom and Despotism, the most clearly marked, the most stupendous, the most impassioned and decisive, ever waged or endured, in the lapse of ages. And,—that being so,—how can we, their survivors, or our posterity, sufficiently praise and honor their names and memories? As the Israelites honored Jephtha's daughter and the fallen heroes at Minnith, or in Gath? Notwithstanding those victories, the Jews are outcasts upon the earth and the Religion, for which they fought and fell is a past thing and a mockery amongst men! As the Greek honored the Dead of Marathon and Thermopyle? In despite of those wonderful achievements, the Greeks of today are and for generations past, have been, no better than the Persian Barbarians, whom they fought, or those they themselves would have been, if they had been conquered! As the Romans honored Scipio and his compatriots, who fought or fell at Zama or Cannae? Why, within a few fleeting years thereafter, the power and the liberties of the Romans were as completely overwhelmed, as they could have been, by that Carthage, which they destroyed and made desolate. As the English, have honored and are honoring the martyrs at Waterloo? England's power was no greater after, than before that event. And France is again supine and under the illegitimate authority of another Bonaparte-adventurer, whose scepter is more absolute over France and more menacing to the peace, and independence of other nations, than whilst swayed by the mighty arm of that first, great one, of Corsica. In a general alliance and War, contracted and waged for the sake of a Dynasty and family, its decisive Battle has proved insufficient to prevent that grand empire, with all its incidents, from a return to the same name as before. *Not* then fellow countrymen, as these Nations have ever honored their valiant Dead, must we honor the sacred dust beneath our feet. Their cause was infinitely higher, holier, and more potential too in the fate of our nation and our race, than was that of either of those famed Contests. And we must glorify them commensurately with that Cause. We must signalize their martyrdom, commensurately with the difficulty of their undertaking, the effects and influences of their victory and with their general personal and social worth as men and citizens, with the dignity and disinterestedness of the special motives, which prompted them to *volunteer* into these frightful dangers and this certain death and, above all, in proportion, to that priceless stake, for which they fought and died. And, intelligently compared in all these respects, with the dead heroes of this our War, how poor and unequal in the review, pass the long line of the Gaths and Ashkelons; or the Marathons; and Thermopyles, or the Zamas and Cannaes and Sanguinettos; or the Portiers and Hastings, or the Blenheims and Waterloos and all the other bloody campaigns and fatal fields or recorded history? But let us, my Countrymen, as rational beings unbiased by personal ambitions or by National vanities, calmly and strongly *assure* ourselves of these historic truths.

And first you will observe that by long hasty marches, wearied and disheartened by late defeats, they were surrounded and assaulted by a much larger Army, recently victorious and sanguine with all the assurance of another victory. Those alone who have experienced these disadvantages can truly estimate them.

They saved two great states with their great Metropolitan cities, from certain capture, pillage, and general conflagration. I do not here ignore the excellent moral character of the commanding General of that Army, nor those of many of his subordinates. Neither do I intend to apply any of these censures or epithets of contumely to such men, nor to the great body of the Southern people. I know too well the many virtues and noble traits of these gentlemen and of that class of our countrymen, so to adjudge them. And, I am sure, I love truth too much to so cruelly asperse them. But in their conduct of this civil war, as in the conspiracy which brought it on, the wicked purposes of vile and desperate politician traitors have overruled the good dispositions and infatuated and misguided the honest impulses of their Army-officers and their people. To them and them alone do I apply these harsh but truthful terms. To return however to our direct topic; when we remember, that of these States and cities, were Pennsylvania and Philadelphia and consider the Geographical positions of Maryland and Baltimore and the peculiar relations, which large numbers of their citizens have to the cause and war of the invading traitors, the influences of that victory must, in countless regards, grow wonderfully in our estimate.

And then again, that campaign and Battle were designed by the Foe and expected by ourselves and the World, to prove decisive of the fate of our National Capitol. That Foe and that World hoped and fully believed also, that its capture would decide and close this grand War, by the establishment and universal recognition of this new National Power of a Slavery-Oligarchy. We know better. We know, that the loss of a capitol in a Democracy, (unlike a similar casualty in Monarchies,) does not reach the seat and life of its governmental power. Our powers of war or peace,—thank God and our fathers— are not concentrated in Washington, or any other city or site. They pervade and flow from the whole body of this great people, throughout the length and breadth of this long and broad land. This is no War of President and Cabinets. The President and his Secretaries, with all the great powers and dignities, with which our Constitution endues them,—are the mere creatures of time and place, the passing official breath of our nostrils—nothing and infinitely less than nothing, when compared either with the fixed deep purpose of the American People for the prosecution of this War, or with those immutable and price-less principles, which justify and make that purpose. The capture of our National Capitol; the burning of its Archives; the interruption, for a few months in the offices of one of its Administrations—these petty, transient casualties of war, indeed!—to make the term and end the being of this Democracy! Why; let them seize and destroy our National City—its wood into ashes and its Marble into sand—Let them imprison—hang—burn our President with all the heads and hands of the Departments;—Let them leave on Earth, no trace, in type or Scroll, of all the Acts of our Congress—of all our Treaties with Foreign nations—nor of the American Constitution. *Yet, are we still a Nation.* Foreign Monarchy must understand,—Domestic Oligarchy must re-learn, that our National Being flows on forever in the stream of moral principles and not through any chain of printed deeds or written charters. And, can they erase from the National *Mind*, that record of those principles, which *Reason* has graven there? Can they burn out from the National *Heart* the traces of that undying love for truth and liberty, which God implanted in his mercy and our Fathers watered with their blood,—our Mothers with their tears? No—indeed can they not! Let what may befall external forms and dead matter; *the eternal soul of Freedom fights this War.* And she *shall* conquer;

> For Freedom's battle once begun
> Bequeathed from bleeding sire to son
> Though baffled oft—is ever *won*!

And it would have been far better for the shallow demagogues, who conspired themselves and us into this War; if they had first ad-vised themselves of its intrinsic nature and its consequent destiny. This Earth will not reverse the courses of its daily rotations upon its axis of calm air, nor its annual circuit through yet calmer space, the free winds will not cease to breathe the balmy breath of flowers through all its vales; Niagara's heavy floods will not hush its roar and stop its swift plunge, Old Ocean's deep breast will never lull the mighty music of his ceaseless throbs and resounding, to please a junta of insane slavery oligarchs! No more will God's equally natural and equally sure laws of Civilization and Liberty in all the stillness and brightness of their beauty and all the genial warmth of their undying life, either pause, of flow backwards, into the chaos of black Barbarism and of red Despotism, at the bidding of these puny and palsied Canutes of South Carolina and Mississippi.

Nevertheless; my countrymen, and although we may not, even in our funereal eulogies, claim for this martyr-blood the actual decision of our National fate, nor the fate of freedom throughout the World, it would be difficult for us, short of these results to overestimate the ruinous consequences of that capture by the Traitor Army.

We come now to consider the *characters* of these Dead. And what manner of men, were they who here fought unto bitter death? Were they professional adventurous mercenaries, who hire out their bodies and the chances of their lives and souls to any leader and any cause of other lands, offering them the highest pay and the most rations? Were they the soldiers, who are impressed or conscripted and dragged unwillingly by their own governments, into the privations and dangers of war? No truly they were not! On the contrary of all this, they were the bravest and the best of the young and old, rich and poor, of our whole people, and the representatives of all its best classes. The honest day-laborers, the skilled and industrious mechanics, the prosperous merchants; the sober, solid farmers; the rising and risen Lawyers, physicians, ministers and Statesmen, the students and professors of our Schools, Colleges, and Universities and the men of greatest wealth and the highest social positions, who, when this War was begun against the interests, principles and life of our Nation, "with wings as swift as meditation, or the thoughts of love," swept into the ranks of the National Army. And when, before this war, was ever seen such a quality of men, acting and suffering as the common soldiers in the field? When before, did their own free wills alone impel the soldiers of an entire Army, consciously and purposely, into longest campaigns and bloodiest Battles? And, if you pass from this comparisons of individual characters and motives, to that of the aggregate results in the respective numbers of different Armies; only think of the stupendous fact—the sublimest of all history,—the spectacle of more than a Million of Freemen, freely fighting for Freedom! Of that grand host, these lowly dead, were a most noble part.

And, what other wars ever disclosed such valuable and holy ends, as these which ennoble and sanctify this grand War of ours? Let us patiently and honestly specify but a few of these many justifications of War, in itself so unnecessary, cruel and unnatural. These soldiers died to save our Nation's life. And what a Life it is? Consider its history and career. A new, fresh, people, for the first time in history started forth as a Nation, *in the fullness of its civilization.* Not rising together with their customs, laws and institutions from a state of barbarism, into the developments of slow experience, into its civilization, but like a modern Minerva, our Nation sprang from the pregnant mind of England, then the freest and most civilized Nation of Earth or Time—full grown and full armed for all the enterprises of her National life. She fixed her home upon this distant, virgin Continent, across the Seas. And what a continent it was? Unbroken and boundless forests; vast and unploughed plains; Mountains of Mineral with the iron frame of the Earth protruding its black skeleton, up through the thick mould of richest valleys, glistening with streamlets; Whose waves were amber and whose sands were Gold,— grand chains and systems of Rivers, Lakes, Bays and Ocean-harbors and every other faculty and facility of Nature, essential to the developments of Agriculture, Manufactures, Navigation & Commerce, composed here a land for the growth and maintenance and happiness of the largest homogenous Nation of history. With such a European Civilization from its Mother-land, as an out start in its career and with such an inheritance from its Father—the God of Nature—as its domain, we cannot fail to perceive peculiar opportunity for the fair and full trial of a new system of Government which such a wilderness with this its isolation, afforded to our fathers. For the first time, again and necessarily, their form of government, could not become, like others, the result of mere usages and precedents—a *growth*. It was, inevitably, a *design & a creation*. This condition of things, directed to the study of the nature and ends of human government, a mass of thought, which as the circumstances of no antecedent population had ever invited, or allowed, and whomsoever, the immigrants and their descendants, could suffice in numbers and development to become independent of the parent-government and people,—as purely a question of time alone, as in the case our natural offspring or of maturing fruits—necessarily, also, that separation in mere space, left that experiment in its practical workings wholly undisturbed, by the neighborships and entangling alliances of unlike governments. Here then was the first and only fair trial of self-government,—of a government of the people, for the people, ever made on earth. And it was also made amidst circumstances, the most favorable for success, which ever concurred or could be imagined. In the light of these simple truths, is it not most plain, that the success of this experiment of a Government of free and equal laws, would prove not only the very highest direct blessing to its own citizens, but a boon beyond estimation, as our example to all other peoples in all future time? What a disaster and disgrace to ourselves and what a calamity and a curse to our race, therefore, if we should destroy all these institutions—the product of such rare opportunity—such combined wisdom and such heroic virtues? But let us *here* recollect that it *was this great ruin,* which that Traitor Army marched *hither* expressly to accomplish and which *these* dead heroes died to prevent.

Do any of my hearers distrust this frequent citation of the value of our experiment in government, in its example to the world, as being only another of the manifold delusions and exaggeration of National vanity? Listen then to the neutral testimony of one, who was at once a great Poet, Scholar, Philosopher and Philanthropist.

> There is a People, mighty in its youth,
> A land beyond the Oceans of the West
> Where, though with rudest rites, Freedom and Truth
> Are worshipped; from a glorious Mother's breast,
>
> XXIII
> That land is like an Eagle, whose young gaze
> Feeds on the noontide beam, whose golden plume
> Floats move less on the storm, and in the blaze
> Of sunrise gleams, when Earth is wrapt in gloom;

An epitaph of glory, for the tomb
Of murdered Europe may thy fame be made,
Great People! as the sands, shalt thou become;
Thy growth is swift as morn when night must fade;
The multitudinous Earth shall sleep beneath thy shade.

XXIV
Yes, in the desert, there is built a home
For Freedom. Genius is made strong to rear
The monuments of man beneath the dome
Of a new Heaven; Myriads assemble there,
Whom the proud lords of man, in rage or fear,
Drive from their wasted homes.

My countrymen, let me repeat, in the cause of *such* an inheritance to ourselves and such a Refuge and Example to our Race, have these inanimate forms yielded up their labors and their lives.

But they fought for far more than an Idea, or the right to try an experiment. Our Nation had made attainments and acquisitions in its short progress, with amazing speed and of incalculable values. What student of history will pretend, that any former nation, within a period of tenfold our time, can be compared with our past progress either in Agriculture, Manufactures, Commerce or, especially in maritime developments? And, although, with equal numbers of the same population, broken into lesser nationalities and under more absolute governments, the sum of its products in several of these departments of labor might possibly be as great as they would be in our Nation undivided, yet is it most certain, that after Disunion and its other consequent disintegrations the maritime powers and resources of this people, for example, would almost disappear, in fact, from the Seas of the World, as well as in name, from the its shipping lists. Amongst these positive acquisitions , and as a specimen again, we must remember, that the champions of this war are fighting for the exercise and enjoyment, by our Nation, now and through coming ages, of its strict rights, to the use of that vast system of the Mississippi—more that thirty thousand miles of Steamboat navigation. And this absolute right and possession, were bought by the Nation proper, with money out of the National Exchequer, and without the least pretext for any States-rights appertaining to the title, either in its origin or its uses. Yet these Traitors, without notice of claim or excuse either for separation or war insolently seized this special National property,—this actual artery of our commercial System and circulation,—choked and blocked it up by fortifications and artillery. And, forthwith, upon the perpetration of these frauds, treasons and insulting outrages, with the curling smoke of actual war drifting over the face of that river, proposed to dictate to us, its *owner*, the terms of our future use of it and all its tributaries. And only think of that insult to our understandings, which alone could surpass that upon our flag;—the basis of our acquiescence was to be our faith in the *honor* of Mississippi; of the wisdom of Louisiana and the moderation and justice of that band of gentlemanly conspirators, plunderers, rebels, and traitors, self-called the Southern Confederacy!

To return to our summary of facts; what Nation on Earth, in the sphere of material interests, could have ever alleged such vast possessions, or such unquestionable rights as its cause of War? For these covenanted rights; for these vast properties of inheritance from and for our Nation, have these men died. But my countrymen they were martyred. They died for rights and interests, far more precious and exalted than those pertaining to material possessions. They died in the cause of our civil and religious liberties. To take only one of the many values, which this point suggests, nothing can be plainer, that that a government of fixed territorial limits, founded on Slavery in order to repress the constantly increasing dangers and horrors of servile insurrections, must necessarily and perpetually maintain, as a branch of its established institutions, a vast standing Army with all its accessories, otherwise the Slaves would cease. These fixed limits for Slaves, cannot be fixed as to the freemen. Hence, the emigration of the latter and the non-emigration of the former class of population, must inevitably, year by year and generation upon generation, so diminish its white and free population and so enhance its black and slave class, as to give it an awful preponderance. As a consequence of this certain truth, that standing army and military organization of this Southern Confederacy, must, *from the nature of its case,* bear such a proportion to the entire population of freemen as never had a parallel in history. Nor is this their own proper affair merely. It is ours as much and as directly. For, no neighbor Republic could trust another, although of like institutions with such an ability and ready preparation for assault, without supplying itself constantly with an equal or superior means of defense. Add now to those general reasons, for our being *perpetually* armed and fortified, we shall also add, these special and peculiar necessities of our case—*Viz*; that, our new Neighbor is to be an Oligarchy, pure and simple, in form and sprit;—that this is a government, which, as a class, is by its intrinsic nature, ambitious, intriguing, cruel, implacable and full of warlike vigor;—that the inheritance and possession of domestic slaves not only enhances and envenoms each one of these vices of abstract oligarchy, but under pretext of the violation of one of our treaties for the return and redelivery of *their* fugitive slaves on account of its expansion of its slavery-limits and of their many other like requirements and demands must furnish multitudinous and virulent causes and provocative to mutual War, And our doom must become apparent to every mind.

A great standing Army, as a constituent portion of any government, is not merely an invariable source of the most heavy and grievous of all taxations and public debts, but—far worse,—it is utterly incompatible with civil liberty. Such a standing Army makes ours a Military Republic. A Military Republic is the most despotic form of Government except alone, an Oligarchy. And so, the sum of all is, that the free Republic of the United States, would eventuate in two forms of government—theirs the Southern and strongest a Slavery-Oligarchy, the worst government tried or imaginable and ours, the Northern and weakest, a Military Republic only less bad than the Southern Confederacy only less weak than Mexico. And all this unparalleled load of taxation, and public debt; all this degradation and loss of liberty, be it observed, will have been made eternal necessities to each portion of the broken and divided Nation from a Disunion, conspired and executed by one section alone, in the *special interests* of Slavery, an institution peculiar to itself! Did ever the rights of property before, find so reasonable and honest a cause of war as these?

Did ever Freedom arm herself against dangers, so many or destruction so sure? It was for civil liberty then, that these martyrs here shed their most precious life-blood.

We are admonished and exhorted by very strange apostles at home and abroad, that—"Blessed are the Peace-makers." Well; my friends we say too, blessed be God! For that truth and its promises. As we pass, however, we only express our astonishment, that Great Britain preaches it, with the ink of the warlike menaces of the Trent-affair, yet moist on her dispatches, or that Napoleon the third, while the sulfurous smoke of Solferino, slow rolls away before our eyes and the thunders of his artillery at Puebla are still resounding in our ears, should so suddenly and so zealously be preaching to us this new gospel of peace. We are for peace. But neither the God of Nature; nor the God of Revelation, has taught us of those changes, in which, Fire shall consist with water; light with darkness;—truth with error;—virtue with vice;—Liberty with despotism—*nor, Loyalty with Treason.* "The good time coming" when the lion and the lamb shall lie down together, can only be when the Lion shall become as a lamb, and not that the Lamb shall become as the Lion. And in brief, if darkness and error and crime and despotism and Treason, or their friends for them, crave peace and respite in their own unending war with Light and Truth and Virtue and Liberty and Patriotism, why let them ground their arms; do works meant for repentance and cease thus to afflict mankind and to insult God.

What offers or promises of peace however did these conspirators tender us in advance of their revolt? What acts or signs of peace, did they show in its beginning? What pacific or honest purpose, have they exhibited in its progress? And, leaving the men and considering things, what prospect of Peace,—A real, permanent Peace,—Peace as an institution—can we perceive, in all the probabilities of this new Foreign Government as our Neighbor? It will have a boundary-line of Twenty five hundred miles for all its accidents of border wars;—the rapacity and arrogance of an Oligarchy, for its spirit of encroachment thousands of fugitive slaves, tens of thousands in all their generations, fleeing across that long line of emancipation, from the lash, the goad, or the brand and each trembling fugitive unconsciously enkindling, as he flies, such many and endless feuds and wars and conflagrations as shall startle "Pale midnight on her starry throne"; What prospect of peace, to yourselves or your children, do you perceive in the future of these conditions? But, my friends, we must look yet further. For I am resolved to justify these Dead, in what they have done and suffered, by specifically disclosing the chief causes and ends of this war. Let no vague generalizations mystify the cleanness of their cause. Let no affectations as to customary funereal rites, silence us from uttering, in their full vindication and their highest honor,—these clear truths of History.

This Southern Confederacy designs and strives to found a separate government, upon Slavery, as a corner-stone. The founders vaunt before Christendom, the originality, wisdom, and benevolence of that foundation. The interests of that property and institution are openly alleged to be the justification for the violent destruction of the former government and in like manner, to be the end of the new. I make no controversy here, upon those propositions. But whatever one may think, or may affect to think about the morality, justice or political economy of Slavery, two results must clearly follow from their success in these enterprises. That people, which in the very outset of their undertaking, suffers so much in behalf of slavery and which moulds the very foundations and framework of their new government mainly for its preservation and propagandism, (instead of in reference to the infinitude of other rights and interests that compose the usual purposes in the founders of all other new governments,) must necessarily, in its future, prize and love that institution of Slavery with an increased estimate and ardor.

Dear is the helpless creature we defend
Against the *World!*

The second result is equally evident. The other fragment of the old Nation, which is without slaves itself, and which will have suffered such infinite losses of property, such insults to personal independence and national love and pride; such wounds, murders, wars and loss of peace and liberty at the hands of Slaveholders, must perforce hate, yes *abhor* Slavery with a unanimity and intensity, before unknown to itself, or any other free people on Earth. Now then; suppose these two Nations arrayed, face to face, across a Continent! What will be the result? Peace or War? We must know that the only result could be a war and nothing else, so far forth as these states of feeling should influence their action. Let us now look beyond and at other motives and probabilities. We shall see that every other of all their conditions would only increase and intensify these horrid tendencies.

They begin their separate national existences, in all the bitterness of their previous malignity and envy. So much for the Past. Their present must evolve yet numerous other unsettled and, *to this hour, unconsidered* grounds of debate and dispute, preliminary to the act of separation. Their Future, amongst other obstacles to a peaceful neighborship, promises only great and rapid changes in the views, passions and conduct of all three of the parties henceforth concerned in the matter of Slavery—viz: the slave-holders, the Slaves, and the new *Anti-Slavery Nation*. Let us note the drift and extent of these changes. The segregation of this nation of mere slaveholders, cut off from its former intercourse of trade education and friendship with their former fellow-citizens of the Free states and from the general society of Christendom and nursing this particular property and its fanaticisms, with increased morbidness in its dreary isolation—will wonderfully enhance that wild self-will and spirit of unrestraint,— that intolerable arrogance,—which so distinctively marks this class of men in all their histories. No wind or current from the free, pure, moving Ocean, or without, can be permitted to stir and to freshen the stagnant waters of their embayed and lifeless societies. The putrid stillness of the Dead Sea, windless and waveless and fatal to the Air above as in the Deep below, were motion and joy, when compared to the existence of such a people in their own home. To deplore their general calamities, however, is not now my office nor desire. How their state shall affect others,—us—is my present aim. It is obvious enough that in such a state of things, or in one anything like it, that those vices of Slave-ownership in King-Cotton proportions, must more and more, become morbid down to a chronic and general fanaticism. Meanwhile, and with equal pace, the bondage and suffer-

ing of the Slaves would become more and more cruel and intolerable.
And see; how again other causes, opportunities and temptations must
unluckily conspire to endanger the peace of these neighbor-Nations.
The increased severity of the Slaveholders must increase the numbers of their fugitive slaves, beyond the proportions of their mere
multitude. That greater loss makes it necessary again to tighten and
harden their fetters. And so on, in this action and reaction of the
enraged master and the desperate slave upon each other, to the end
of those relations. But we must also remind ourselves,—that there
can be then no fugitive slave law to capture and return the escaping
slaves to slavery—better or worse—to deter the much greater number
from the attempt to escape when Freedom to the bondsmen will have
been brought from the great, cold distance, across states and over
the Lakes, in Canada, *within their sight—aye, to their touch—yes—
only across an Air*-line! What increased motives to fly? What temptations and opportunities will draw them to Freedom? But there is a
third party to this business—The people of these and yet *other* Free
States—yourselves. How will they and you feel and act in and after
these many rapid and wide changes of opinion, feeling, and legal relations towards Slavery? Let us consider yourselves. First, you will have
no constitutional compact, nor fugitive-Slave-Law, commanding you
to do, or to forbear, towards Slaves, or Masters. This latter class will
have adroitly discharged you all from any, the least, obligations or
law towards them in these regards. You will stand upon the precise
legal platform of the British and Canadians in all that matter. Next,
The promised non-intercourse in trade and society, will leave here no
class, whose avarice or vanity would make them Kidnappers for, or
of your loving brethren or sisters. Thirdly, you will have no large and
able class of politicians deriving all their wealth, powers and fame,
wholly from their political alliances with *their* Southern brethren,
as the consideration of helping them, by your own misguided votes.
Fourthly: You would have all the hatreds and loves, I have mentioned,
to impel you to help the fugitive and to hinder and resist his pursuer.
And, in general is it not self-evident, that the public peace of these
two nations would become the sport or accident of every casual flight
of the slave; of every word, or act of arrogance of the Slavehunter

with or without his bloodhounds and of every throb of pride or love of liberty upon that line between Slavery and Freedom, which is as long as the continent and narrower than a hair? Do you not perceive, that the worse the slave-holders shall become, that the more their increased despotisms shall frighten, or drive away their slaves and the more you shall improve in morality, Christianity and in love of independence for yourselves and of liberty to others, *each necessary result*—that the more and more, *forever,* would fresh causes of War spring up, like saurian dragon teeth, to afflict these new Nations. And what a *frightful* consequence; that *God's* inspired love for your own Liberty and pity for the oppressed and hatred for the oppressors, should bring down endless and bitter wars and woes upon you an innocent and a Foreign Nation?

There is another point of this subject, which ought to be noticed in this connection. It is alledged, that these are great dangers to be apprehended by the Northern States, in case of a general emancipation, from an inundation by a tide of black barbarism. In consequence the white laboring population may be greatly injured by this new competition and in addition, to this special trouble, our whole property being made to bear the heavy burdens of a new pauper-tax. These cases seem to me very easy of solution. If the Southern Confederacy shall be established, then so long as Slavery exists, the Northern people and government will be actually infested and cursed by alien and heterogeneous multitudes of fugitives. The evils of this calamity to the Northern society and government it will be scarcely possible to exaggerate by language. If Slavery should be abolished, however, throughout the south, then there will be no slaves to fly nor any possible motive for the enfranchised individuals to migrate hither. On the contrary; every motive, as climate, custom, society, with their likes and equals etc. will conspire to withhold the absent and to withdraw from us even those who are now here. And so seriously do I estimate those evils—of such black immigrations and colonization amongst us, that if all or *other* causes of war against the establishment and recognition of the Southern Confederacy of Slave states, could be obviated and removed, I do really think that these dangers from having

our land converted into a vast Cloaca Maxima for their overflowing
filth, would constitute a just and sufficient cause of war, to the end
of the century. But there is one middle course. It is in reunion, either
with, or without Slavery.

We may be all willing, as the least of two evils or of two doubts,—I
am willing—to tolerate this monster-disease and crime *within the
Union,* until Providence may, in his own good time and way, mit-
igate or remove it. With the Union restored and its political powers retrenched in fact, as they already have been in the progress of
this, its own war, it seems to me better for us to bear with slavery,
in its unquestionable constitutional rights, than for us,—beyond the
point of the Union restored,—to press this cruel War for other ends
of doubtful, perhaps vain benevolence. But Slavery *in an adjacent
Foreign State, must* be fought without respite or forbearance, so long
as it is cruel, crafty, and despotic, or as this Free people have sense,
or courage or virtue or love of Peace.

And lastly let it suffice on this head to say, as a perfect justification
for our resolution to conquer peace, by restoring our Union, that we
think it to be the only road to Peace. It is the generic law of separate
and neighbor Republics that they cannot dwell together in amity. As
the thoughts and passions of the people in a *Representative* Form of
Government, are *also* represented in its legislation, all the feuds, for-
ays, mobs, conflagrations, and murders of the respective populaces,
necessarily and directly culminate into National public Wars. Then
again; Wars breed Wars. And to all these certain and terrible causes
of ferocious war, must be, once more, added those peculiar circumstances of these two particular Republics already indicated Oh! My
friends, what infinite blessings of Peace did our glorious Union ensure us? Oh! What endless sufferings and crimes from War—Wars—
Horrid Wars—must Disunion entail upon us thru all the coming
years and ages? And to perpetuate those blessings of Peace, to avert
those ruins and curses and woes of War, these heroes have died on
this now glorious Battlefield.

Such then, my dear fellow Patriots (I am not ashamed *here* to call
myself a patriot) are some of the grand issues of this War. And such
were the rights and interests, for which these mute forms have poured

out their life-blood. Our *fathers* of the first Revolution have *alone* shed blood in a cause so great and so good. They—the few and feeble colonists of 76, all naked and unarmed, first encountered the mailed and gauntleted legions of Despotic power and broke into slivers those shackles of steel, in which old Europe had enchained young America. They indeed, alone opened to the Human Race, a new career, not only in the enjoyments of public liberty, but in all the enterprises, arts and delights of private Life. They by their wisest words and bravest deeds, first aroused Mankind,—like another Sampson sleeping in the lap of Delilah,—to the highest visions, the high hopes and the earnest passions of the new Era. We may not compare ourselves, or these our dead, with our dead *Fathers*. Our wars cannot be claimed, to have initiated a new career for our Race. But, if their mission and want, were to create and to and inaugurate, It must be ours, to conserve and transmit. Accordingly, this War, will decide,—the one way or the other,—for our Country and our Kind, for the time present and the times to come;—whether, or not, this youthful Giant of American Liberty shall be re-enthralled by the Old World's ideas, usages, and powers? Whether the risen dawn of this better Era shall at once be quenched in eternal gloom, or shall spread and shine and glow, within all the encircling Skies and around all the enclosed Earth, until the black night of all Barbarisms and Despotisms shall blanch and lighten into an unending Day of universal Liberty and of calmest Peace?

Let us, therefore, my friends, ever honor these our martyred fellow countrymen, above all the dead heroes of other lands and ages and next only to our Fathers of the Revolution, who lived and died to establish that general Liberty, which American Treason in *rebellion* now strives to slay and which these, their worthy sons here died in arms to defend.

ACKNOWLEDGMENTS

Nearly ten years ago I came across a blog posting by a controversial antiracism activist. Tim Wise was infuriated at what he called the "men of their times" defense of slavery and other apologies for America's legacy of racism. Wise cited Charles Anderson's brave speech against a doctrine of white supremacy that was accepted as fact by nearly all white U.S. citizens in the nineteenth century. I had just published a study of free blacks in New Hampshire and was developing several other projects, so I dropped Anderson into my "ideas" file and forgot about him. A few years later I returned to Anderson as a potential story candidate. I was astonished at what I discovered.

Indiana University's Rob Tolley had stumbled upon the original manuscript of Anderson's oration that concluded the Gettysburg cemetery dedication events. As I pieced together Anderson's remarkable life story, Rob was always on call, introducing me to local contacts and directing me to archives where he had donated the remainder of Anderson's personal papers. Without Rob's passion and dedication, this small piece of Gettysburg lore might have remained lost forever. Anderson is certainly one of many "B-list" characters in U.S. history who merits more attention.

Many people deserve special mention for their cheerful assistance and patience as I slogged through innumerable letters, diaries, photographs, and other treasures. Olga Tsapina and the efficient staff at the Huntington Library in San Marino, California, did an incredible job cataloguing and preserving the largest collection of Anderson papers and ephemera. Archivists at the Ohio Historical Society, Cincinnati Historical Society, Cincinnati Public Library, Dayton Metro Library, and especially Robert Schmidt and his staff at the Miami University Archives helped make my research trips to the Buckeye State worthwhile and productive. Sally Whittington of the Lyon County (Kentucky) Historical Society offered me gracious Southern hospitality in abundance. James Holmberg's archivists at the Filson Historical Society in Louisville were friendly and helpful. The fine folks at the Dolph Briscoe Center for American History at the University of Texas at Austin assisted me in every way imaginable, as did the staff at the Texas State Library and Archives and the Institute for Texan Cultures in San Antonio. Finally, James B. Lewis and his exceptional cadre of park rangers at the Stones River National Battlefield took great pains to help me understand the challenges and horrors inherent in the duties of Civil War soldiers. All of these people and many others are the true unsung heroes of the history profession.

I am heavily indebted to friends and colleagues who helped me during the course of this project. Dan Roper, editor of *Georgia Backroads*, published six of my articles while providing substantive advice and encouragement in my transition to a full-time writing career. Dan read the entire manuscript and offered countless suggestions that improved the work measurably. Holly Farmer also gave the drafts plenty of red ink, combing through the paragraphs line by line and challenging me to think more clearly about my protagonist, his unique talents and character traits. Dr. Julie Winch, eminent professor of history at the University of Massachusetts, sparked my interest in both African American history and biography with her incisive intellect, keen sense of humor, and unwavering mentorship. Dave McGuire read early drafts of the manuscript, contributed important insights, and asked excellent questions. Dr. Alan Ebenstein of the University of California at Santa Barbara and Andrea Hartman were notable among my readers for their comments and suggestions on the book and its marketing. Kate McMillan, my web guru, and Peter

O'Connor, who designed the book cover, are young entrepreneurs who are already masters of their respective crafts. Copyeditor Amy Smith Bell's attention to detail helped me find the hidden little mistakes that too often embarrass independent authors. The terrific tag team of book designer David Peattie and proofreader Tanya Grove gave the book visual elegance while eliminating distracting errors of grammar and format. Finally, my wife, Jeanne, lived with the ghost of Charles Anderson for several years, displaying patience with my history obsession. She is also a knowledgeable and helpful reader when the spirit moves her.

Notes

ONE: PATRIOT LEGACY

1. Chief manuscript sources for Richard C. Anderson (1750–1826) are found in the Richard Clough Anderson Papers, Huntington Library, San Marino, California, and in the Anderson-Latham Papers, Filson Historical Society, Louisville, Kentucky. Most of Anderson's papers relating to his position as surveyor (and those of his son-in-law and successor, Allen Latham) are found in the Anderson-Latham Collection, 1777–1881, Personal Papers Collection, Library of Virginia and the Richard Clough Anderson Papers, William L. Clements Library, University of Michigan.

2. George Washington to John A. Washington, December 18, 1776, George Washington Papers, Library of Congress, Washington, D.C.

3. Edward L. Anderson, *Soldier and Pioneer: A Biographical Sketch of Lt.-Col. Richard C. Anderson of the Continental Army* (New York: G. P. Putnam's Sons, 1879), 20.

4. Charles Anderson, "Ye Andersons of Virginia and Some of Their Descendants bye One of Ye Familie," *The "Old Northwest" Genealogical Quarterly* 11 (October 1908): 231–288.

5. Marquis de Lafayette, *Memories, Correspondence and Manuscripts of General Lafayette* (New York: Saunders and Otley, 1837) vol. 1, 264.

6. Anderson, *Soldier and Pioneer*, 39–60.

TWO: BEAR GRASS LESSONS

1. For an interesting perspective on the migration of settlers from Virginia to Kentucky, and eventually to Ohio, see John V. H. Dippel, *Race to the*

Frontier: "White Flight" and Westward Expansion (New York: Algora Publishing, 2005).

2. Edward L. Anderson, *Soldier and Pioneer: A Biographical Sketch of Lt.-Col. Richard C. Anderson of the Continental Army* (New York: G. P. Putnam's Sons, 1879). Charles Anderson, "Ye Andersons of Virginia and Some of Their Descendants bye One of Ye Familie," *The "Old Northwest" Genealogical Quarterly* 11 (October 1908): 231–288. Thomas McArthur Anderson, *A Monograph of the Anderson, Clark, Marshall, and McArthur Connection* (printed by author, 1900). Edward L. Anderson, *The Andersons of Gold Mine, Hanover County, Virginia* (Cincinnati, Ohio, 1913). William Pope Anderson, *Anderson Family Records* (Cincinnati, Ohio: Press of W. F. Schaefer & Company, 1936).

3. Primary source for scenes and quotations in this chapter are from Charles Anderson, "The Story of Soldier's Retreat: A Memoir," unpublished manuscript, Filson Historical Society, Louisville, Kentucky.

4. Anderson, *Soldier and Pioneer*, 56–60.

5. Anderson, "Ye Andersons of Virginia," 251–288.

THREE: BORN TO LEAD

1. Larz Anderson to William Marshall Anderson, April 18, 1825; and Larz Anderson to Maria Latham, July 26, 1826, Anderson Family Papers, Huntington Library, San Marino, California.

2. Larz Anderson to Maria Latham, August 27, 1827; September 4, 1827; November 18, 1828, Anderson Family Papers, Huntington Library.

3. Larz Anderson to Maria Latham, November 7, 1829, Anderson Family Papers, Huntington Library.

4. Walter Havighurst, *Men of Old Miami 1809–1873: A Book of Portraits* (New York: Putnam, 1974), 49–63. Walter Havighurst, *The Miami Years 1809–1984* (New York: Putnam, 1984). Miami University, *Recensio* (Oxford, Ohio: Miami University, 1905), 120–124.

5. Charles Anderson, "An Oration on the Influence of Monumental Records upon National Morals," speech delivered at Miami University, Oxford, Ohio, September 25, 1833, Walter Havighurst Special Collections, Miami University Library, Oxford, Ohio.

6. Charles Anderson to Allen Latham Anderson, February 17, 1893, Charles Anderson Family Papers, Ohio Historical Society, Columbus.

7. Charles Anderson as quoted in Hudson Strode, *Jefferson Davis: American Patriot 1808–1861* (New York: Harcourt, Brace and Co., 1955), 78–99, 222–223.

8. William Marshall Anderson, *The Rocky Mountain Journals of William Marshall Anderson: The West in 1834* (San Marino, California: Huntington Library Publications, 1967).

FOUR: DEVILISH WHISPERS

1. Quotations in this section from letter of Larz Anderson to Charles Anderson, December 30, 1840, Richard Clough Anderson Papers, Huntington Library, San Marino, California.

2. Charles Anderson to Maria Latham, September 8, 1841, Anderson-Latham Papers, Filson Historical Society, Louisville, Kentucky.

3. Lewis B. Gunkel, *The Bench and Bar of Dayton* (Dayton, Ohio: Dayton Historical Society, 1900).

4. J. H. Battle, W. H. Perrin, and G. C. Kifflin, *Kentucky: A History of the State*, third edition (Louisville, Kentucky: F. A. Battey & Co., 1886).

5. David S. Heidler and Jeanne T. Heidler, *Henry Clay: The Essential American* (New York: Random House, 2010).

6. Eliza Anderson to Sarah Marshall Anderson, January 20, 1844, Richard Clough Anderson Papers, Huntington Library.

7. *Journal of the Senate of the State of Ohio, 43rd General Assembly*, Vol. 43 (Columbus, Ohio: Scott & Co., 1845). *Western Empire* (Dayton, Ohio), February 13 and 20, 1845.

8. Salmon P. Chase to Charles Anderson, March 1, 1845, Richard Clough Anderson Papers, Huntington Library. *Weekly Ohio State Journal*, March 12, 1845.

9. Larz Anderson to William Marshall Anderson, October 11, 1845, Anderson Family Papers, Huntington Library.

10. *Journal of the Senate of the State of Ohio, 44th General Assembly*, Vol. 44 (Columbus, Ohio: Scott & Co., 1846). *Ohio State Journal*, February 28, 1846.

11. George F. Drake to Charles Anderson, June 14, 1877, Richard Clough Anderson Papers, Huntington Library.

12. Joseph S. Stern, *Cincinnati's Little Known Renaissance Man* (Cincinnati, Ohio: The Literary Club, 1999). Jacob D. Cox, "Rufus King," reprinted from *The Green Bag* (March 1891).

13. Charles Anderson to William Marshall Anderson, June 19, 1849, Anderson Family Papers, Huntington Library.

14. Robert Anderson, *An Artillery Officer in The Mexican War 1846–7: Letters of Robert Anderson, Captain 3rd Artillery, U.S.A.* (New York: G. P. Putnam's Sons, 1911). To understand the rarity of Anderson's public stance on Anglo-Saxon political ideology, see Reginald Horsman, *Race and Manifest*

Destiny: The Origins of American Racial Anglo-Saxonism (Cambridge, Massachusetts: Harvard University Press, 1981), 260–271.

15. Larz Anderson to Orlando Brown, February 5, 1850, Orlando Brown Papers, Filson Historical Society.

16. Charles Anderson, *An Address on Anglo Saxon Destiny; Delivered before the Philomathesian Society, of Kenyon College, Ohio, August 8th, 1849, and Repeated before the New England Society of Cincinnati; December 20th, 1849* (Cincinnati, Ohio: John B. Thorpe, 1850). The speech was published under a different title by the same publisher in the same year as *Anglo Saxons: Their Origin, Character, Identity, and Connection with the English and American People and Their Destiny.*

17. Elias Longley, *Report on the Trial of William R. Winton, M.D., on a Charge for Seducing Harriet Keever, in Preble Com. Pleases, on the Third and Fourth of June, 1850* (Cincinnati, Ohio: T. Wrightson, 1851).

18. Charles Anderson to William Marshall Anderson, November 3, 1850, and January 21, 1851, Anderson Family Papers, Huntington Library. *Cincinnati Enquirer*, September 27, 1851.

19. *Anti-Slavery Bugle* (Salem, Ohio), May 22, 1852.

20. Charles Anderson, *A Funeral Oration on the Character, Life, and Public Services of Henry Clay* (Cincinnati, Ohio: Ben Franklin Office Print, 1852).

FIVE: POLITICAL OUTCAST

1. John Aston Warder and James W. Ward, ed., *The Horticultural Review and Botanical Magazine* (Cincinnati, Ohio: H. W. Derby, 1854), vol. 4, frontispiece, 141.

2. Rufus King to Sarah Worthington King, January 14, 1855, Rufus King Papers, Cincinnati Historical Society Library, Ohio.

3. *Daily Ohio State Journal*, September 3 and 27, 1855; and October 1, 2, and 13, 1855.

4. *Daily Ohio State Journal*, June 14 and 26, July 25 and 29, 1856. *Dayton Gazette*, as quoted in the *Daily Ohio State Journal*, June 23, 1856.

5. Charles Anderson to Orlando Brown, November 3 and 25, 1856, Orlando Brown Papers, Filson Historical Society, Louisville, Kentucky.

SIX: TEXAS FEVER

1. *Daily Ohio State Journal*, September 8 and 23, 1857; and October 12, 1857.

2. Rufus King to Sarah Worthington King, May 15 and June 9, 1857, Rufus King Papers, Cincinnati Historical Society Library, Ohio.

3. Charles Anderson to Allen Latham Anderson, January 2, 1894, Charles Anderson Family Papers, Ohio Historical Society, Columbus, Ohio.

4. Frederick Law Olmsted, *A Journey through Texas* (New York: Dix, Edwards & Co., 1857), 148–160.

5. Catherine Longworth to Ellen Ryan, November 8, 1858, Anderson Family Papers, Huntington Library, San Marino, California.

6. Eliza Anderson to Maria Latham, April 18, 1859, Anderson Family Papers, Huntington Library.

7. Stephan Schwartz, *Twenty-two Months a Prisoner of War* (St. Louis, Missouri: A. F. Nelson Publishing Co., 1892).

8. City of San Antonio to Charles Anderson, May 10, 1860, Bexar County Deed Records, Book "S," 121, Texas State Library, Austin. The land had been donated by the city of San Antonio to the U.S. government for a planned arsenal, which was begun and later abandoned. The land was recovered by the city and sold at auction.

9. Zenas R. Bliss, "Reminiscences of Zenas R. Bliss," *Southwestern Historical Quarterly* 110, no. 1 (July 2006): 85–107.

10. Charles Anderson, *A Paper Read before the Cincinnati Society of Ex-Army and Navy Officers, January 3d, 1884* (Cincinnati, Ohio: Peter G. Thomson, 1884).

11. Joseph H. Holt to Larz Anderson, February 16, 1860, Richard Clough Anderson Papers, Huntington Library.

12. Charles Anderson, unidentified manuscript, Charles Anderson Family Papers, Ohio Historical Society. This appears to be a draft of Anderson's speech delivered at Cooper Union in New York City in January 1862.

13. *Goliad Messenger,* March 31, 1860.

14. Charles Anderson to Elizabeth Gwalthney, July 4, 1860. *Daily Ledger and Texan* (San Antonio), June 20, 1860.

15. Donald E. Reynolds, "Texas Troubles," in *Handbook of Texas Online,* Texas State Historical Association (http://www.tshaonline.org/handbook/online/articles/vetbr), accessed December 31, 2014.

16. Charles Anderson to Rufus King, November 13, 1860, Rufus King Papers, Cincinnati Historical Society Library, Ohio.

SEVEN: DEBATE AT ALAMO SQUARE

1. Charles Anderson, *Speech of Charles Anderson, Esq., on the State of the Country, at a Meeting of the People of Bexar County, at San Antonio, Texas, November 24, 1860* (Washington, D.C.: Lemuel Towers, 1860). Charles

Anderson, *A Paper Read before the Cincinnati Society of Ex-Army and Navy Officers, January 3d, 1884* (Cincinnati, Ohio: Peter G. Thomson, 1884).

2. Charles Anderson to Rufus King, December 2, 1860, Rufus King Papers, Cincinnati Historical Society Library, Ohio. *San Antonio Ledger and Texan*, December 1, 1860. *Cincinnati Daily Enquirer*, December 18, 1860. George W. Pendleton to Rufus King, December 25, 1860, Rufus King Papers, Cincinnati Historical Society Library.

EIGHT: TREACHERY AND TREASON

1. Charles Anderson to Rufus King, December 7, 1860, Rufus King Papers, Cincinnati Historical Society Library, Ohio.

2. Bickley explained the aims of the KGC at a public meeting held in San Antonio. *Alamo Express* (San Antonio, Texas), November 5, 1860.

3. Zenas R. Bliss, "Reminiscences of Zenas R. Bliss," *Southwestern Historical Quarterly* 110, no. 1 (July 2006): 85–107.

4. Charles Anderson, *A Paper Read before the Cincinnati Society of Ex-Army and Navy Officers, January 3d, 1884* (Cincinnati, Ohio: Peter G. Thomson, 1884).

5. Charles Anderson to Thomas Corwin, January 21, 1861, Richard Clough Anderson Papers, Huntington Library, San Marino, California.

6. David Detzer, *Allegiance: Fort Sumter, Charleston, and the Beginning of the Civil War* (New York: Harcourt, 2001), 150–152.

7. Charles Anderson to Rufus King, February 9, 1861, Rufus King Papers, Cincinnati Historical Society Library, Ohio.

8. Anderson, *A Paper Read before the Cincinnati Society*.

9. Charles Anderson to Rufus King, February 9 and March 24, 1861, Rufus King Papers, Cincinnati Historical Society Library.

10. Bliss, "Reminiscences of Zenas R. Bliss."

11. James P. Newcomb, *Sketch of Secession Times in Texas and Journal of Travel from Texas through Mexico to California* (San Francisco, 1863). See also the James Pearson Newcomb Sr. Papers, 1835–1941, Center for American History, University of Texas at Austin.

12. *Cincinnati Daily Press,* June 1, 1861.

NINE: CAPTURE

1. *Congressional Globe,* 37th Congress, 3rd Session, 205 (1863). Charles and Eliza Anderson to William McLane, May 6, 1862, Bexar County Deed

Records, Book "S," 285, Texas State Library, Austin. Anderson sold the house and surrounding ranch lands to McLane for ten thousand dollars.

2. The primary source for this chapter is *Kitty Anderson Civil War Diary*, 1861, Dolph Briscoe Center for American History, University of Texas at Austin.

3. *Richmond Enquirer* (Richmond, Virginia), October 24, 1861.

4. Henry Eustace McCulloch to Charles Anderson, October 4, 1861, Anderson Family Papers, Huntington Library, San Marino, California; and Henry Eustace McCulloch to Paul O. Hébert, October 4, 1861, in *The War of the Rebellion: Official Records of the Union and Confederate Armies, 1861–1865* (Washington, D.C.: Government Printing Office, 1880–1901), ser. 1, vol. 4, 114–115.

TEN: EXODUS

1. Eliza Anderson to "brother," October 30, 1861, Skinner collection, Pinedale, Wyoming.

2. *Kitty Anderson Civil War Diary*, 1861, Dolph Briscoe Center for American History, University of Texas at Austin.

ELEVEN: ESCAPE

1. Zenas R. Bliss, "Reminiscences of Zenas R. Bliss," *Southwestern Historical Quarterly* 110, no. 1 (July 2006): 85–107. *Kitty Anderson Civil War Diary*, 1861, Dolph Briscoe Center for American History, University of Texas at Austin.

2. De Witt C. Peters to Adjutant General Lorenzo Thomas, October 20, 1861, in *The War of the Rebellion: Official Records of the Union and Confederate Armies, 1861–1865* (Washington, D.C.: Government Printing Office, 1880–1901), ser. 2, vol. 1, 65.

3. Ann S. Ludlum to Charles Anderson, October 7, 1865; Ann S. Ludlum to Eliza Anderson, July 15, 1866, Richard Clough Anderson Papers, Huntington Library, San Marino, California. Charles Anderson to Lorenzo Shearwood, September 26, 1865; Charles Anderson to Nelson Sayler, October 24, 1865; and Charles Anderson to Florida Tunstall, October 25, 1865, Charles Anderson Papers, Ohio Historical Society, Columbus.

4. J. C. Houzeau, *La Terreur Blanche au Texas et Mon Evasion* (Brussels: Ve Parent & Fils, 1863), 44–56.

5. William Bayard to Charles Anderson, December 9, 1865, Richard Clough Anderson Papers, Huntington Library. Samuel J. Bayard, *The Life of George Dashiell Bayard* (New York: G. P. Putnam's Sons, 1874), 304–306.

6. *Kitty Anderson Civil War Diary*, 1861.

7. *Texas State Gazette* (Austin), November 9, 1861. *Dallas Herald*, November 13, 1861.

8. Colonel John S. Ford to Captain D. C. Stith, November 9, 1861, in *War of the Rebellion*, ser. 2, vol. 1, 93.

TWELVE: HOMEWARD

1. *Kitty Anderson Civil War Diary*, 1861, Dolph Briscoe Center for American History, University of Texas at Austin.

2. Charles Anderson to Eliza Anderson, November 9, 1861, Richard Clough Anderson Papers, Huntington Library, San Marino, California.

3. *Cincinnati Daily Press*, December 13, 1861, and January 9, 1862. *New York Times*, December 11, 1861.

THIRTEEN: HERO

1. *New York Times*, December 21, 22, and 24, 1861.

2. Charles Anderson to Major General Henry Halleck, January 7, 1862, in *The War of the Rebellion: Official Records of the Union and Confederate Armies, 1861–1865* (Washington, D.C.: Government Printing Office, 1880–1901), ser. 2, vol. 1, 70. Charles Anderson to General Lorenzo Thomas, February 7, 1862, in *War of the Rebellion*, ser. 2, vol. 1, 79. Charles Anderson to Edwin Stanton, February 7, 1862, in *War of the Rebellion*, ser. 2, vol. 1, 79–81.

3. *Gallipolis* (Ohio) *Journal*, January 23, 1862.

4. Charles Anderson to Eliza Anderson, January 18, 1862, Richard Clough Anderson Papers, Huntington Library, San Marino, California.

5. James Russell Lowell to Mary A. Clarke, May 17, 1890, *The Century Illustrated Monthly Magazine*, vol. 51 (1896): 545.

6. Gordon H. Warren, *Fountain of Discontent: The Trent Affair and Freedom of the Seas* (Boston, Massachusetts: Northeastern University Press, 1981).

7. Charles Anderson to Eliza Anderson, March 28 and 29, May 16 and 21, and June 23, 1862; Charles Anderson to Kitty Anderson, May 13 and 30, 1862; and Charles Anderson to Charles Francis Adams, April 24, 1862, Richard Clough Anderson Papers, Huntington Library.

FOURTEEN: RANK AMATEURS

1. Enlistment broadside of Charles Anderson, Ninety-Third Ohio Volunteer Infantry, 1863. Charles Anderson Family Papers, Ohio Historical Society, Columbus. Robert W. Steele and Mary Davies Steele, *Early Dayton* (Dayton, Ohio: U. B. Publishing House, 1896), 205. *Cincinnati Daily Enquirer,* July 10, 1862.

2. Charles Hill, Adjutant General, to Charles Anderson, August 8, 1862, Richard Clough Anderson Papers, Huntington Library, San Marino, California. *New York Times,* August 9, 1862.

3. Historical context for this chapter is taken principally from James Lee McDonough, *War in Kentucky: From Shiloh to Perryville* (Knoxville: University of Tennessee Press, 1991), 61–87, 104–127, 144–157, 182–245, and 296–325.

4. *Dayton* (Ohio) *Journal,* August 16, 1862.

5. *The War of the Rebellion: Official Records of the Union and Confederate Armies, 1861–1865* (Washington, D.C.: Government Printing Office, 1880–1901), ser. 1, vol. 16, part 1, 908–909.

6. Samuel B. Smith, *Autobiography of Samuel B. Smith transcription by Paul D. Cameruci,* unpublished manuscript, undated, Dayton Metro Library.

7. Henry Richards, *Letters of Captain Henry Richards of the Ninety-Third Ohio Infantry* (Cincinnati: Wrightson and Company, 1883). Alfred Demoret, *A Brief History of the Ninety-Third Regiment Ohio Volunteer Infantry: Recollections of a Private* (Ross, Ohio: 1898). Companion J. T. Patton, *Personal Recollections of Four Years in Dixie* (Detroit: Winn & Hammond, 1892).

8. A. T. Babbitt to Eliza Anderson, September 11, 1862, Richard Clough Anderson Papers, Huntington Library, San Marino, California.

9. Hiram Strong, *Inventory, Calendar, and Index of the Hiram Strong Papers, 1862–1863 by Ronald Jan Plavchan,* unpublished typescript, 1964, Dayton Metro Library.

10. Charles Anderson to Eliza Anderson, September 30, 1862, Richard Clough Anderson Papers, Huntington Library.

11. Charles Anderson to Kitty Anderson, October 7, 1862, Richard Clough Anderson Papers, Huntington Library.

12. Charles Anderson to Eliza Anderson, October 16, 1862, Richard Clough Anderson Papers, Huntington Library.

13. Charles Anderson to Kitty Anderson, October 26, 1862, Richard Clough Anderson Papers, Huntington Library.

14. A. T. Babbitt to Eliza Anderson, October 29, 1862, Richard Clough Anderson Papers, Huntington Library. Rosecrans's army was officially called the Fourteenth Army Corps until after the Battle of Stones River, but this was

a temporary designation. Most historians refer to this army by its later name, the Army of the Cumberland.

15. Charles Anderson to Eliza Anderson, October 29 and November 3, 1862, Richard Clough Anderson Papers, Huntington Library.

16. Strong, *Inventory, Calendar, and Index of the Hiram Strong Papers. Dayton Daily Empire*, December 15, 1862. *War of the Rebellion*, ser. 1, vol. 20, part 1, 34–37.

17. Charles Anderson to Eliza Anderson, December 7, 1862, Richard Clough Anderson Papers, Huntington Library.

18. Charles Anderson to Eliza Anderson, December 23, 1862, Richard Clough Anderson Papers, Huntington Library.

19. David R. Logsdon, ed., *Eyewitnesses at the Battle of Stones River* (Nashville, Tennessee: David R. Logsdon, 2002).

FIFTEEN: BLOOD AND BUTTONS

1. For detailed accounts of the Battle of Stones River used in this chapter, see Peter Cozzens, *No Better Place to Die* (Chicago: University of Illinois Press, 1990); James Lee McDonough, *Stones River: Bloody Winter in Tennessee* (Knoxville: University of Tennessee Press, 1980); Matt Spruill and Lee Spruill, *Winter Lightning: A Guide to the Battle of Stones River* (Knoxville: University of Tennessee Press, 2007), and *Blue & Gray Magazine* 28, no. 6.

2. *The War of the Rebellion: Official Records of the Union and Confederate Armies, 1861–1865* (Washington, D.C.: Government Printing Office, 1880–1901), ser. 1, vol. 20, part 1, 336–347, 445.

3. Ibid., 558–563, 570–571.

4. Bragg's telegram to Richmond as printed in *Charleston Mercury*, January 3, 1863.

5. Poem from Nicholas L. Anderson, *The Letters and Journals of Nicholas Longworth Anderson* (New York: Fleming H. Revel, 1942).

6. Frank Moore, ed., *The Rebellion Record: A Diary of American Events* (New York: G. P. Putnam, 1863), vol. 6, 160. Abraham Lincoln, *The Collected Works of Abraham Lincoln*, ed. Roy P. Basler (New Brunswick, New Jersey: Rutgers University Press, 1953), 424–425.

7. Charles Anderson to Eliza, Kitty, and Belle Anderson, January 7, 1863, Richard Clough Anderson Papers, Huntington Library.

8. David R. Logsdon, ed., *Eyewitnesses at the Battle of Stones River* (Nashville, Tennessee: D. R. Logsdon, 1989), 86–89.

9. Charles Anderson to Kitty Anderson, January 2, 1863, Richard Clough Anderson Papers, Huntington Library, San Marino, California.

10. Charles Anderson to Eliza, Kitty, and Belle Anderson, January 7, 1863; Charles Anderson to Belle Anderson, January 9, 1863, Richard Clough Anderson Papers, Huntington Library. *Dayton Daily Empire*, February 5 and 28, 1863.

SIXTEEN: A DANGEROUS MAN

1. James L. Vallandigham, *A Life of Clement L. Vallandigham* (Baltimore, Maryland: Turnbull Brothers, 1872), 478–479.

2. Clement L. Vallandigham, *Speeches, Arguments, Addresses, and Letters of Clement L. Vallandigham* (New York: J. Walter and Co., 1864), 305.

3. Frank L. Klement, *The Limits of Dissent: Clement L. Vallandigham and the Civil War* (Louisville: University Press of Kentucky, 1970), 105.

4. Klement, *The Limits of Dissent*, 102–116.

5. Clement L. Vallandigham, *The Record of Hon. C. L. Vallandigham* (Cincinnati, Ohio: J. Walter and Co., 1863). Anderson's personal copy of this work includes extensive penciled margin notes in his own hand (Skinner collection, Pinedale, Wyoming).

6. From George H. Porter, *Ohio Politics during the Civil War Period* (New York: AMS Press, 1911).

7. Charles Anderson, *Letter Addressed to the Opera House Meeting, Cincinnati*, Loyal Publication Society No. 21 (New York: W. C. Bryant & Co., 1863).

8. Porter, *Ohio Politics*, 177.

9. Klement, *The Limits of Dissent*, 116–213.

SEVENTEEN: SEVERING THE HEAD OF THE SNAKE

1. The poem "Vallandigham: The Bastilled Hero" and other facts in this passage are largely from Frank L. Klement, *The Limits of Dissent: Clement L. Vallandigham and the Civil War* (Louisville: University Press of Kentucky, 1970), 213–256.

2. George H. Porter, *Ohio Politics during the Civil War Period* (New York: AMS Press, 1911), 177.

3. *Cincinnati Daily Enquirer,* June 17,1863.

4. John Caldwell to Charles Anderson, June 18, 1863; William Johnston to Charles Anderson, June 19, 1863, Richard Clough Anderson Papers, Huntington Library, San Marino, California. *Cincinnati Daily Enquirer,* July 7, 1863.

5. Larz Anderson to Charles Anderson, June 26 and July 4, 1863; John Caldwell to Charles Anderson, July 1, 1863, Richard Clough Anderson Papers, Huntington Library. *Jeffersonian Democrat*, July 24, 1863. *Ohio Statesman*, July 11, 1863.

6. Porter, *Ohio Politics*, 167–199.

7. Joseph H. Geiger to Charles Anderson, July 10, 1863, Richard Clough Anderson Papers, Huntington Library. *Dayton Empire*, March 27, 1863.

8. Joseph Leeds to Liberty Ball, October 13, 1863, Cincinnati Historical Society Library, Ohio. *Cleveland Morning Leader*, October 8, 1863.

9. *Daily Ohio Statesman*, August 27, 1863. *Daily Empire* (Dayton, Ohio), August 29 and September 2, 1863. *Belmont* (Ohio) *Chronicle*, October 1, 1863.

10. This telegram, repeated in countless histories as addressed to either Tod or Brough, is not found in the voluminous records of Lincoln correspondence.

EIGHTEEN: THE PIT BULL AND THE PRESIDENT

1. William P. Wellen to Charles Anderson, October 19, 1863, Richard Clough Anderson Papers, Huntington Library, San Marino, California.

2. David Tod to Charles Anderson, October 27, 1863 in *Documents Accompanying the Governor's Message of January, 1864* (Columbus, Ohio, 1864), 285–287.

3. *Daily Ohio Statesman*, November 19, 1863. *Cincinnati Enquirer*, November 9, 1863.

4. Three studies of the Gettysburg consecration ceremonies were used as key sources to frame this chapter: Martin P. Johnson, *Writing the Gettysburg Address* (Lawrence: University Press of Kansas, 2013); Gabor Boritt, *The Gettysburg Gospel: The Lincoln Speech That Nobody Knows* (New York: Simon & Schuster, 2006); and Garry Wills, *Lincoln at Gettysburg: The Words That Remade America* (New York: Simon & Schuster, 1992).

5. For Everett's speech and details of the event, see Edward Everett, *Address of the Honorable Edward Everett at the Consecration of the National Cemetery at Gettysburg 19th November, 1863, with the Dedication Speech of President Lincoln and the Other Exercises of the Occasion* (Boston: Little, Brown, 1868).

6. Earl W. Wiley, "Colonel Charles Anderson's Gettysburg Address," *Lincoln Herald* 54, no. 3 (Fall 1952): 14–21. Wiley relied on newspaper reports that included less than half of the speech. Frank L. Klement dedicates an entire chapter to Ohio's participation in the event in *The Gettysburg Soldiers' Cemetery and Lincoln's Address* (Shippensburg, Pennsylvania: White Mane Publishing Company, 1993). Klement incorrectly assumes that the text in the

Cincinnati *Commercial* represents Anderson's complete speech. A close reading of that report reveals that large sections of the speech were paraphrased or omitted.

7. Bret Harte, *The Poetical Works of Bret Harte* (New York: Houghton Mifflin Company, 1899), 1–4.

8. *Ohio State Journal,* November 23, 1863.

9. The delivery manuscript of Anderson's oration is in the Charles Anderson Family Papers, Ohio Historical Society Archives, Columbus. Extant draft pages of the speech are in the Skinner Collection, Pinedale, Wyoming.

10. Audience reaction to Anderson's speech is found in numerous pro-administration newspapers cited by Wiley, "Colonel Charles Anderson's Gettysburg Address." The meeting of the Ohio delegation was a partisan affair with distinctly political purposes. The November 25, 1863, edition of *Crisis* (Columbus, Ohio) described how "Seward and Charles Anderson mingled their abolition hate and destructiveness" in what was clearly a boisterous gathering. Martin P. Johnson (in his *Writing the Gettysburg Address*, 238) relates the opposition newspaper *New York World*'s claim that Lincoln slept through Anderson's speech. This is highly unlikely.

NINETEEN: UNFORTUNATE MISSTEP

1. Nicholas L. Anderson, *The Letters and Journals of Nicholas Longworth Anderson* (New York: Fleming H. Revel, 1942).

2. *Xenia* (Ohio) *Sentinel*, April 26, 1864. Anderson's speech in Lexington, Kentucky, was seen by radicals as a betrayal of the antislavery principles he had espoused during the gubernatorial campaign.

3. Doris Kearns Goodwin, *Team of Rivals: The Political Genius of Abraham Lincoln* (New York: Simon & Shuster, 2005), 621–666.

4. Oliver Perry Morton to Charles Anderson, August 22, 1864; and Charles Anderson to Godwin Volney Dorsey, August 22, 1864, Richard Clough Anderson Papers, Huntington Library, San Marino, California.

5. *Richmond Examiner,* September 5, 1864. Lincoln's words to a soldier friend regarding his election prospects have been quoted in numerous secondary sources by authors such as James M. McPherson, *Tried by War: Abraham Lincoln as Commander in Chief* (New York: Penguin Press, 2008).

6. Richard C. Anderson to Charles Anderson, January 28, 1865, Richard Clough Anderson Papers, Huntington Library.

7. J. Markley to Charles Anderson, February 25, 1865; William Dennison to Charles Anderson, February 27, 1865; James Speed to Charles Anderson, February 27, 1865; Thomas Corwin to Charles Anderson, February 28, 1865; John Sherman to Charles Anderson, March 6, 7, and 13, April 3, 1865;

Rutherford B. Hayes to Charles Anderson, March 25, 1865; and Joseph Holt to Charles Anderson, March 27, 1865—all in Richard Clough Anderson Papers, Huntington Library.

8. David Detzer, *Allegiance: Fort Sumter, Charleston, and the Beginning of the Civil War* (New York: Harcourt, 2001), 317–320. William A. Spicer, *The Flag Replaced on Sumter: A Personal Narrative* (Providence, Rhode Island: Providence Press Co., 1885).

9. William G. Deshler to Charles Anderson, April 22, 1865, Richard Clough Anderson Papers, Huntington Library.

10. As reported in *Daily Sentinel* (Indianapolis), June 17, 1864.

11. William T. Sherman to Charles Anderson, July 28, 1865, Richard Clough Anderson Papers, Huntington Library.

12. George H. Porter, *Ohio Politics during the Civil War Period* (New York: AMS Press, 1911), 200–220.

13. William Dennison to Charles Anderson, June 17 and July 20, 1865; Robert C. Schenck to Charles Anderson, July 6, 1865; Charles Anderson to Andrew Johnson, July 10, 1865; Rutherford B. Hayes to Charles Anderson, July 12, 1865; Sidney Maxwell to Charles Anderson, July 19, 1865—all in Richard Clough Anderson Papers, Huntington Library.

14. Robert C. Schenck to Charles Anderson, July 20, 1865; Benjamin Franklin Wade to Charles Anderson, July 29, 1865; William Dennison to Charles Anderson, August 1 and 15, 1865; John Sherman to Charles Anderson, August 2, 1865; and Charles Anderson to William H. Seward, August 14, 1865—all in Richard Clough Anderson Papers, Huntington Library.

15. Benjamin Cowen to Charles Anderson, August 26, 1865; William Dennison to Charles Anderson, August, 1865; and George Henshaw to Charles Anderson, September 1, 1865—all in Richard Clough Anderson Papers, Huntington Library. *New York Times*, September 1, 1865.

16. *Message and Annual Reports for 1865, Made to the Fifty-Seventh General Assembly of Ohio, at the Regular Session, Begun and Held in the City of Columbus, January, 1, 1866* (Columbus, Ohio: Richard Nevins, 1866), part 1, 161, 211–212, 272–295, and 300–302.

17. Charles Anderson to Henry B. Payne, October 31, 1865, Charles Anderson Papers, Ohio Historical Society, Columbus.

18. Charles Anderson, *Annual Message of the Governor of Ohio, to the Fifty-Seventh General Assembly, at the Regular Session Commencing January 1, 1866* (Columbus, Ohio, 1866).

19. William T. Sherman to Charles Anderson, January 4, 1866, Richard Clough Anderson Papers, Huntington Library. *New York Times*, January 1, 1866.

20. Ephraim George Squier to Charles Anderson, January 9, 1866, Richard Clough Anderson Papers, Huntington Library.

TWENTY: DREAMS LOST AND FULFILLED

1. Charles Anderson to J. B. McCullough, *Cincinnati Daily Enquirer*, October 6, 1866.

2. Eric Foner, *Reconstruction: America's Unfinished Revolution, 1863–1877* (New York: Harper & Row, 1988).

3. Charles Anderson to William Marshall Anderson, March 30, 1867; and Charles Anderson to John Sherman, July 22, 1867—both in Charles Anderson Family Papers, Ohio Historical Society, Columbus.

4. Abraham Rencher to Charles Anderson, February 4, 1867, Richard Clough Anderson Papers, Huntington Library, San Marino, California.

5. Charles Anderson to A. G. Curtin, November, 1869, Richard Clough Anderson Papers, Huntington Library. Charles Anderson to Peter Cooper, September 4, 1876, Charles Anderson Family Papers, Ohio Historical Society.

6. Lyon County, Kentucky Deeds, Book "P," 286–292, Lyon County Courthouse, Eddyville, Kentucky; W. W. Martin and E. Y McNeill, *Tale of Two Cities* (Kuttawa, Kentucky, 1901); *Memorial Record of Western Kentucky* (Chicago and New York: Lewis Publishing Co., 1904); and J. P. Barnum to Charles Anderson, April 30, 1890, plat map of Kuttawa, Kentucky, warranty deed by Charles Anderson, December 30, 1879, Charles Anderson Family Papers, Ohio Historical Society.

7. Charles Anderson to Nelson Saylor, October 24, 1865; Charles Anderson to Florida Tunstall, October 25, 1865; Charles Anderson to Penelope Phillips, October 30, 1865—all in Charles Anderson Papers, Ohio Historical Society. George W. Paschall to Charles Anderson, September 18 and 29, 1865; William Bayard to Charles Anderson, December 9, 1865; Ann Ludlum to Charles Anderson, December 12, 1865; William Dennison to Charles Anderson, November 10, 1865; P. J. Edwards to Charles Anderson, January 20, 1870; and Warwick Tunstall to Charles Anderson, February 6, 1868—all in Richard Clough Anderson Papers, Huntington Library.

8. Charles Anderson to William Marshall Anderson, December 8, 1872, October 6, 1873, and January 10, 1879; and William Marshall Anderson to Charles Anderson, December 26, 1878—all in Charles Anderson Family Papers, Ohio Historical Society.

9. S. N. Leonard to Charles Anderson, July 14, 1876; and Charles Anderson to Kitty Anderson, October 12, 1876—both in Richard Clough Anderson Papers, Huntington Library.

10. Charles Anderson to Kitty Anderson, November 16, 1876, Richard Clough Anderson Papers, Huntington Library.

11. Charles Anderson to Larz Anderson Jr., July 4, 1891, Charles Anderson Family Papers, Ohio Historical Society.

12. Charles Anderson to Larz Anderson Jr., August 11, 1891; and Will of Charles Anderson, 1895—both in Charles Anderson Family Papers, Ohio Historical Society.

AFTERWORD: AMERICAN SACRED SCRIPTURE RECONSIDERED

1. To understand the story of the Gettysburg Address and its wartime political context, read Martin P. Johnson's *Writing the Gettysburg Address* (Lawrence: University Press of Kansas, 2013) alongside Doris Kearns Goodwin's *Team of Rivals: The Political Genius of Abraham Lincoln* (New York: Simon & Schuster, 2005) and Eric Foner's *The Fiery Trial: Abraham Lincoln and American Slavery* (New York: W. W. Norton, 2010).

2. Gabor Boritt, *The Gettysburg Gospel: The Lincoln Speech That Nobody Knows* (New York: Simon & Schuster, 2006), 59–62. *Crisis* (Columbus, Ohio), November 25, 1863.

3. Johnson, *Writing the Gettysburg Address*, 85.

4. David Tod to Charles Anderson, October 27, 1863, in *Documents Accompanying the Governor's Message of January, 1864* (Columbus, Ohio, 1864), 285–287.

5. Charles Anderson, *Letter Addressed to the Opera House Meeting, Cincinnati*, Loyal Publication Society No. 21 (New York: 1863). Charles Anderson, *The Cause of the War, Who Brought It on and for What Purpose?* Loyal Publication Society No. 17 (New York: 1863).

6. Abraham Lincoln, quoted in Johnson, *Writing the Gettysburg Address*, 84.

7. Anderson, *Cause of the War*, 10. Garry Willis makes a strong argument that the famous phrasing "of the people, by the people, for the people," which Anderson also used in his speech, was the genius of the Transcendentalist and patriot Theodore Parker. See Garry Willis, *Lincoln at Gettysburg*, (New York: Simon & Schuster, 1992), 105–120.

8. *Daily Republican of Springfield* (Massachusetts), November 21, 1863. *Crisis* (Columbus, Ohio), November 25, 1863. Adam Gurowski, quoted in Boritt, *Gettysburg Gospel*, 141. *Wabash Express*, November 18, 1863.

9. *Washington Daily Chronicle*, November 20, 1863. *Cincinnati Enquirer*, December 3, 1863.

10. Boritt, *Gettysburg* Gospel, 131–135. S. A. Hine to Charles Anderson, December 3, 1863, Richard Clough Anderson Papers, Huntington Library.

11. Springfield (Ohio) *Republic*, November 30, 1863. *The Portage County* (Ohio) *Democrat*, November 25, 1863. *Crisis* (Columbus, Ohio), November 25, 1863. Abraham Stagg to Charles Anderson, November 17, 1864, Richard Clough Anderson Papers, Huntington Library.

Index

About the Author

PHOTO BY DAVID ROTH

David T. Dixon earned his M.A. in history from the University of Massachusetts. He has published in numerous scholarly journals and magazines. He lives in Santa Barbara, California with his wife, Jeanne.

By uncovering little-known historical figures with compelling stories, David challenges us to think critically about the way that history, especially American Civil War history, has been presented in the past. Find their stories at B-List History, www.davidtdixon.com.